THE COPENHAGEN BOHUN MANUSCRIPTS

The Copenhagen Bohun Manuscripts

WOMEN, REPRESENTATION, AND RECEPTION IN LATE FOURTEENTH-CENTURY ENGLAND

Marina Vidas

MUSEUM TUSCULANUM PRESS

The Copenhagen Bohun Manuscripts: Women, Representation and Reception in Late Fourteenth-Century England
Marina Vidas

Cover design: Pernille Sys Hansen
Set in Baskerville and printed in Denmark by Narayana Press
ISBN 978 87 635 4324 8

Cover illustration: Thott 547, 4°, f. 1. Historiated Initial "D" at Matins: Annunciation. Borders: Portrait of the Book-Owner, Angel Musicians. *Bas-de-Page*: Legend of the Unchaste Abbess.

Published with financial support from
Ny Carlsberg Foundation

MIX
Paper from responsible sources
FSC® C010651

Museum Tusculanum Press
Dantes Plads 1
DK-1556 Copenhagen
Denmark
www.mtp.dk

Contents

List of Plates and Figures 9
Plates 9
Figures 11

Acknowledgements 13

Introduction 15
State of the Research on the Bohun Manuscripts: Style, Production, Programs, and Dating 16

The Historical Background 23

The Illuminators 33

Part One

Chapter One 39
Description of Thott 547, 4° 39
Collation, Page and Text Block Dimensions, Condition 39
The Hours of the Virgin (Sarum Use), ff. 1–31v 40
The Historiated Initials in the Text 42
The Background Panels 43
The *Bas-de-Pages* 43
The *Haut-de-Pages* 44
The Heraldry 44
The Secondary Decoration 44
The Borders 44
The Ornamental Initials 45
The Line Fillers 46
The Seven Penitential Psalms, ff. 32v–38v 46
The Litany, ff. 38 v–41 46
The Collects, ff. 42–42v 47
The Office of the Dead, ff. 43–66v (Sarum Use) 48
The Paleography 48
The Binding 48
The Provenance 49

Chapter Two 51
Principal Illuminations in Thott 547,4°: Historiated Initials, *Bas-de-Page*, *Haut-de-Page*, and Heraldry 51
Miracles of the Virgin: Texs and Images 52
Plate 1. Folio 1. Matins. Historiated Initial "D": Annunciation (Luke 1:26–38) 54
Border: Portrait of the Book Owner 56
Bas-de-Page: Legend of the Unchaste Abbess 58
Plate 2. Folio 6v. Lauds. Historiated Initial "D": Visitation (Luke 1:39–56) 61
Armorials 62
Bas-de-Page: Legend of Theophilus 63
Plate 3. Folio 14v. Prime. Haut-de-Page: Annunciation to the Shepherds (Luke 2:8–14) 65
Historiated Initial "D": Nativity (Luke 2:7) 66
Bas-de-Page: Legend of the Jew of Bourges 68
Plate 4. Folio 17v. End of Prime. Three-line initial "C": Shield with the arms of St. George (*argent a cross gules*) 71
Plate 5. Folio 18. Terce. Historiated Initial "D": Adoration of the Magi (Matthew 2:9–11) 73
Bas-de-Page: Legend of the Child Image taken Hostage 74
Jacobus de Voragine, *The Golden Legend* 74
Plate 6. Folio 20. Sext. Historiated Initial "D": Presentation of the Child in the Temple and the Purification of the Virgin (Luke 2:22–34) 76
Bas-de-Page: Legend of the Monk and the Roses 78
Plate 7. Folio 22v. None. Historiated Initial "D": Crucifixion (Matthew 27:33–55, Mark 15:22–41, Luke 23:26–49, John 19:16–37) 82
Bas-de-Page: The Soul Saved 84
Plate 8. Folio 24. Vespers. Historiated Initial "D": Resurrection (Matthew 27:62–66) 86
Bas-de-Page: Legend of the Drowned Sacristan 87
Jacobus de Voragine, *The Golden Legend* 87
Plate 9. Folio 28v. Compline. Historated Initial "C": Coronation of the Virgin 89
Bas-de-Page: Legend of the Jew and the Merchant 90
Plate 10. Folio 32. Seven Penitential Psalms. Haut-de-Page: The Just in the New Jerusalem (Revelation 21). Historated Initial "D": Last Judgement (Psalm 9:8–9, Matthew 19:28; 22:31–46, 24:30–31, 25:31–46, Mark 13:24–37, John 5:21–30; Acts 17:30–31; 2 Corinthians 5:10, Revelation 20:11–15). *Bas-de-Page*: The Dead are Raised, Separation of Souls 93

Plate 11. Folio 43. Office of the Dead. Historiated Initial "D": Job and Satan before God (Job 1:6–8) 98
Bas-de-Page: The Misfortunes that befall Job, Job rends his Garments (Job 1:15–21, 2:9) 99
Conclusion 101

Part Two

CHAPTER THREE 111
Description of Thott 517, 4° 111
The Collation, Page and Text Block Dimensions, Condition 111
The Texts 112
The Historiated Initials 112
The Background Panels of the Historiated Initials 113
The Secondary Decoration 113
The Borders 113
The Ornamental Initials 114
The Line Fillers 115
The Scribe 115
The Illuminators 115
The Binding 115
The Relationship between Thott 547, 4° and Thott 517, 4° 116

CHAPTER FOUR 121
Principal Texts and Illuminations in Thott 517, 4° 121
The Texts 121
I. *Transitus mariae* (The Passing of Mary), ff. 1–10v 122
II. A. The Life and Passion of St. Margaret, ff. 10v–22v 124
II.B. Antiphon, Versicle and Prayer, f. 22v 129
III. The Apostolic and Eremitic Life of Mary Magdalene, ff. 22v–38 130
The Major Illuminations in the Copenhagen Bohun *Lives* 133
Plate 12. Folio 1. Historiated Initial "Q": Assumption of the Virgin 134
Plate 13. Folio 10v. Historiated Initial "S": St. Margaret Delivered from the Dragon 135
Plate 14. Folio 22v. Historiated Initial "A": Mary Magdalene Borne Up by Angels 136
The Intended Reader 138

CONCLUSION 143

Plates Following p. 144

Notes 145

Appendix 183

Bibliography 187

Index of Names, Places, and Manuscripts 203

List of Plates and Figures

Plates

Plate 1. Thott 547, 4°, f. 1. Historiated Initial "D" at Matins: Annunciation. Borders: Portrait of the Book-Owner, Angel Musicians. *Bas-de-Page*: Legend of the Unchaste Abbess.

Plate 2. Thott 547, 4°, f. 6v. Historiated Initial "D" at Lauds: Visitation. Two-line initial "D": Shield with the Bohun Arms, Earls of Hereford and Essex (*azure a bend argent two cotises and between six lions rampart or*). *Bas-de-Page*: Legend of Theophilus.

Plate 3. Thott 547, 4°, f. 14v. *Haut-de-Page*: Annunciation to the Shepherds. Historiated Initial "D" at Prime: Nativity. Three-line initial "D": Shield with the Bohun Arms. Borders: Seven Medallions with Angel Musicians. *Bas-de-Page*: Legend of the Jew of Bourges.

Plate 4. Thott 547, 4°, f. 17v. End of Prime. Three-line initial "C": Shield with the arms of St. George (*argent a cross gules*).

Plate 5. Thott 547, 4°, f. 18. Historiated Initial "D" at Terce: Adoration of the Magi. *Bas-de-Page*: Legend of the Child Image taken Hostage.

Plate 6. Thott 547, 4°, f. 20. Historiated Initial "D" at Sext: Presentation of the Child in the Temple and Purification of the Virgin. *Bas-de-Page*: Legend of the Monk and the Roses.

Plate 7. Thott 547, 4°, f. 22v. Historiated Initial "D" at None: Crucifixion. *Bas-de-Page*: Miracle of the Soul Saved. Borders: Longinus, Two Angels, Head of God.

Plate 8. Thott 547, 4°, f. 24v. Historiated Initial "D" at Vespers: Resurrection. *Bas-de-Page*: Legend of the Drowned Sacristan. Border: Soldier Guarding Christ's Sepulcher.

Plate 9. Thott 547, 4°, f. 28v. Historated Initial "C" at Compline: Coronation of the Virgin. *Bas-de-Page*: Legend of the Jew and the Merchant. Border: Angel Musicians.

Plate 10. Thott 547, 4°, f. 32v. *Haut-de-Page*: The Just in the New Jerusalem. Historiated Initial "D" at the Seven Penitential Psalms: Last Judgement. *Bas-de-Page*: The Dead are Raised. Separation of the Saved from the Damned. Borders: Angels, Souls, Devils.

Plate 11. Thott 547, 4°, f. 43. Historiated Initial "D" at the Office of the Dead: Job and Satan before God. *Bas-de-Page*: Three Scenes from the Book of Job (1:18, 19, 15, 20, 21, 2:9).

Plate 12. Thott 517, 4°, f. 1. Historiated Initial "Q": Assumption of the Virgin.

Plate 13. Thott 517, 4°, f. 10v. Historiated Initial "S": St. Margaret Delivered from the Dragon.

Plate 14. Thott 517, 4°, f. 22v. Historated Initial "A": Mary Magdalene Borne Up by Angels.

Plate 15. Thott 547, 4°. Front Binding.

Plate 16. Thott 547, 4°. Back Binding.

Plate 17. Thott 517, 4°. Front Binding.

Plate 18. Thott 517, 4°. Back Binding.

Figures

Figure 1. Thott 547, 4°, f. 1. Detail. Historiated Initial "D" at Matins: Annunciation.

Figure 2. Thott 547, 4°, f. 1. Detail. Border: Portrait of the Book Owner.

Figure 3. Thott 547, 4°, f. 1. Detail. *Bas-de-Page*: Legend of the Unchaste Abbess.

Figure 4. Oxford, Bodleian Library, MS Auct.D.4.4, f. 181v. Virgin and Child with Mary Magdelene and a kneeling woman clad in arms of England and Bohun.

Figure 5. Thott 547, 4°, f. 6v. Detail. Historiated Initial "D" at Lauds: Visitation.

Figure 6. Thott 547, 4°, f. 6v. Detail. *Bas-de-Page*: Legend of Theophilus.

Figure 7. Thott 547, 4°, f. 14v. Detail. *Haut-de-Page*: Annunciation to the Shepherds.

Figure 8. Thott 547, 4°, f. 14v. Detail. Historiated Initial "D" at Prime: Nativity. Detail. *Bas-de-Page*: Legend of the Jew of Bourges.

Figure 9. Thott 547, 4°, f. 18. Detail. Historiated Initial "D" at Terce: Adoration of the Magi.

Figure 10. Thott 547, 4°, f. 18. Detail. *Bas-de-Page*: Legend of the Child Image taken Hostage.

Figure 11. Thott 547, 4°, f. 20. Detail. Historiated Initial "D" at Sext: Presentation of the Child in the Temple and Purification of the Virgin. Detail. *Bas-de-Page*: Legend of the Monk and the Roses.

Figure 12. Thott 547, 4°, f. 22v. Detail. Historiated Initial "D" at None: Crucifixion.

Figure 13. Thott 547, 4°, f. 22v. Detail. *Bas-de-Page*: Miracle of the Soul Saved.

Figure 14. Thott 547, 4°, f. 24v. Detail. Historiated Initial "D" at Vespers: Resurrection. Detail. *Bas-de-Page*: Legend of the Drowned Sacristan.

Figure 15. Thott 547, 4°, f. 28v. Detail. Historiated Initial "C" at Compline: Coronation of the Virgin.

Figure 16. Thott 547, 4°, f. 28v. Detail. *Bas-de-Page*: Legend of the Jew and the Merchant.

Figure 17. Thott 547, 4°, f. 32v. Detail. *Haut-de-Page*: The Just in the New Jerusalem. Historiated Initial "D" at the Seven Penitential Psalms: Last Judgement, Christ Displays His Wounds.

Figure 18. Thott 547, 4°, f. 32v. Detail. *Bas-de-Page*: the Dead are Raised.

Figure 19. Thott 547, 4°, f. 43. Detail. Historiated Initial "D" at the Office of the Dead: Job and Satan before God.

Figure 20. Thott 547, 4°, f. 43. Detail. *Bas-de-Page*: Three Scenes from the Book of Job (1:18, 19, 15, 20, 21, 2:9).

Figure 21. Thott 517, 4°, f. 1. Detail. Historiated Initial "Q": Assumption of the Virgin.

Figure 22. Thott 517, 4°, f. 10v. Detail. Historiated Initial "S": St. Margaret Delivered from the Dragon.

Figure 23. Thott 517, 4°, f. 22v. Detail. Historiated Initial "A": Mary Magdalene Borne Up by Angels.

Acknowledgements

THIS BOOK COULD NOT have been written without the support of Jonathan J. G. Alexander who has never failed to help me with my professional endeavors. Kathryn A. Smith deserves special thanks for reading the text and making many detailed and valuable suggestions. I would like to express my most sincere gratitude to Ian Mortimer for his careful and critical reading of selected parts of the Introduction and of Chapter Two as well as to extend my deep appreciation to Keith Busby for reading Chapter Four and for his comments. Lucy Freeman Sandler has been a source of inspiration with her scholarship and I greatly appreciate her generosity in sending me a copy of her then unpublished essay "Mary de Bohun's *Livret de saintes* in Copenhagen." I gratefully acknowledge the generous grants I received from the Danish National Endowment for the Humanities, the Novo Nordisk Foundation, the Carlsberg Foundation as well as from the Ny Carlsberg Foundation, which provided subvention funding toward the costs of publishing the book. I am grateful to the Danish Academy in Rome for a one-month fellowship that permitted me to consult documents at the Archivio degli Agostiniani, Rome.

I am also greatly indebted to the Royal Library, Copenhagen where I researched and wrote this book and especially to Erland Kolding Nielsen, John T. Lauridsen, and Ivan Boserup who have helped me enormously in numerous ways. Additionally, I wish to thank Knud Ottosen for kindly reading an early draft of this book and, in particular, for his comments on the liturgical components of Thott 547, 4°. I am also much indebted to Bent Boel for his insightful comments. Thanks are also due to Michael H. Gelting and Ivan Boserup for help with Latin texts, to Anders Toftgaard for his assistance with Anglo-Norman French transcriptions and English translations, and to Karsten Christensen for giving me his opinion on the date of the manuscripts' bindings.

I received help on particular points from: Katherine Ludwig Jansen, Jenny Stratford, Jean-Louis Gabriel Benoit, Wendy Reardon, Elisa Brilli, Sven Rune Havsteen, Bea Gottlieb, Anna Russakoff, and Susan Boynton, and I thank them. My research was facilitated by the helpful staff at the libraries and archives where I researched this publication. Special thanks are due to: Kathleen Doyle and Justin Clegg at the British Library, London; Peter Greenhalgh and Nicholas Robinson at the Fitzwilliam Museum, Cambridge; Martin Kauffmann and Rigmor Batsvik at the Bodleian Library,

Oxford; Dorothee Feldmann at Kunstsammlungen Graf von Schönborn; Juliet Chadwick at Exeter College, Oxford; and the staff of the Archivio degli Agostiniani, Rome.

I would like to thank Nora Berend, Phillipp Schofield, and Erik Petersen for their advice and help as well as my student Susanne Aasted, with whom I have had interesting discussions about the Copenhagen Hours.

Finally, I would like to dedicate this book to my family: my sons, Sebastian Boel-Vidas and Mathias Boel-Vidas, my husband, Bent Boel, my aunt, Dubravka Kustec, my parents, Vlasta and Ljudevit Vidas, my brother, Neven Vidas, my sister-in-law, Denise Lender Vidas, my niece, Maya Vidas, my nephews, Nicolas Vidas and Nathan Murguia, as well as to Laura Juul Jensen and her family.

Introduction

THOTT 547, 4° AND Thott 517, 4° are two exquisitely illuminated fourteenth-century English manuscripts in the collection of the Royal Library in Copenhagen. Thott 547, 4°, containing many of the components of a Book of Hours, has an elaborate pictorial program that includes heraldic decoration and a portrait of its intended reader, while Thott 517, 4°, a volume comprising the legends of the Virgin, St. Margaret, and Mary Magdalene, is more sparsely decorated. On the basis of manuscript evidence, it has been shown that the two volumes now in Copenhagen were owned originally by a member of the Bohun family. The Bohuns were important patrons and collectors of illuminated books as well as one of the wealthiest families in England in the period and were related by descent and intermarriage to the royal family. Humphrey de Bohun, the seventh Earl of Hereford, sixth Earl of Essex, and second Earl of Northampton (1342–1373), was the grandson of Elizabeth Plantagenet, a daughter of Edward I, and Humphrey de Bohun, 4th Earl of Hereford and Essex, while his wife Joan Fitzalan (1347–1419) was the granddaughter of Blanche d'Artois, Queen of Navarre and Edmund "Crouchback," Earl of Lancaster, the second surviving son of Henry III. Humphrey and Joan de Bohun's elder daughter Eleanor (1367–1399) married Thomas of Woodstock (1355–1397), Edward III's youngest son, in 1376, while in 1381 their younger daughter Mary (1370–1394) wed Edward's grandson, Henry of Bolingbroke, the future Henry IV.

Scholars have attributed ten illuminated manuscripts to the patronage of the Bohuns in the second half of the fourteenth century. Most of these volumes have been judged to have been produced or completed predominantly by the family's atelier, and after the death of Humphrey, the seventh earl and the last direct male descendent of the family.[1] Stylistic, iconographic, paleographic, and codicological similarities between the two Copenhagen manuscripts and other books made for the Bohuns support the manuscripts' connection to this family. Furthermore, Thott 547, 4° displays the family's heraldic devices and armorials of their relatives as well as a portrait of a young female member of the family. It is generally held that the two books in Copenhagen were made for the seventh earl's younger daughter, Mary de Bohun, either around the time she wed Henry of Bolingbroke or sometime in the period between her marriage and her death.

State of the Research on the Bohun Manuscripts: Style, Production, Programs, and Dating

The importance of the ten books commissioned by the Bohuns has been acknowledged by many writers, and a large body of scholarship concerned with these exceptional manuscripts has been produced.[2] In this study, I will limit my summary of the literature to publications dealing with Thott 547, 4° and Thott 517, 4° and to those concerned with issues of the Bohun family's patronage and the production of their manuscripts, as it is these studies which have a bearing on the understanding of the images and texts in the two Copenhagen volumes. The scholars who have discussed Thott 547, 4° and Thott 517, 4° in earlier studies have shed light on the manuscripts' style, date, and their place in the chronology of production of Bohun manuscripts, as well as on the identification of scribal and artistic hands.

Christian Bruun was the first to describe the principal illuminations in Thott 547, 4° and to identify many of their subjects.[3] On the basis of the coats of arms present in Thott 547, 4°, which he stated were connected to those of Bohun, Hereford, and Lancaster, and the depiction of a female donor painted against a background decorated with Bohun arms, he conjectured that the manuscript could have been made for Mary de Bohun.[4] Bruun, furthermore, concluded that the two Copenhagen manuscripts were produced in the same atelier because the same colors were used in Thott 517, 4° as in Thott 547, 4°, and because both books were executed in the same manner.[5]

In a study of saints' legends written in French, Paul Meyer briefly discussed the three Anglo-Norman texts in Thott 517, 4°. He noted that there were five other manuscripts known to him containing the *Transitus mariae* found in Thott 517, 4° in various French dialects.[6] He also pointed out that the version of the *vita* of the Magdalene in the Copenhagen volume corresponds to a Picard one found in a manuscript containing miscellaneous texts (Paris, Bibliothèque Nationale de France, français 25532).[7] No other copies of the Anglo-French translation of the life of St. Margaret in Thott 517, 4° were known to Meyer.[8]

M. R. James, in a monograph concerned with five manuscripts made for members of the Bohun family (Vienna, Österreichische Nationalbibliothek, MS 1826; Oxford University, Exeter College, MS 47; Oxford, Bodleian Library, MS Auct.D.4.4.; Cambridge, Fitzwilliam Museum, MS 38–1950; and Thott 547, 4°), provided more detailed descriptions of the subject matter of the historiated initials, *haut-de-pages*, and *bas-de-pages* in Thott 547, 4° than

Bruun. He also presented alternative identifications of two of the subjects of the lower marginal illuminations.[9] James noticed that the program of illustration of Thott 547, 4° closely resembles that of the Hours of the Virgin in the Bodleian Library's Psalter-Hours. Eric Millar, in the introduction, judged that four of the discussed books were executed for Humphrey, the seventh earl, while MS Auct.D.4.4. was finished for Mary de Bohun and MS Thott 547, 4° was made for her.[10]

In one of her early publications concerned with the Bohun manuscripts that were made during the second half of the fourteenth century, Lucy Freeman Sandler argued that they are the work of a single group of artists, some of whose hands recur in two or more of the volumes.[11] Until Sandler's study was published, the Bohun volumes were thought to have been the work of anonymous artists. She uncovered the names of two Augustinian friars who worked as their illuminators, John de Teye and Henry Hood, in documents published by Francis Roth. Her judgment that de Teye and Hood worked at Pleshey Castle led her to make conclusions about the dates, origins, and stylistic continuity of the Bohun manuscripts and about the circumstances of their patronage.

In her survey of English Gothic illuminated manuscripts, Sandler catalogued the until then known Bohun volumes. She sensitively described the illuminations in Thott 547, 4° and Thott 517, 4°, which she believed at that time were the work of one hand.[12] She also brought attention to the fact that the format and size of Thott 517, 4° was similar, though not identical, to the Bodleian Psalter-Hours and the Fitzwilliam Psalter. She dated the Copenhagen manuscripts to the period of 1380–1394.

Lynda Dennison, in her doctoral dissertation, analyzed in great detail the group of books illuminated for the Bohuns between c. 1340–1400 and cast new light on their dating, production, localization, and ownership.[13] She charted the artistic development of the illuminators and found that some of the manuscripts, like the two Copenhagen volumes, were the products of a single campaign of work while others were worked on for successive members of the family. Dennison dated Bohun patronage to three distinctive phases. She dated the first phase, in which the English sources of the Bohun style lie, to the 1340s, and argued that the activity of these probably Cambridge-based illuminators was curtailed by the Black Death. She judged the second phase, which was more homogeneous than the first and spanned from the early 1350s to the mid 1380s, to be comprised of the work of two artists who made manuscripts exclusively for the Bohuns at Pleshey Castle, Essex. Dennison called them the "English Artist" and the "Flemish Hand," a painter whose origins she localized to Tournai and Ghent. It is to this period that she assigns the production of Thott 517, 4° and Thott 547, 4°. In Dennison's view, the Fitzwilliam Psalter and the Bodleian Psalter-Hours were painted c. 1370–1372/3, primarily by the Flemish Hand, and it was the English Artist who painted the Beatus pages in the Fitzwilliam Psalter and the Bodleian Psalter-Hours as well as the full page miniatures on single leaves in the Psalter-Hours. She judged that the latter paintings are probably marginally later in date. The stylistic ambivalence represented by the English Artist's miniatures in Pommersfelden suggest to her that this work stands chronologically between the single inserted leaves in the Bodleian Psalter-Hours and the two manuscripts in Copenhagen, while still showing attachment to the Vienna Exeter tradition. The Copenhagen manuscripts, in Dennison's opinion, embody a new stylistic phase and were executed c. 1380–1384.[14] The third phase of Bohun authorized manuscript production, which she dated to c. 1385–1400, took place in the aftermath of the demise or departure of the resident miniaturists.

In several articles, Dennison further developed ideas put forth in her thesis.[15] She argued that Oxford, Exeter College MS 47 was executed in three campaigns between c. 1360 and 1400.[16] Her analysis of the codicology and style of two other manuscripts made for the Bohun family, the Psalter in Vienna and the Psalter-Hours in the British Library, showed that they, too, were products of interrupted campaigns of work.[17] Dennison hypothesized that the reason the Egerton and Exeter manuscripts were not immediately completed after the sixth earl's death may have been due to a shift in fashion to smaller format books, reflected in the taste of the seventh earl. After the seventh earl's death, work on the three manuscripts was taken up again in the 1380s. Dennison argued that the major illuminator of the British Library's Egerton manuscript was Henry Hood, and she dates the final campaign of work to between c. 1384/5 and 1389.

In 1989 Felix Heinzer published his discovery of a fragmentary Psalter (Baden-Baden, Lichtenthal Abbey, Archiv, MS 2), which on historical and stylistic grounds, he argued, was written and illuminated for a member of the Bohun family around 1380.[18] He judged that the volumes in Lichtenthal, Copenhagen, and Pommersfelden were part of a single manuscript.[19] In the same year, John Rees Smith published a partial transcription of the Apostolic and Eremitic Life of Mary Magdalene in Thott 517, 4°, ff. 29–38, and discussed its Latin antecedents.[20]

In a number of articles, Lucy F. Sandler has analyzed the pictorial programs of three of the family's Psalters, illuminated with historiated initials at the opening of every Psalm, namely those in Vienna, Oxford, and London.[21] Sandler demonstrated how the small group of artists inventively translated texts into images and designed pictorial programs that are significantly different from one another. The Vienna Psalter illustrates the Psalms according to their words, while the Exeter College and British Library manuscripts use a historic mode of illustration of the Old Testament. She also argued that the images in Psalters associated with Humphrey, the seventh earl, and his wife, Joan de Bohun, communicated political views very similar to those in *The Prophecy of John of Bridlington*, a work dedicated to the earl.[22] Sandler showed that the importance of the Bohuns in the fourteenth century is reflected in allusions to contemporary politics in the depictions of Old Testament subject matter. Sandler also hypothesized that after the seventh earl's death, it was Joan de Bohun who commissioned additional work on unfinished Bohun manuscripts as well as on new devotional books.

In another important article, Sandler studied the armorials represented in a number of personal devotional books (Copenhagen Hours, Egerton Psalter-Hours, Fitzwilliam Psalter, Bodleian Psalter-Hours, Pommersfelden MS 348, *Lichtenthal Psalter*) made for the Bohuns in the second half of the fourteenth century and judged that some had been incorrectly identified in studies earlier than her own.[23] Sandler's examination of one of the shields in the Copenhagen Hours led her to conclude that it displayed the arms of the heir apparent and not those of John of Gaunt, as had been postulated in earlier studies. Sandler also argued that the destined owners of the Copenhagen Hours and four other manuscripts of the Bohun group were Mary de Bohun and/or Henry of Bolingbroke.[24] The coats of arms in the Copenhagen Hours, in Sandler's view, project the dynastic vision of Joan de Bohun.[25]

Sarah Glover, in her unpublished dissertation focusing on the pictorial representations of miracles of the Virgin appearing in fourteen manuscripts, included a discussion of the iconography of the Marian legends depicted in three mansucripts she considered were owned by Mary de Bohun: the Bodleian Library's Bohun Psalter-Hours, the British Library's Psalter-Hours, and the *bas-de-page* in Thott 547, 4°.[26] Like a number of Sandler's articles, Glover's study pointed out the relationship between texts and images in Bohun manuscripts. She argued that the Bodleian Psalter Hours were given to Mary de Bohun as a coming of age gift and marked her transformation from girl to woman and from child to penitent, and that it might have been Mary herself who commissioned the Copenhagen manuscript.[27]

In the *Lichtenthal Psalter*, Sandler analyzed in detail the iconography of the illuminations and the division of artistic and scribal hands, and placed the Psalter in the wider context of extant manuscripts produced for the Bohuns.[28] Sandler judged that the Lichtenthal manuscript was executed by John de Teye and two other individuals, and that de Teye was responsible for both the principal illluminations of the Psalter as well as those of the Copenhagen Hours.[29] She concluded that the scribe of the *Lichtenthal Psalter* was also responsible for writing the text of Thott 517, 4° and Thott 547, 4°, except f. 1.[30] Although Sandler found that the illustrations in the Copenhagen Hours were more developed in style, with more "tricks" of illusion and figures clothed in fashionable garments of a later date, she did not date the Copenhagen books nor the *Lichtenthal Psalter* any more precisely than 1380–1394.[31] Her analyisis of the iconography of the illumnations led her to conclude that the artists had a high degree of literacy and Biblical knowledge.

Erik Drigsdahl's transcription of the texts found in Thott 547, 4°, and his commentary on its liturgical content, are available on the web.[32] Full digital facsimiles of the two Copenhagen manuscripts under discussion here are available on the Royal Library's site.[33]

Shortly after a chance meeting in 2007 with Lucy Freeman Sandler at the British Library in London where I was doing research on the two Copenhagen Bohun manuscripts, Professor Sandler kindly sent her unpublished contribution to Nigel Morgan's festschrift concerning the Copenhagen Lives. I have profited from reading it and on those occasions where I have drawn on information in her essay, and of which I was previously unaware, I have footnoted her now published article.[34]

In sum, the literature to date dealing with the two Copenhagen manuscripts is substantial and the observations of the authors in these scholarly works are important and provide the foundations for this study. In the first chapter, I chart the history of the circumstances of the Bohuns, focusing on the period after the death of the seventh earl. It is hoped that such a detailed analysis of the historic record will shed light on the situation of the Bohuns, important for understanding the family's patronage, as well as on the place and circumstances of production of the Bohun manuscripts, particularly on the two works that are the focus of this study. Thott 547, 4°, the more elaborately and extensively illuminated of the two manuscripts, is presented first. In light of the information I shed on the provenance of the Copenhagen Hours, it can no longer be taken for granted that Mary de Bohun was its original owner. Therefore, the possibility that Eleanor de Bohun is represented on folio 1 of Thott 547, 4° will be explored. I then discuss the components of Thott 517, 4°. Possible meanings that the texts and images would have had for their intended reader are suggested. I also address the identity of the patron of the Copenhagen volumes.

The Historical Background

IN 1359, JOAN FITZALAN, then aged twelve, married seventeen-year-old Humphrey de Bohun, heir of William de Bohun, first Earl of Northampton.[1] Joan was the eldest daughter of Richard Fitzalan, Earl of Arundel (c. 1306–1376), and his second wife, Eleanor Plantagenet, daughter of Henry, third Earl of Lancaster, and Maud Chaworth. The marriage was negotiated by the two fathers of the bride and the groom, and they also arranged for Joan's brother, Richard, to wed Humphrey's nine-year-old sister, Elizabeth (born c. 1350). By marrying his heir to the other's daughter, each father ensured a strong bond with an influential wealthy family, and, additionally, did not have to pay a marriage portion, which was not a dowry but rather a price for a husband.[2] These were not the only unions with distinguished and wealthy families arranged for Richard Fitzalan's children. For his youngest daughter, Alice (1352–1416), the earl negotiated a match in 1364 with Thomas Holland, later Earl of Kent, the young heir and half-brother of the future Richard II.[3] An advantageous marriage was also orchestrated for John Fitzalan (born c. 1348) who by 1357 had wed Eleanor (born 1345), a co-heiress of the baronial house of Mautravers.[4] For his son, Thomas (1353–1414), Richard Fitzalan obtained the see of Ely.[5]

Humphrey de Bohun was a minor when his father died in 1360 and when his uncle, the sixth earl, died without issue in 1361. He did not inherit their titles, his father's properties, and his uncle's vast estates until 1363.[6] Shortly afterwards, in c. 1365, he became a knight of the Garter. In 1367, eight years after Humphrey's marriage to Joan, a daughter, Eleanor, was born to them; and three years later, in 1370, Joan gave birth to her second daughter, Mary.[7] Not long afterwards, on January 26, 1373, Humphrey de Bohun died. And so, at the age of twenty-five and after fourteen years of marriage, Joan de Bohun became a widow.

In February 1374, King Edward III ordered a survey to be made of the Bohun properties.[8] Inheritance of feudal lands in medieval England was determined by primogeniture: the eldest son was his parents' sole heir. However, in the absence of a male heir, any surviving female children inherited equal portions of the estate. When Eleanor and Mary, Joan's two daughters, were around fourteen years old, and married, they were entitled to a third of their father's lands. Before then, their inheritance was in the hands of the king.[9] Their widowed mother received a dower, the life use of roughly one third of the deceased's estates.[10] By March 9, 1373 Joan de Bohun had taken the oath of fealty to the king, promising not to remarry without his permission.[11] The king issued orders after this to deliver in dower castles, manors, lands, etc., in Essex, Huntingdonshire, Buckinghamshire, Middlesex, Wiltshire, London, and Surrey.[12] Joan was also assigned knight's fees and advowsons.[13] Humphrey's will was proved on May 7, 1373.[14]

Joan de Bohun, née Fitzalan, was a member of the highest nobility and still young at the time of her husband's death. Her lineage and her share of his husband's estates as well as her family's connections would have made her a desirable bride.[15] Yet she did not remarry. A contributing factor in the countess remaining a widow may have been that Joan's father died in 1376, shortly after her husband. Had Richard Fitzalan lived he might have pressured his daughter to remarry for the sake of an alliance with a family from which he might have derived political or economic benefits. It is also likely that Joan herself did not wish to remarry, or to enter a nunnery at that stage of her life. Widowhood had advantages. According to Joel T. Rosenthal, the data on remarriage indicates that many wealthy widows were free to avoid remarriage and exercised this freedom.[16] For wealthy noblewomen, widowhood could lead to a life of unprecedented freedom, power, influence, and financial independence, especially if they were capable of managing their household and estates.[17] Joan appears to have exhibited managerial skills during her married life, and as a young widow, since her husband and her father both named her as one of the supervisors of their wills, a sign of their confidence in her competence to carry out their wishes.[18]

After the earl's death, in 1373, Edward III granted Humphrey de Bohun's executors the right to have his castles, manors, lordships, and lands, etc., in England and the march of Wales for one whole year.[19] The following year, in 1374, the king assigned "the wardship of the castle and manor of Plessis" as well as other properties to Thomas de Maundevill until Eleanor and Mary came of age.[20]

The right of custody of minor children did not belong to the mother but rather to the feudal overlord, who could decide to sell or give away the guardianship of the heir. Mary and Eleanor were thus the king's wards and Edward III held their estates during their minority.[21] Wardship of an heir was potentially a lucrative business. As custodian of the land, the guardian enjoyed the entire profits of the estate and was obligated only to maintain the child. Wardship of the body carried with it the right to negotiate the heir's marriage, which in many cases resulted in the arrangement of a match with one of the guardian's own children. While very young, a small percentage of children were left at home with their mother who was paid for their maintenance, often a pittance in comparison to the overall sum paid to the guardian.[22] The period the child remained with the mother varied according to the guardian's wishes, but usually came to an end when the child was betrothed or married at the age of six or seven.[23] The child would then begin a life with their future spouse, either in their own home, or at the home of their prospective parents-in-law.[24]

With their vast inheritance and illustrious lineage, Eleanor and Mary were highly desirable brides. Not surprisingly, the king quickly found the eldest daughter, Eleanor, a prospective husband – namely, his own son, Thomas of Woodstock. As the youngest of Edward's five surviving sons, Thomas could not look forward to much of an inheritance so it was essential for Thomas's finances and status that he married a wealthy woman. In April 1374, a little over a year after Humphrey's death, and in anticipation of his marriage to Eleanor, Edward III granted Thomas of Woodstock a number of the manors that were part of her inheritance.[25] He also granted the couple 300 pounds until the girl came of age.[26]

By June of 1374, Eleanor and Thomas were married. Evidence of the wedding can be found in a document dating from June 1374 recording John of Gaunt's gift of a goblet and an ewer to his sister-in-law, Eleanor, on the day of her marriage.[27] According to canon law, in order for a couple to be considered married it was required that the bride and groom freely consent to the union and that they were old enough to express their willingness to be married. The age of consent was interpreted generally as twelve for girls and fourteen for boys, but in practice children in England were married much younger.[28] Secondly, a marriage needed to be consummated.[29] However, it was not required that intercourse between the couple take place immediately after the exchange of vows. Sexual relations were usually postponed in the case of girls until they reached the age of at least fourteen because of the dangers childbirth posed to them. Both Joan Fitzalan and her sister-in-law, Elizabeth de Bohun, did not bear any children until after their fifteenth birthday, suggesting that consummation of their marriages had been delayed. Eleanor de Bohun's first child, Humphrey Plantagenet, was born around 1381, after she had proved her age, so it is imaginable that she and Thomas of Woodstock had waited to consummate the marriage.[30]

Edward III was masterful in his use of wardships and marriages to reward his favorites and relatives, and particularly his own children.[31] The king also arranged the union between his second surviving son, Lionel of Antwerp (1338–1368) and the heiress, Elizabeth de Burgh (1332–1363), daughter of William de Burgh, 3rd Earl of Ulster (d. 1332).[32] On May 19, 1359 the king's third surviving son, John of Gaunt (1340–1399), married Blanche of Lancaster (c. 1345–1369) who two years later became co-heiress with her older sister, Maud, to the earl of Lancaster's estates.[33] In 1362 Maud died, leaving no surviving children and making Gaunt an immensely wealthy man.[34] Edward III also wanted to arrange a marriage between his fourth son, Edmund of Langley, and the widowed Margaret, heiress of Louis II, Count of Flanders. However, his hopes were dashed when a more advantageous match was found for Margaret who married Philip, Duke of Burgundy, brother of the French king, in 1369.[35]

After Thomas of Woodstock's marriage to Eleanor de Bohun, Edward III continued to provide his son with further sources of income.[36] On June 10, 1376 Thomas was appointed Constable of England, an office that had been hereditary in the Bohun family and that had been held by Humphrey, Eleanor's father.[37] Two months later the king visited his son at Pleshey and advanced him 1,000 marks out of the lands of the late Humphrey de Bohun.[38] Thomas was awarded additional support from Eleanor's manors, including the Bohun family's principal residence, Pleshey Castle.[39]

It is imaginable that once Thomas of Woodstock was installed at Pleshey in 1376, Joan was no longer living there. Dowagers were expected to retire to their lands, although they might be invited to marriage celebrations, baptisms, and religious feasts at their married children's homes. On June 21, 1377 Edward III died and his ten-year-old grandson, Richard, became king of England. Thomas of Woodstock was created Earl of Buckingham in 1377 and in the same year the young king's uncle was granted £1,000 a year for life should his wife, Eleanor, die without issue.[40] Thomas also served Richard in a naval expedition.[41] During Eleanor's minority, the Earl of Buckingham, however, was still underendowed and dependent on crown grants.[42]

But what of Mary de Bohun? As far as can be gathered from the existing record, her guardian had not made any arrangements for finding her a husband. It is possible that Edward III might have seen advantages in Mary remaining unmarried so that the Bohun estates would not be partitioned and his son, Thomas, could eventually come into sole control of Humphrey de Bohun's lands, and so until that time he would enjoy the profits of Mary's estates. Edward had, on at least one occasion, been involved with having a wealthy co-heiress placed in a nunnery, thus enabling her married sister to inherit the entire estate.[43]

No payments have been found for Mary de Bohun's maintenance until two and a half years after Edward III's death, so her whereabouts until that time are not known. The first record of a payment is dated March 10, 1380 when Joan de Bohun was granted 100 marks retroactively from January 16, 1380 during the reign of Edward III's successor.[44] Around the time Joan was allocated funds for Mary's maintenance, preparations were being made for new military undertakings in France under the command of Thomas of Woodstock.[45] On May 3 of that year, he was appointed to lead the expedition. The expenses he would have incurred might have prompted the earl to look for additional sources of income.[46] On May 8, 1380 Thomas of Woodstock was granted custody without rent of Mary's share of her inheritance.[47] By June, Eleanor had come of age and on June 22, 1380 orders were given to escheators to give Thomas and Eleanor seisin of her moiety of the Bohun inheritance.[48] Thomas must have believed that he had put his financial and other affairs in order before leaving for Brittany. However, immediately after Thomas's departure his brother John of Gaunt, on July 27, 1380, bought from the king, to the value of 5,000 marks that were owed to him for his services in war, the right to arrange Mary de Bohun's marriage.[49] Jean Froissart, who had served in the household of Edward III's queen, Philippa of Hainault, from 1361–1368, and who returned to England in 1395, provides in his chronicles a description of the events leading to Mary de Bohun's marriage:

> There fell out about this time, in England, an event that gave great displeasure to the earl of Buckingham when he heard of it. I will explain to you what it was. Humphrey earl of Hereford and Northampton, constable of England, was one of the greatest lords and landholders in that country; for it was said, and I, the author of this book, heard it when I resided in England, that his revenue was valued at fifty thousand nobles a-year. From this earl of Hereford there remained only two daughters as his heiresses; Blanche the eldest, and Isabella her sister. The eldest was married to Thomas of Woodstock, earl of Buckingham. The youngest was unmarried, and the earl of Buckingham would willingly have had her remain so, for then he would have enjoyed the whole of the earl of Hereford's fortune. Upon his marriage with Eleanor, he went to reside at his handsome castle of Pleshy, in the county of Essex, thirty miles from London, which he possessed in right of his wife; He took on himself the tutelage of his sister-in-law, and had her instructed in doctrine; for it was his intention she should be professed a nun of the order of St. Clare, which had a very rich and large convent in England. In this manner was she educated during the time the earl remained in England, before his expedition into France. She was also constantly at-

tended by nuns from this convent, who tutored her in matters of religion, continually blaming the married state. The young lady seemed to incline to their doctrine, and thought not of marriage.

Duke John of Lancaster, being a prudent and wise man foresaw the advantage of marrying his only son Henry, by his first wife Blanche, to the lady Mary: he was heir to all the possessions of the house of Lancaster in England, which were very considerable. The duke had for some time considered he could not choose a more desirable wife for his son than the lady who was intended for a nun, as her estates were very large, and her birth suitable to any rank; but he did not take any steps in the matter until his brother of Buckingham had set out on his expedition to France. When he had crossed the sea, the duke of Lancaster had the young lady conducted to Arundel castle; for the aunt of the two ladies was the sister of Richard, earl of Arundel, one of the most powerful barons of England. This lady Arundel, out of complaisance to the duke of Lancaster, and for the advancement of the young lady, went to Pleshy, where she remained with the countess of Buckingham and her sister for fifteen days. On her departure from Pleshy, she managed so well that she carried with her the Mary to Arundel where the marriage was instantly consummated between her and Henry of Lancaster. During their union of twelve years, he had by her four handsome sons, Henry, Thomas, John and Humphrey, and two daughters, Blanche and Philippa. The earl of Buckingham, as I said, had not any inclination to laugh when he heard these tidings; for it would now be necessary to divide an inheritance which he considered wholly as his own, excepting the constableship which was continued to him. When he learnt that his brothers had all been concerned in this matter, he became melancholy, and never after loved the duke of Lancaster as he had hitherto done.[50]

Froissart was not in England at the time these events took place but the account appears credible. There are only a few verifiable inaccuracies in this story, none serious enough to cast doubt on it. Initially, in the version of Froissart's Chronicles translated by Thomas Johnes but no longer extant, Humphrey's daughters are mistakenly called Blanche and Isabella. Shortly after introducing them by these names they are then correctly called Eleanor and Mary.

In this version, the lady who takes Mary from Pleshey is called "Lady Arundel" and is described as "the aunt of the two ladies" and "sister of Richard, earl of Arundel." No historical person exactly fitting these descriptions was known as Lady Arundel. Mary and Eleanor did have an aunt, Alice, who like their mother was a sister of Richard, Earl of Arundel. Alice Fitzalan, however, would not have been known as Lady Arundel. Upon her marriage in 1364, Alice was styled as Lady Holland, and after her husband became earl in 1381, as Countess of Kent. The Earl of Arundel's other sister was the girl's mother, Joan de Bohun, who was known as Countess of Hereford, Essex, and Northampton, or Countess of Hereford. Froissart's chronicles also state that the marriage between Mary and Henry was consummated at Arundel. However, information in John of Gaunt's register suggests that the marriage took place at Joan de Bohun's manor of Rochford.[51] Adding further credibility to the marriage being consummated at Joan's castle is that it was quite common for consummation of the marriage to take place in the home of the bride's parents following the wedding. It is, therefore, likely that the woman called Lady Arundel in Froissart's Chronicles was in fact Joan de Bohun, sister of Richard, Earl of Arundel, and that the marriage was consummated at her castle.[52]

Froissart's account – in which he describes Thomas of Woodstock residing at Pleshey Castle upon his marriage, and then in the following sentence introduces the fact that Buckingham had Mary de Bohun instructed in doctrine and attended by nuns – suggests that the girl could have lived for a longer period at Pleshey with her sister and brother-in-law, perhaps from 1376. Although conferring custody of a minor co-heiress to an elder sister and her spouse unfairly benefited one party over the other, this type of arrangement was not without parallel.[53]

Mary de Bohun married Henry of Bolingbroke before March 6, 1381, the date on which payments were recorded for expenses incurred by John of Gaunt for gifts and entertainment for his son's wedding.[54] By the time Thomas of Woodstock returned from France in the spring of 1381, there was little he could do.[55]

In the first few years of her marriage, Mary de Bohun did not live with her husband. This is evident from a record, dated January 31, 1382, of an annuity of 100 marks granted to the dowager countess by Gaunt for the girl's maintenance until she was fourteen.[56] Consummation was key to the marriage formation and made it indissoluble. Therefore, in order for Henry to guarantee Mary's inheritance, sexual intercourse might, as Froissart states, have taken place immediately following the marriage but afterwards it might have been thought too risky for the girl to continue to be sexually active. In a study by John Carmi Parsons focusing on the matrimonial and maternal careers of members of the noble houses of Plantagenet, Mortimer of March, and Holland of Kent, between 1150 and 1500, only in seven of eighty-seven documentable cases was marriage followed by childbirth when the mother was younger than fifteen.[57] Parson judges that consumation of marriage was usually delayed because of the high risks of childbirth associated with very young mothers.

Froissart's story about Thomas planning to place Mary with the Clares is not far-fetched. Girls could not make their professions before a suitable age, twelve or later, when they were given the veil, and had to wait even later until they could be solemnly professed by the bishop. Woodstock had a close connection to the Franciscan nuns and had his own daughter, Isabelle (born c. 1385/6), donated to the house of the Minoresses without Aldgate when she was a baby.[58]

Joan de Bohun would have been close enough to Gaunt to carry out a plan to take Mary away from Pleshey, like the one described by Froissart. The motives, according to Froissart, of "lady Arundel, [who] out of complaisance to the duke of Lancaster, and for the advancement of the young lady" for facilitating Henry of Bolingbroke to wed Mary de Bohun seem likely ones. The dowager countess was Gaunt's kinswoman: they were both descendents of Henry III. She was a first cousin of Henry of Bolingbroke's mother, the duke's first wife, Blanche of Lancaster.[59] Gaunt was also related to Joan's husband, the seventh earl, with whom he had had a good relationship.[60]

The marriage of Mary to Henry had a number of advantages for Gaunt. By marrying his son to a wealthy heiress, Gaunt ensured his son's financial future without giving up much of his own fortune. He also recovered the 5,000 marks owed to him, albeit that it was a generous amount for Mary's marriage. The arrangement also made sense for the crown since allowing Mary to enter a nunnery would not have benefitted the king's purse and would have made Thomas of Woodstock a very rich man.

For Joan, the marriage would have had advantages as well. She was reinforcing the bond between herself and Gaunt, and her daughter would become the wife of the heir to one of the largest fortunes in England and one day be elevated to the title of Duchess of Lancaster. In the case of Henry's death, Mary would have been a very wealthy woman. Another attraction of marrying Mary to the son of John of Gaunt, which must have appealed to Joan de Bohun's dynastic ambitions, was Gaunt's place in the line of succession to the English throne.[61]

In 1376, following the death of the Black Prince, the eldest son and heir of Edward III, the sixty-four-year-old king laid down the order of succession.[62] His wishes were recorded in a document known only to men in his immediate circle. The English king had the right to choose his successor if the matter was in doubt. Richard of Bordeaux, the Black Prince's heir, was only nine years old in 1376. The prospect of the succession of a child was not without its pitfalls and had led in the past to political unrest.[63] While Edward I laid down the order of succession, commencing with his surviving son, Edward of Carnarvon, and any subsequent sons, and continuing with his two surviving daughters and any subsequent daughters, Edward III created an entail in the male line.[64] He named his grandson, Richard, and his three surviving sons, John, Edmund, and Thomas, in turn. Those who knew of the document were aware that it made Gaunt the heir apparent, and after him, his son, Henry of Bolingbroke. The consequence of the declaration was to bar Philippa (d. 1378), daughter and heir of Edward III's third son, Lionel, Duke of Clarence (d. 1368), and mother of Roger Mortimer (1374–1398), fourth Earl of March and sixth Earl of Ulster, from the order of succession. Although this document was not known publicly, Michael Bennett judges that the potential beneficiaries of the declaration, John of Gaunt and Edward's other sons, were privy to its contents and that Richard II would have been made aware of the document early in his reign, if not before.[65] An important reason why the declaration in which Edward III had determined that John of Gaunt was Richard's heir was not made public was that Gaunt was extremely unpopular in the years 1376–1381. Had the contents of the document been widely known there might have been a public uproar. The issue of the succession was only relevant if Richard had no children, and in Bennett's opinion there would have been no point in drawing public attention to this document and stirring up the anti-Gaunt discontent while Richard's ability to father an heir was still unknown.

In 1385, or possibly 1386, the teenaged king made an announcement, naming Roger Mortimer heir to the throne. However, Ian Mortimer has argued that this was never an official position.[66] Richard made the declaration, in Mortimer's view, to challenge the Lancastrian position in the order of succession as laid down by Edward III's entail. The context for Richard's announcement was that after the 1386 parliament the king was threatened with deposition and would have had to abdicate in favor of an heir. By naming a twelve-year-old child as his successor, Richard hoped to divide and rule. He was also flexing his muscles, making a point that he could remove Henry of Bolingbroke from the succession at will. Mortimer judges that the announcement of 1386 was only a notional or temporary elevation of the Mortimers.[67] In December 1387, at the persuasion of the Lords Apellant – a group of nobles that included Thomas of Woodstock, so-called because they appealed or accused of treason some of the king's favorites – Richard acknowledged Gaunt as his heir in line with Edward's entail.[68]

If there was a rift between Thomas of Woodstock and his brother and mother-in-law created by the marrige of Mary and Henry, it was mended not long afterwards. Gaunt and Woodstock exchanged presents in 1382 and Thomas sent a squire to Henry to announce the birth of his son.[69] In 1383, Joan and Thomas dined together at the home of Bishop Arundel, Joan's brother.[70] In December 1384, after Mary's age had been proved, Henry and Mary started to receive part of her share of her father's castles, manors, and lands, as well as of the knight's fees, and parts of fees and advowsons assigned to her.[71]

The Illuminators

I WILL NOW CONSIDER the question of the location of the Bohun atelier after the death of the seventh earl, and will begin by summarizing the scholarship. On the basis of stylistic analysis, it has been proposed in the literature and generally accepted that the painted decorations in the two Copenhagen manuscripts made for the Bohun family were executed by two artists. In Lynda Dennison's opinion, their work is first seen in the second campaign of the Vienna Psalter, which she dates as taking place in the 1350s.[1] The hands of the two artists, who Dennison has called "the English Artist" and "the Flemish Hand," are also visible in a number of the Bohun manuscripts, including the Exeter Psalter, the British Library's Psalter-Hours, the Fitzwilliam Psalter, the Bodleian Library's Psalter-Hours, the Pommersfelden fragment, and the *Lichtenthal Psalter*. Beside these two painters, other artists did contribute to illuminating and embellishing the Bohun manuscripts – for example, parts of the British Library's Psalter-Hours, the folia inserted in the Bodleian Library's Psalter-Hours, the overpainted miniatures in the *Romance of Lancelot*, and in the *Lichtenthal Psalter*.[2] During the 1390s, the Bohuns turned to commercial illuminators in London.[3]

As has been pointed out by Lucy Sandler, one of the illuminators working for the Bohuns appears to have resided at the family's chief residence, Pleshey Castle in Essex, during the lifetime of Eleanor and Mary's great-uncle, Humphrey de Bohun, sixth Earl of Hereford and Essex (1309–1361).[4] In the sixth earl's will, dated 1361, an Augustinian friar, John de Teye, called "our illuminator," was bequeathed £10 to pray for Humphrey's soul.[5] This bequest is stated after detailed instructions for the earl's burial and masses for his soul, bequests to religious institutions, and directly after gifts and provisions for Brother William de Monkelane, the sixth earl's confessor and one of the executors of his will. The rather substantial sum of the bequest, its placement in the will, plus the fact that in the same will John "Luminour" is left an additional 40s., suggest that de Teye played a role of some note in the household.[6]

From evidence in another document, it can be deduced that de Teye was still involved in manuscript illumination in 1384.[7] Bartholomeus Venetus, the prior general of the Augustinian friars in Rome, on May 20, 1384 gave Brother John de Teye written permission to summon Brother Henry Hood and instruct him in the art of manuscript illumination.[8] Francis Roth, who published the document, judged that because dispensation for Brother

Henry's training was needed, John de Teye must not have been staying at a friary.[9]

The contents of the sixth earl's will of 1361, and of the 1384 document giving Brother John permission to summon Brother Henry, led Sandler to conclude that in 1384 John de Teye was working at Pleshey Castle, where he most likely had lived in 1361 when the sixth earl made his will. However, neither Pleshey Castle nor the Bohuns are mentioned in the 1384 document. Although it is possible, as Sandler suggests, that de Teye lived and worked at Pleshey in 1384, it is equally possible that he lived and worked elsewhere.

There is manuscript evidence to support Sandler's hypothesis that John de Teye was still working for the Bohuns in 1384. The most compelling is that there are two hands which continuously appear in manuscripts made for members of the family between the 1350s and 1380s. Dennison and Sandler have argued that one of these hands is John de Teye's.[10]

Dennison, but not Sandler, believes that the British Library's Psalter-Hours (London, BL, MS Egerton 3277), a work judged to have been mostly illuminated in the 1380s, includes several pages painted by a close follower of one of the chief painters of the Bohun atelier and that this close follower was probably Henry Hood.[11] The problem with identifying the Egerton Hand as Hood is that all we know about this friar is that he was trained by de Teye "for a period of a year." We cannot, therefore, be certain that Hood continued to work with de Teye after that interval of time.

What can be surmised from the documentary and stylistic evidence is that in 1384 someone thought highly enough of the miniature painting of John de Teye to engage him to teach Brother Henry Hood. Another observation that can be made is that not just any man was apprenticed to de Teye. Henry Hood was an Augustinian friar. The reasons for this interest in training a friar as an illuminator can only be guessed.[12]

If the Bohuns were behind the request for de Teye to train Hood then perhaps a reason for the petition, and probably for the Prior General's consent, was the family's longstanding close connection to the order of St. Augustine.[13] Humphrey, the sixth earl, had not only employed Augustinian friars in his household but more importantly was a generous patron of the order.[14] It is likely that the sixth earl's illuminator, John de Teye, who was asked to pray for his employer's soul, had other functions in the household, most likely of a religious nature. Humphrey, the seventh earl, and his wife, Joan de Bohun, are also known to have had ties to the friars.[15] Both of the Bohun co-heiresses had connections to the priory of Augustinian canons of

LLlanthony, which their family had patronized since the twelfth century.[16]

I would like to take up Lynda Dennison's important observation that "Many of the Bohun manuscripts were illuminated in several campaigns, reflecting the circumstances of the family."[17] From the conclusions drawn by Dennison and Sandler about the chronology of the extant Bohun manuscripts, it appears that there was not much painting carried out during the 1370s. It might be concluded from this observation that after Humphrey's death the Bohun artists were not engaged in the production of manuscripts, or that their work from this period is lost. Documentary evidence suggests that a reason for a lull in activity could be attributed to the family's situation. Pleshey Castle, where the atelier was presumably located at least until 1373, was no longer held by the family after the earl's death.[18] In 1376, two years after Thomas of Woodstock's marriage to Eleanor de Bohun, the twenty-one-year-old Thomas received Pleshey Castle from his father.[19] Thomas of Woodstock, at the time of his arrest and confiscation of his property, had a library of eighty-four books and, additionally, forty-two books for chapel.[20] Although it was on a much smaller scale than those of male bibliophiles on the continent – such as the French king Charles V, for example, who owned about 1,000 books, or of Gian Galeazzo Visconti, Duke of Milan (d.1402), whose library was even more extensive – Woodstock's collection was one of the largest in private hands in England.[21] How many of the books in total in the library in Pleshey Castle were added by Thomas, and how many stemmed from the collection of his wife's family is not known.[22] As pointed out by Sandler, Thomas and Eleanor were very young when they came into possession of the family castle and were not likely to be that interested in buying or commissioning books. Nevertheless, it is not impossible that the Bohun artists worked at Pleshey in the decade that followed the seventh earl's death.

Another possibility is that the illuminators, who had a past connection to Joan de Bohun, might have left Pleshey and entered her household. The two principal painters had worked for the seventh earl while he and his wife lived at the castle.[23] Completed manuscripts were likely to have been considered Thomas of Woodstock's property when he took over Pleshey Castle and probably remained there. However, if Joan left the family residence with the illuminators, it is possible that incomplete manuscripts (for example, quires from the Vienna Psalter, the Exeter Psalter, Pommersfelden MS 348, the British Library's Psalter-Hours, and the Bodleian's Psalter-Hours) might have been removed from the atelier and later completed at the dowager countess's command.

With the exception of the period in which there was a break in the relationship between Thomas of Woodstock and Joan de Bohun, if such a break did occur, in principle the painters could have produced manuscripts for the earl's widow or the co-heiresses and their husbands, regardless of the atelier's location. It is also worth noting that the year Hood began his apprenticeship with John de Teye was the same year Mary de Bohun came of age and began living with her husband, Henry of Bolingbroke. It is, therefore, possible that Hood may have been summoned to help with the production of manuscripts for Mary.

Part One

Chapter One

Description of Thott 547, 4°

THOTT 547, 4° in its present state contains the Hours of the Virgin (ff. 1–31v), the Seven Penitential Psalms (ff. 32v–38v), a Litany (ff. 38v–41), as well as an Office of the Dead (ff. 43–66v). It has an extraordinarily beautifully executed pictorial program, consisting of a cycle of ten six-line historiated initials depicting events from the Infancy, the Passion, and the Last Judgment, two *haut-de-pages* showing Christological events, and ten *bas-de-pages*, eight of which show Miracles of the Virgin. The manuscript is further handsomely embellished with rectilinear borders, one of which encompasses a portrait of its intended owner, heraldic shields, and decorative initials as well as abstract, zoomorphic, and vegetal line endings.

In this chapter, the different parts of Thott 547, 4° are presented and analyzed. I begin with a codicological assessment, continue with an examination of the manuscript from front to back starting with the Office of the Virgin, and end with a discussion of the binding. Lengthy descriptions of the miniatures and analysis of their narratives are provided in the following chapter.

Collation, Page and Text Block Dimensions, Condition

In its present state, Thott 547, 4° contains 66 folios measuring 129 × 179 mm. The manuscript consists of eight quaternions and two extra leaves.[1] The vellum is of very fine quality; it is white, thin, smooth, and well prepared. The hair and skin sides of the folia are nearly indistinguishable from each other. The text block of twenty lines of script, measuring 67/68 × 108/9 mm, is surrounded by broad margins. The folios have been trimmed. The size of the manuscript makes it easily portable and the page design easy to read.

The Hours of the Virgin (Sarum Use), ff. 1–31v

The Office or Hours of the Virgin was intended to be recited throughout the day and night at the eight canonical hours (Matins, Lauds, Prime, Terce, Sext, None, Vespers, and Compline). The focus of devotions of the Office is on Mary and is largely composed of prayers that affirm the Virgin's role in the mystery of salvation. The text is organized according to a traditional structure and the Psalms and Readings are interspersed with Verses and Responses. The Hours of Prime and None each have an Antiphon to the Psalms and a Capitulum that are not standard, variations which point to local custom and use in a particular diocese, which the Hours follow.[2] In Thott 547, 4° the Office of Prime contains the Antiphon "O admirabile" and the Capitulum "In omnibus" while the Office of None includes the Antiphon "Germinavit" and the Capitulum "Et radicavi," indications that the manuscript was made for Sarum use.[3] These rites, developed and used at the Cathedral and Diocese of Salisbury, were widespread in southern England.

The Hours of the Virgin is the quintessential element of a Book of Hours, a type of prayer book that was fashionable in the period in which the Copenhagen manuscript was executed. Books of Hours were used by both laymen and laywomen for private devotion and spiritual contemplation. Many of the surviving English Books of Hours were made, like Thott 547, 4°, for women.[4] The program of devotions in these manuscripts imitated the cycle of daily prayers, Psalms, Hymns, and Antiphons recited by the clergy, but the Book of Hours is shorter, simpler, and almost unchanging with the seasons.[5] The contents of these manuscripts, made outside formal religious supervision and for private use, vary.[6] Aside from the Hours of the Virgin, components usually found in this type of book are a Calendar, the Seven Penitential Psalms, a Litany, and an Office of the Dead. In English Books of Hours prayers to individual special saints – called the commemorations of saints, *memoriae*, or suffrages – are found at the end of Lauds and Vespers of the Office of the Virgin, while in continental manuscripts they are usually a separate section.[7] Other Offices such as the short Hours of the Holy Cross, Hours of the Holy Spirit, Hours of the Trinity, and Hours of the Passion might also be included in a Book of Hours. Thott 547, 4° does not have any of the additional Offices, but none of the components generally found in a Books of Hours are missing from Thott 547, 4° other than a Calendar. It is, therefore, possible that Thott 547, 4° was envisioned to be a book of this kind. In comparison to other English Books of Hours of this period, the components of Thott 547, 4° are rather standard.[8]

In Thott 547, 4° most of the canonical Hours, the Seven Penitential Psalms, and the Office of the Dead are introduced by Anglo-Norman French rubrics, words in red identifying types of texts, which often appear in manuscripts for readers who need guidance with Latin texts. There are, however, no prayers, collects, or other type of material in the vernacular.[9] The Office of the Virgin, the Seven Penitential Psalms, the Litany, and the Office of the Dead, as was common, are in Latin.

Thott 547, 4° is not the only Bohun manuscript lacking a Calendar. Manuscripts that belonged to this family which are in fragmentary or incomplete states – such as the ones in Pommersfelden and in a private collection, as well as more complete manuscripts like the Exeter College Psalter and Bodleian Library's Psalter-Hours – have Calendars that were not executed by the Bohun atelier.[10] That Bohun manuscripts are missing Calendars, or have ones that post-date the rest of the components, suggests that these folios were often executed last by the workshop.[11]

It is possible, as Lucy Sandler has suggested, that Thott 547, 4° was envisioned to be a Psalter-Hours, and that its extant components were intended to be placed alongside the text of the Psalter.[12] Psalter-Hours combine two different sorts of books that were made for private use in the late Middle Ages. They contain the text of the 150 Psalms alongside the Hours of the Virgin and might include other Offices. Since the Bohuns are known to have commissioned two Psalter-Hours, one in the collection of the Bodleian Library, and the other in the British Library, it would not be unreasonable to presume that the patron of Thott 547, 4° may have wished to commission yet another devotional book of this type. The historiated initials within the Office of the Virgin in the Copenhagen manuscript are illuminated with the same subjects as the initials placed at the opening of each of the canonical hours in the Bodleian Psalter-Hours, an iconographic kinship which may be taken as evidence that Thott 547, 4° was intended to form part of a Psalter-Hours. However, Thott 547, 4° is smaller than the British Library's Psalter-Hours (340 × 235 mm) and the Bodleian's Psalter-Hours (169 × 118 mm), and easily portable. It is thus equally possible that the Copenhagen manuscript was intended as a Book of Hours, a type of manuscript that was fashionable at the time.

The Historiated Initials in the Text

Thott 547, 4° has ten six-line letters containing Christological narrative scenes which provide a marker for the divisions in the manuscript. Eight of the historiated initials are placed at the opening of each canonical hour, one at the opening of the Seven Penitential Psalms, f. 32v, and the last marks the Office of the Dead, f. 43. Like the selection of supplementary texts, the choice of subject matter at the main divisions in English devotional books varied considerably, giving a highly individual quality to the manuscript.[13] Like more than half of the late thirteenth- and fourteenth-century illuminated English Books of Hours, the Office of the Virgin in Thott 547, 4° contains a mixed Infancy and Passion cycle. The Christological subject matter, which is ordered chronologically, opens with an illumination of the Annunciation. The Infancy scenes continue until the Hour of None, at which point the Passion cycle is introduced with an image of the Crucifixion, followed by one of the Resurrection at Vespers. Here the Passion cycle ends and Compline, the final Hour of the Office of the Virgin, is accompanied by an illumination of the Coronation of the Virgin. Aside from the Crucifixion and Resurrection the events chosen to mark the canonical Hours of the Office of the Virgin in Thott 547, 4° are not dissimilar from those subjects marking the divisions of the core text of continental Books of Hours.[14]

All the stunningly painted historiated initials are the work of a single illuminator. He employed a wide palette of colors, ranging from red, light and dusty pink, orange, dark and light green, dark and light blue, light blue-grey, purple, brown, grey black, and white. The artist had a distinctive figure style. His principal figures are tall, slim, and long-limbed. Most of the faces of the individuals he painted have round black eyes, small mouths, and long narrow noses. Grey shadows and lines painted on faces, necks and exposed white skin create a sense of three-dimensionality of the figures. For individual characterization, he used different patterns and various arrangements of draperies; the textiles appear to cling to the figures' legs or be wrapped around them and fall into a series of deep folds. The body language and the facial expressions of the figures are usually composed; rarely are they placed in awkward positions or showing violent emotions.

Elements of the representations within the historiated initials spill into some of the interstices, formed by the outlines of the letters, as well as onto some of the background panels and into the borders. On a number of folia the scenes continue beyond the background panels into other areas of the page – for example, the episodes from the Last Judgment, f. 32v (plate 10), represented in the historiated initial extend into all four borders.

The shape of the letter may encompass details from the central scene or alternatively be filled with tooled gold, abstract, vegetal, or figurative forms. For example, in the vertical stem of the letter "D" f. 1 there are lion heads, which repeat the leonine motif represented in the armorials in the background panel, while on f. 28 a shield with the arms of Bohun is placed inside the shape of the letter "C." Extensions of the letters form medallions, some of which are filled with hybrids, angels, and/or vegetal forms.

Gold leaf is lavishly used. It is thickly applied, highly burnished, and tooled in most of the backgrounds of the historiated initials.[15] It is also employed for embellishing the stems and/or bowls of the letters, e.g. f. 14v, f. 18, etc.

The Background Panels

The historiated initials are placed on rectangular panels, completely surrounded on three sides by a tooled gold rectilinear framing device while some letters are also encompassed partially or completely on the forth side. The spandrels, created by the placement of the initial on the backgrounds, contain heraldic motifs, figures, architecture, floral, vegetal, and/or geometric patterns.

The *Bas-de-Pages*

Bas-de-page, an unframed narrative cluster placed at the bottom of the page beneath the text, appeared in devotional manuscripts from the second half of the thirteenth century. In the part of Thott 547, 4° containing the Hours of the Virgin, the subjects of the superbly painted *bas-de-pages* are Marian miracles. The narrative cluster found in the lower margin of the folios at the opening of the last two liturgical divisions of the manuscript, at the Seven Penitential Psalms, f. 32v and at the Office of the Dead, f. 43 depict the saved and the damned and episodes from the Book of Job, respectively.

The *Haut-de-Pages*

Two folios in the manuscript are decorated with unframed narrative scenes in the area above the text block. The first is drawn from the Gospel of St. Luke while the second is from the Apocalypse. The subjects of the *haut-de-pages* on f. 14v and f. 32v are dramatic continuations of those of the historiated initials.

The Heraldry

In Thott 547, 4°, arms are found in shields, in the backgrounds of miniatures, as well as on clothing solely within the section devoted to the Office of the Virgin.[16] The most often displayed arms are those of the book owner's family, the Bohuns, Earls of Hereford and Essex (*azure a bend argent two cotises and between six lions rampart or*). They are found on folia with the opening texts of the first three hours, Matins, f. 1, Lauds, f. 6v and Prime, f. 14v and at Compline, f. 28v. In close proximity to the first two historiated initials are arms associated with the crown, those of pre-1340 England, f 1, the post-1340 arms of England, f. 6v, and those of the heir apparent to the throne, f. 6v. The arms of St. George, f. 17v, are not inserted on a folio with a historiated initial but rather inside the three-line initial of the closing collect at the end of Prime.

The Secondary Decoration

All the pages of the manuscript are sumptuously decorated with gold borders, ornamental initials, and, with a few exceptions, with line fillers. Except on some of the folia with historiated initials, the secondary decorations were painted handsomely by Hand Two who employed a more limited range of colors than Hand One. While Hand One used bright, highly burnished gold for the folios with historiated initials, Hand Two used a duller type of this precious metal.[17]

The Borders

Full borders in gold and colors, outlined in black, surround the text block of folios with historiated initials. The rectilinear form of the four-sided border is interrupted by medallions with scalloped edges containing angels, grotesques, shields, and vegetal motifs. Five star foliage in tooled gold, orange, pink, or blue with white veins, some attached to the border, alternate with small gold balls on three or four sides of the page. Thin black irregular lines extend from the small gold studs and lobes of the leaves.

A more elaborate border is found at the opening of the Hours of the Virgin than at the other nine liturgical divisions of the manuscript. In the center of the border are entwining pink and blue lines with white strokes atop of them, imitating the appearance of two twisted cords – one blue and the other pink. The illusion is created that the blue and pink strands unwind to encompass the quatrefoils surrounding angels and then are twisted together again in the rectilinear portions of the border. Unlike the Egerton Psalter-Hours which has borders inhabited by animals, hybrids, and/or people, Thott 547, 4° has few decorations of this type. The exceptions are a hybrid winged man wearing a miter in the border, f. 1, and a composite creature chewing on a vine, f. 6v.

All other borders are three-sided in colors and gold with scalloped medallions. They are outlined in black and terminate in a spray of leaves. One of the portions of the left border of f. 5v, which extends partway in the margin, terminates in a stork.

The Ornamental Initials

A hierarchical arrangement is evident in the size and decoration of the letters of the text. Beside the ten six-line historiated initials, there are over one hundred three-line decorated initials, fifteen two-line decorated initials as well as over one thousand one-line initials marking different sections of text. Each letter is outlined in black and set against a highly burnished gold background which encompasses it and echoes its form. This uniform treatment of initials throughout the manuscript creates a sense of order, while the various motifs used to decorate the letters enliven the pages of text. Some of the three-line letters are composed of zoomorphic elements; for example, the initial is made up of canine and asinine components, f. 25v, f. 30v, f. 36, while on f. 18v the stem of the "A" is marlin-like. Inside some of the three-line initials are figurative motifs such as shields, masks (f. 10), human heads in profile or three-quarter view (black man f. 21, women, knights), animal heads (donkey f. 45v, birds: pelican, f. 20v), animals (squirrels, rabbits f. 15v, f. 30v), a harp (f. 18v), dragons, grotesques, as well as spiraling vines terminating in different types of leaves and rectilinear motifs with vegetal elements. The colors employed are white, pink, blue, orange, tan, greenish grey, and black. The two-line initials are similarly composed of zoomorphic, vegetal, and anthropomorphic elements and contain armorial shields (f. 6v), humans (a monk, f. 14), animals (dog, f. 3v), etc. The one-line versal initials alternate in pink and blue and are additionally decorated with white lines and dots. The interior of the letter is painted with foliate or floral tendrils in contrasting colors.

The Line Fillers

Gold line fillers, outlined in black, are either left unadorned or decorated with geometric, foliate, floral, and/or zoomorphic motifs. The decorations are painted blue, white, pink, and orange. The zoomorphic forms are the most animated. They include pairs of creatures appearing to be either chasing or confronting each other and creatures biting themselves. This type of decoration fills the space from where the text ends to the edge of the text block.

The Seven Penitential Psalms, ff. 32v–38v

The Seven Penitential Psalms (6, 31, 37, 50, 101, 129, and 142) are one of the standard texts of Books of Hours, recited for purely devotional reasons and as a means of doing penance for one's sins.[18] They were also uttered by the laity during special times of the year, such as Lent and on specific occasions such as pilgrimages. As was customary, the Seven Penitential Psalms are followed by a Litany.

The Litany, ff. 38 v–41

Litanies, consisting of invocations for mercy and deliverance, were conventional components of personal devotional books like Psalters, Books of Hours, or Psalter-Hours. As was common in Litanies, the opening text of the one found in this manuscript is comprised of calls for mercy addressed to the Trinity, for Christ to hear us and for intercession by Mary, the archangels, the blessed spirits, John the Baptist, the patriarchs and prophets, the apostles, evangelists, and holy innocents.[19] The next part of the text in which various martyrs, confessors, and virgins are invoked, ff. 39v–41, follows Sarum use.[20]

The Litany has some unusual omissions and the hierarchy of the saints is not entirely conventional. Augustine of Hippo, one of the major confessors, is not present, for example.[21] Such an omission in the Litany of Thott 547, 4° is somewhat surprising given that Augustine is included in all the original Litanies found in Bohun devotional manuscripts. An additional reason to find the exclusion of Augustine in the Litany particularly odd is that the Bohuns were important patrons of the Augustinian order and at least one of those involved in the execution of the manuscript was an Augustinian friar. Another unusual feature of the Litany in Thott 547, 4° is the placement of St. Francis and St. Dominic. The founders of the mendicant orders are untraditionally invoked before St. Ambrose and St. Benedict in the sequence of saints.[22]

As was common in lay devotional manuscripts of the time, local saints are recorded in the Litany. In Thott 547, 4° eight English saints are named: Alban, protomartyr of Britain; Edmund, King of East Anglia; Thomas Becket, Archbishop of Canterbury; Oswald, Archbishop of York; Alphege, Archbishop of Canterbury; Dunstan, Archbishop of Canterbury; Cuthbert, Bishop of Lindisfarne; and Botulph, Abbot of Icanho. St. George, whose cult was particularly strong in England in this period, is also included.[23] This Litany invokes more local saints than any other Bohun devotional manuscript.

The final section of the Litany concludes with petitions of the three types, *Ab*, *Per*, and *Ut*, and is followed by the *Agnus Dei*, *Kyrie*, Lord's Prayer, etc., and ends with the *Domine exaudi*.

The Collects, ff. 42–42v

After the text of the Litany are a number of collects, short prayers, asking the Lord to hear the devotee's petitions, and in particular to have mercy upon the souls of the dead and to forgive them their sins. The short prayer for the souls of the owner's mother and father, ff. 42–42v, is not unusual and the presence of this collect does not exclude either of the Bohun heiresses, whose mother outlived them, as the intended owner of Thott 547, 4°. The dowager countess of Hereford, like other individuals living in the Middle Ages, would have assumed that death could come at anytime. It would have been considered natural that once deceased she would be included in her daughter's prayers.

The Office of the Dead, ff. 43–66v (Sarum Use)

The Office of the Dead is a prayer cycle of the liturgy said to help the soul after death. Usually placed at the end of personal devotional books, it comprises three hours, Vespers, Matins, and Lauds, and is mainly composed of different Psalms, scripture, and prayers. The Office of the Dead was read during the night preceding a burial, on a death anniversary, or on particular feast days of the liturgical year. It was also held that the Office should be read whenever possible because without the prayers of the living, souls would be trapped in purgatory. The contents of the Office of the Dead in personal devotional books are the same as in Breviaries and Antiphonaries used by the clergy and follows the custom of a particular diocese. The Office of the Dead in Thott 547, 4° follows Sarum use.[24] Having this text in personal manuscripts, which could be brought to church or chapel, allowed the owners to follow the liturgy performed there.

Usually after the collects there are a few short concluding verses (*requiescant in pace* and an Amen), similar to those found after the *vigilie*, ff. 46–46v. Omissions of such standard texts are not unusual if a scribe had only a few available blank lines to complete the manuscript.[25]

The Paleography

The text of the manuscript is written in Gothic semi-quadrata, a style that is somewhat less formal than quadrata used in the larger and earlier Bohun manuscripts.[26] It was executed by one scribe – with the exception of f. 1, which was written out in a firmer hand.[27] The brown color of the ink on many of the folios complements the gold leaf used in the borders, initials, and line fillers.

The Binding

The manuscript has a gold-tooled red morocco binding. Pressed into the front and back covers are decorative motives. On the front one are two rectangles composed of alternating circles and squares between ovals. In the four corners of the smaller rectangle are fans, topped by acorns. The centerpiece is made up of drawer handles, acorns, leaves, circles, and vegetal motifs. The composition of the back binding is almost the same, except for the central motif which is smaller. This type of tooled ornament is found on bindings dating from the late seventeenth century to the early eighteenth century. On the spine are five raised bands, decorated with gilt fillets and stamps. The four words of the spine title "MATM DE NOST DAME" appear one below the other in between the top two raised bands.

The binder inserted marbled end papers and marbled the edges of the folios. The paper inserted before and after the quires of the fourteenth-century folia do not have watermarks. On the front pastedown in the top left hand corner, the handwritten number four is crossed out and next to it the number thirteen is written. Mirjam Foot has judged that the manuscript was bound in The Hague by the Drawer Handle/Fleuron/Pieterson bindery.[28]

The Provenance

The heraldic garments in which the owner of the manuscript is portrayed on folio 1 indicate that it was intended for a young female member of the Bohun family. The subsequent provenance of the manuscript is unknown prior to its entry into the collection of Samuel van Huls (1655–1734), a Hague magistrate and avid collector of books and pictures.[29] Afterwards it was owned by a Danish nobleman, Count Otto Thott (1703–1785).[30] Count Thott bought many of his books on the international market and he may have obtained the manuscripts at the Huls sale of 1720.[31] The manuscript was bequeathed by the count to the Copenhagen Royal Library.

Chapter Two

Principal Illuminations in Thott 547,4°: Historiated Initials, *Bas-de-Page*, *Haut-de-Page*, and Heraldry

In this chapter, each of the folia in Thott 547, 4° on which the principal illuminations appear are presented, and the significance of the arms of St. George at the end of Prime is also discussed. In order to help the reader discern the degree to which texts influenced the design of the Christological illuminations in the historiated initials, translated passages from the Vulgate, the commonly used text of the Bible in the fourteenth century, and the Apocrypha, which unlike the Gospels provide information about Mary's life, are cited. Then a description of the scene in the historiated initial is presented. The choice of subject matter to mark the liturgical division is examined and, thereafter, an analysis of the images' iconography is provided. The role pictorial tradition and established symbolism played in the contents and design of these images is evaluated.

When present, armorials, displayed in background squares and three-line initials, are noted. Next we turn to the *bas-de-page*. Firstly, a translated excerpt from a short version of the legend is quoted, or, in the case of long texts, a summary of the work, which the reader can compare with the narrative in the *bas-de-page*. Each scene is described in detail and afterwards its subject matter is examined. It will be shown that many of the subjects of the compositions in the lower borders are those identified by C. Bruun and M. R. James. The visual rendition of the Marian miracles is then compared to written accounts of the legend. Works such as the *Golden Legend* or Miracles of Our Lady, which the illuminators might have consulted or recalled from memory to design the *bas-de-page* scenes, are also discussed.[1] It will be demonstrated that, unlike the textual sources for the Christological imagery of the historiated initials, those from which the imagery of the Marian legends are drawn are less easy to discern.

Miracles of the Virgin: Texs and Images

It may be useful for some readers to very briefly review the growth of interest in the legends of the Virgin from the twelfth through the fourteenth century to provide a context for the literary works cited below and to demonstrate the richness of the textual tradition and the interest in England in representing Mariam miracles in the visual arts.

Twelfth-century England is where the earliest Mariales were composed and it was there that the interest in and enthusiasm for these tales continued to rise. The assembling of large collections of Marian legends, primarily drawn from earlier writings or oral tradition, parallels the increasing focus on the mother of Jesus in Christian devotion in England, as well as western Europe, in the twelfth and thirteenth centuries.[2] The earliest collection, consisting of thirty-five Marian legends, has been ascribed to Anselm the Younger (d. 1148), abbot of Bury St. Edmunds.[3] Dominic, Prior of Evesham (d. in or before 1150), is associated with a set of fourteen stories believed to have been compiled in the 1120s and which were shaped by Anselm the Younger's miracles of the Virgin.[4] William of Malmesbury (d. c. 1143) knew Anselm's and Dominic's works and eight of the legends he relates in his collection of fifty-one miracles of the Virgin, *De miraculis beatae virginis*, are adaptations of the narratives in these earlier collections.[5]

The three separate English collections were brought together by Master Alberic, a canon of St. Paul's in London, and made generally accessible around the mid-twelfth century.[6] Alberic's copy of the combined collections was the source for the first assemblage of miracles in Anglo-Norman French, *Le Gracial*, a poem by William Adgar (f. 1150–1200).[7] Adgar's poem, recounting forty-nine miracles, was composed for an audience of laymen and women.[8] A second Anglo-Norman collection of miracles of the Virgin in verse was a close derivative of the Latin texts found in earlier Mariales.[9]

As the cult of the Virgin grew, an ever increasing number of Marian miracles were composed and written down. One of the most extensively circulated collections, called Pez, dates from the twelfth-century and is of French origin.[10] A number of the widely transmitted works containing Marian legends were used for instruction. Caesarius of Heisterbach composed a guidebook, the *Dialogue of Miracles* (c. 1225) for young Cistercian monks at Heisterbach.[11] Gautier de Coinci's vast collection of miracles (c. 1230) was of interest to both monastic and lay audiences.[12] *La Vie de Pères*, a very popular collection of pious tales and miracles, includes a number of Mary legends. The original series dates from around the 1220s. Additions were twice made to the first text during the course of the thirteenth century. Like Gautier's *Miracles de Nostre Dame*, the text speaks out against Jews, heretics, and clerical abuses.[13]

Vincent de Beauvais's *Speculum historiale* included a large number of Marian miracles. The *Speculum* was a part of Vincent's ambitious compendium known as the *Speculum maius*, initially composed for an ecclesiastic audience, but sometime after 1244 Vincent began to take into account some of the interests of King Louis IX, the author's then patron.[14] A number of Marian miracles were included in Jacobus de Voragine's widely disseminated *Legenda Aurea* (The Golden Legend) of c. 1260, a work that primarily consisted of 176 saint's legends and meditations on religious holidays, ordered according to the Church calendar.

In England miracles were depicted in ecclesiastic settings, including sculpture, wall painting, and stained glass.[15] Illuminations of Miracles of the Virgin do not appear in manuscripts with any frequency until the thirteenth century.[16] After the production of a series of illustrated Gautier de Coinci manuscripts in the second half of the thirteenth century, the imagery of Marian miracles expanded significantly in the successive hundred-year period.[17] Most of the image cycles of the miracles of the Virgin from the fourteenth century are English and are located in the *bas-de-page* or historiated initials of Psalters and Books of Hours.[18] Tinted drawings of the miracles of the Virgin situated beneath the text are found in the *Queen Mary Psalter* (London, British Library, MS Royal 2.B.vii, c. 1320), ff. 204v–232, and the *Carew-Poyntz Hours* (Cambridge, Fitzwilliam 48, c. 1350–c. 1360, end of the fourteenth century and fifteenth century).[19] In the *Madresfield Hours* (Madresfield Court, MS M, c. 1320–1330), five miniatures depicting Marian miracles appear in the Office of the Virgin, while in the *Taymouth Hours* (London, British Library, MS Yates Thompson 13, c. 1325–1335) miracle scenes accompany the text of the Office of the Dead, ff. 151v–179.[20] In the *Neville of Hornby Hours* (London, British Library, MS Egerton 2781), c. 1335–40, a number of historiated initials represent various miracles of the Virgin, ff. 21v–25v.[21]

In addition to the Copenhagen Hours, which will be discussed below, two other Bohun manuscripts contain miracles of the Virgin. The Bodleian Library's Psalter-Hours has eight large miniatures located at the opening of each of the canonical hours, ff. 182–219v.[22] In the British Library's Psalter-Hours, three legends are represented: the legend of the Child Image Taken Hostage, f. 123, Theophilus, f. 126v, and two scenes of the miracle of the (usurer's?) soul, f. 129.[23] We now turn our attention to the principal illuminations in the Copenhagen Hours.

Plate 1. Folio 1. Matins.
Historiated Initial "D": Annunciation (Luke 1:26–38)

> Luke 1:26 And in the sixth month, the angel Gabriel was sent from God into a city of Galilee, called Nazareth, 27 To a virgin espoused to a man whose name was Joseph, of the house of David; and the virgin's name was Mary. 28 And the angel being come in, said unto her: Hail, full of grace, the Lord is with thee: blessed art thou among women. 29 Who having heard, was troubled at his saying, and thought with herself what manner of salutation this should be. 30 And the angel said to her: Fear not, Mary, for thou hast found grace with God. 31 Behold thou shalt conceive in thy womb, and shalt bring forth a son; and thou shalt call his name Jesus. 32 He shall be great, and shall be called the Son of the most High; and the Lord God shall give unto him the throne of David his father; and he shall reign in the house of Jacob for ever. 33 And of his kingdom there shall be no end. 34 And Mary said to the angel: How shall this be done, because I know not man? 35 And the angel answering, said to her: The Holy Ghost shall come upon thee, and the power of the most High shall overshadow thee. And therefore also the Holy which shall be born of thee shall be called the Son of God. 36 And behold thy cousin Elizabeth, she also hath conceived a son in her old age; and this is the sixth month with her that is called barren: 37 Because no word shall be impossible with God. 38 And Mary said: Behold the handmaid of the Lord; be it done to me according to thy word. And the angel departed from her.

> Isaiah 7:14 Therefore the Lord himself shall give you a sign. Behold a virgin shall conceive, and bear a son, and his name shall be called Emmanuel.

Within an open architectural structure with gables, towers, and turrets, the kneeling, nimbed Archangel Gabriel addresses the crowned Virgin who is seated on a golden throne. The nimbus and body of the angel sent by God emanate rays of light. In his right hand Gabriel holds a scroll with the words of his greeting "aue maria gracia" (Luke 1:28: Hail Mary [full of] grace). The Virgin, dressed in a rose-colored gown and a blue cloak with white and gilt geometric decorations, holds down the page of the manuscript on the reading stand at her side. With her left hand she gestures, an indication that she is speaking. She is probably represented responding to the angel's message that she will bear a son (Luke 1:31–33) with the words

(Luke 1:34): "How shall this be done, because I know not man?" Between Mary and the angel is a vase with a lily, a traditional symbol of her purity, and a basket, perhaps meant for wool (Protevangelium 10:1–2. Gospel of the Pseudo-Matthew 6: And she occupied herself constantly with her wool-work). Rays of light emanate from the window of a turret and terminate near Mary's head.

The rectangular frame around the six-line historiated initial "D" is decorated with the pre-1340 arms of England (*gules three lions passant guardant or*) quartered with Bohun, Earls of Hereford and Essex (*azure a bend argent between two cotises and six lions rampart or*).[24] These arms also appear in the background of the adjacent marginal scene in which a young noblewoman kneels before a reading stand. A shield, six lines beneath the historiated initial, inside the three-line initial "U," introducing Psalm 94:6, displays once again the Bohun arms.

The selection of the subject, the Annunciation, to mark Matins, the first canonical hour of the Office of the Virgin, is standard. The Annunciation was the moment of Christ's incarnation, the first event in Christ's life on earth and the central moment of the Virgin's life. The subject matter is additionally appropriate for this Hour since the devotee is meant to utter the angel's salutation, "Ave maria gracia plena dominus tecum," between the five sections of Psalm 94, ff. 1–2.

The inclusion of a reading stand and an opened book suggest that before Gabriel's arrival, the Virgin had been reading. The representation of Mary with a book was rather common in works of art depicting the Annunciation in this period and its significance is multifold. The Virgin was believed to have started occupying herself with prayer while still a child in the Temple (Gospel of the Pseudo-Matthew 6). That she devoted herself to prayer or holy reading emphasizes her wisdom, goodness, and devotion.[25] The book could also represent the Christ Gabriel is sent to announce and the fulfillment of the prophecies of the Old Testament by the birth of Mary's son (e.g. Isaiah 7:14). The rays of light terminating near the Virgin's head illustrate the belief that as Mary heard the word of God, she conceived.[26]

In representations of the Annunciation, Mary was often shown with royal attributes since it was believed that she descended from King David.[27] Here she is depicted crowned and seated on a golden throne. Mary was also thought of as a throne herself. From Early Christian times, she was often referred to by theologians as the "throne of God," and medieval authors linked this image to the throne of David's son, Solomon, renowned for his wisdom.[28] The throne in the miniature may also call to mind the words uttered by the Annunciate angel (Luke 1:32–33): "He shall be great, and shall be called the Son of the most High; and the Lord God shall give unto him the throne of David his father; and he shall reign in the house of Jacob forever. 33 And of his kingdom there shall be no end."

Border: Portrait of the Book Owner

In an open tower-like structure in the border is a young kneeling noblewoman, gazing in the direction of the Annunciate Virgin (fig. 2). Before her is a reading stand. Each of her hands is placed on a page from her open book. She wears a short surcoat with the arms of pre-1340 England that covers the upper portion of her long blue gown decorated with the Bohun arms. Her clothing could be understood as hierarchically arranged since the surcoat with the armorials of England is above the gown with the Bohun arms.

Because of the placement of the young aristocrat near the opening of the first Hour and because she is praying, it can be concluded that she is the intended reader of the manuscript. Following the earlier practice in Psalters of representing the person for whom a manuscript was made near God, Christ, or the Virgin Mary, in Books of Hours the depiction of the manuscript's owner was often situated on the folio with the opening of the Office of the Virgin, or on the folio prefacing this section.[29] The owner is often shown at prayer, sometimes with a devotional book. The image of the praying devotee is made in response to the opening of the text of the first Hour of the Virgin: "Domine labia mea aperies. Et os meum annunciabit laudem tuam" (O Lord, thou wilt open my lips: and my mouth shall declare thy praise.) This is the only Hour that has this incipit. The image of the praying book owner also underlines the purpose for which the manuscript was made.

Similarities exist between the physical appearance and actions of the female owner and the Virgin. They are given attributes associated with the ideals of beauty in the period. Both are young, slender, aristocratic in bearing, have long necks and very white skin.[30] Mary's long unbound golden hair is a sign of her maidenhood and because the girl also wears her tresses in this way she too is probably an adolescent and perhaps still a virgin.[31] Both the girl and the Virgin Mary wear rose and blue-colored garments with gilt decoration, albeit the girl's blue gown is decorated with gold rearing lions while the Virgin's blue cloak has geometric motifs. Although there are similarities between the spaces the young aristocrat and the

Holy Mother occupy, both are situated in an interior before a lectern with a book, they inhabit different realms. This is emphasized by the fact that they are situated in two separated architectural structures and in different places on the page, the reader in the left margin and the Virgin within the initial of the opening of the Hour.

The young noblewoman gazes past the opened pages of her book and focuses her attention on the Annunciate Virgin. Her quiet and attentive manner is in juxtaposition to the Virgin's questioning and animated air. The young aristocrat is in the temporal world, pondering the words in her prayerbook and visualizing the Virgin caught up in the unfolding drama in the sacred realm. Although Mary does not pay attention to the supplicant, there are elements creating a connection between the book owner and the Virgin to whom this Office is devoted. The intended reader and the Mother of God are represented on the same scale, on the same plane, and facing each other.

The portrait of the book owner in the book could instruct the viewer how to use the illuminations. Like the young aristocrat in the margin, the book owner could use the images as aids to meditation, and ponder the implications of the moment of the Incarnation. The portrait of the intended recipient of the manuscript is not only flattering and didactic, but it also would have had a commemorative quality when used by later owners of the manuscript. It would have been hoped that they would continue to say prayers for her soul.

But who is the young noblewoman? As noted above, the placement of her portrait in the manuscript indicates that she is the intended recipient of the book. The way in which she wears her hair implies that she is young, and perhaps still a minor. The arrangement of her clothes and the manner they are decorated suggests that she is married. Because her gown is embellished with the arms of Bohun and her surcoat with the arms of the kingdom, she must be a member of one family by blood and the other by marriage.

In the visual arts, when married women are shown wearing heraldic garments, more commonly the arms of their husband's family are impaled with those of their father. For example, in the lower margin of f. 2v of the *Pabenham-Clifford Hours* (formerly *Grey Fitzpayn Hours*, Cambridge, Fitzwilliam Museum, MS 242, 1315–30) are portraits of Joan Clifford of Frampton and her husband, John de Pabenham.[32] The veiled Joan wears a heraldic garment on which her husband's arms (*Barry argent and azure, on a bend gules three molets or*) are placed next to those of her father (*Chequy or and azure, on a bend gules three lions passant argent*).[33]

If the young lady in the Copenhagen Hours is intended to represent either one of the seventh earl's daughters, then the arms of her husband are not painted completely accurately.[34] The arms of Eleanor de Bohun's spouse, Thomas of Woodstock, were those of France and England quarterly.[35] Neither on this folio nor anywhere else in the Copenhagen Hours are the post-1340 arms of the crown impaled, quartered, or shown directly above the armorials of the Bohuns. Mary de Bohun's husband, Henry of Bolingbroke, who since 1377 was styled as Earl of Derby, bore, in his mother's right, the arms of the Duchy of Lancaster, England, with a label of France, or more correctly, *gules three leopards or, a label of three points azure floretty or*.[36] The label that was part of Bolingbroke's arms is not present on the young noblewoman's surcoat. Furthermore, the areas of the page in which the pre-1340 arms of England appear in conjunction with those of Bohun (the background of the historiated initial and of the adjacent marginal scene in which the girl is depicted) do not show any marks of differencing.

There may be practical reasons for the absence of the *fleur-de-lis* or the label of *three points azure floretty or*, perhaps due to the small scale of the areas in which the lions of England occur. However, in another book owner portrait of larger dimensions found in the Bodleian Library's Psalter-Hours (fig. 4) there are similarly no marks of differencing on the girl's surcoat.[37] Artists may have taken liberties with representations of armorials on these types of surfaces, as for example in the depictions of the jupons of the princes in St. Stephen's chapel, Westminster.[38] The absence of marks of differencing on the surcoat might have permitted the girl to see likenesses between herself and her great-grandmother, Elizabeth of Rhuddlan, daughter of Edward I and wife of Humphrey de Bohun, fourth Earl of Hereford and Essex, whose arms were those of pre-1340 England impaled with Bohun.[39]

Bas-de-Page: Legend of the Unchaste Abbess

Gautier de Coincy, *Miracles of the Virgin Mary*

There once was an abbess, who very much loved the lady from paradise. She put her entire heart and good sense into serving her and tried very hard to keep the rules of her order and to manage the convent, so much so that her nuns spoke ill of her and viciously complained about her [...]. The devil made her break the seal of virginity which she had vowed and

> promised the king of truth. After a very short time the lady felt in her flanks a seed that germinated and grew […]. The nuns secretly sent word of this matter in briefs and letters to the bishop. [In a letter] he promised them that he would bring shame upon her if he could prove the matter and that he would be at their chapter house the next day. The abbess rose in the morning without knowing anything about this. The good lady had a solemn Mass said for Our Lady. After Mass she remained alone and sighed and cried, all heartbroken. The lady, kneeling and praying, fell asleep in front of the altar. Holy Mary came to her with two angels […]. Then the sweet lady told the two angels to approach and to deliver the lady of her child and to take it to her friend, the saintly hermit […].The bishop who had been informed of her condition by the nuns arrived at the abbey all fired up with doing her harm […].To make sure of the facts, the bishop sent two mature clerks after the abbess […].The two clerks prodded her here and there […] but all for nothing. They returned to the bishop to tell him […].The bishop was not pleased […] "I want to see her myself. My eyes will tell me the truth." When she had taken all her clothes off the bishop saw her sides and stomach all slim and smooth, he was overcome by great pity for her and fell down by her feet crying. "My lady," the bishop said, "I have been badly tricked and deceived […]." The abbess confessed to the bishop who, astonished by the miracle, praised God and later took charge of the child himself […].[40]

In the lower border of the folio are three scenes: a bishop in an orange cope with a broad gold edging and gold miter, attended by a boy in surplice and two clerics in caps and capes, is shown with three nuns in black habits, their heads covered by wimples, veils, and black hoods (fig. 3). Flanking them is a single aisle building with a clearstory, and a red clay tiled roof. In the doorway stands a bearded man in a grey hooded cloak, pointing at the seated sleeping abbess in the center of the *bas-de-page*. A nimbed angel, holding a naked infant, turns his head to the left to gaze at the crowned, nimbed Virgin seated on a mound before a tree and dressed as in the historiated initial above. The Virgin gestures at the angel with her left hand and returns his gaze. With her right hand she supports the head of the abbess leaning against her. In the third scene a group of five nuns stand behind their abbess. A bishop, attended by two clerks, places the fingers of each of his hands around one of the exposed breasts of the abbess before him.

The episodes of the tale narrated in the lower border of the Copenhagen manuscript appear in a number of versions of the Miracle of the Unchaste

Abbess, one of the most popular of all Mary-legends and included in many of the great Latin collections.[41] The events depicted in the first and middle scenes of the *bas-de-page* are similar to incidents recounted by Vincent de Beauvais and Gautier de Coinci in the central parts of their narratives.[42] There are only small differences between the textual sources and the visualization of the narratives in the *bas-de-page*. In the Copenhagen Hours the nuns are shown with their bishop, informing him that their abbess has been unchaste. (In Vincent's and Gautier's tale they contact the bishop by letter.)[43] Evidence of an image/text divergance is also evident in the representation of the final *bas-de-page* scene. In Vincent's and Gautier's tales the bishop, after being told the outcome of the examination of the abbess for signs of pregnancy by the clerks, decides to inspect her body himself.[44] In Vincent's account the author does not specify the nature of the bishop's examination of the abbess, while in Gautier's poem the bishop's behavior is much more aggressive: he insults her and forces her to completely undress.[45] In the final scene of the *bas-de-page* the bishop squeezes the abbess's exposed breasts to determine whether or not she is lactating.[46]

The choice of placing this story on the same folio as the Annunciation invites the viewer to compare the Annunciate Virgin, pure in body and spirit, and the abbess, who has broken her vow of chastity. The placement of the book owner in the vicinity of the chaste Virgin and the resemblances between the two women also suggest that the young aristocrat is above the kind of behavior demonstrated by the abbess. The manuscript owner is presented as a picture of piety, purity, and beauty.

But while the arrangement of the figures on the page invites criticism of the abbess, it also casts her accusers in an unsympathetic light. In the *bas-de-page* the vengeful and disloyal sisters are placed on either side of the second scene, in which the abbess, placed in the center of the lower marginal episodes, is protected by the compassionate and maternal Virgin. She supports the head of the abbess in an analogous manner to the angel supporting the head of the baby. While the nuns enlist the aid of the bishop to have the abbess punished, the Virgin directs her helpers to remove the evidence of the abbess's guilt and thereby restores her innocence. Thus the nuns appear to embody qualities opposite to those associated with Mary.

The need for the Virgin to intervene suggests that the male authority would have dealt with the abbess's transgressions in a severe, punitive manner. Although it would seem that Mary subverts male clerical authority, the medieval viewer would also have known that the Virgin is Ecclesia and understood that the church has qualities lacking in some of its individual members.[47] The inclusion of a hybrid bat-winged man wearing a miter at the top of the page, a derisory portrayal of a bishop, might allude to such an idea (fig. 1).

Scenes from the legend of the unchaste abbess are also represented in the Oxford Psalter-Hours. They are placed in the miniature prefacing the historiated initial at the opening of Lauds, on f. 188.[48] The episodes from the legend are in juxtaposition to the representation of the Visitation, which shows the meeting of the pregnant Mary and St. Elizabeth.

Plate 2. Folio 6v. Lauds.
Historiated Initial "D": Visitation (Luke 1:39–56)

> Luke 1:36 And behold thy cousin Elizabeth, she also hath conceived a son in her old age; and this is the sixth month with her that is called barren: 37 Because no word shall be impossible with God. 38 And Mary said: Behold the handmaid of the Lord; be it done to me according to thy word. And the angel departed from her. 39 And Mary rising up in those days, went into the hill country with haste into a city of Juda. 40 And she entered into the house of Zachary, and saluted Elizabeth. 41 And it came to pass, that when Elizabeth heard the salutation of Mary, the infant leaped in her womb. And Elizabeth was filled with the Holy Ghost: 42 And she cried out with a loud voice, and said: Blessed art thou among women, and blessed is the fruit of thy womb. 43 And whence is this to me, that the mother of my Lord should come to me? 44 For behold as soon as the voice of thy salutation sounded in my ears, the infant in my womb leaped for joy. 45 And blessed art thou that hast believed, because those things shall be accomplished that were spoken to thee by the Lord. 46 And Mary said: My soul doth magnify the Lord. 47 And my spirit hath rejoiced in God my Saviour. 48 Because he hath regarded the humility of his handmaid; for behold from henceforth all generations shall call me blessed. 49 Because he that is mighty, hath done great things to me; and holy is his name. 50 And his mercy is from generation unto generations, to them that fear him.

Through a door, the crowned Virgin enters a bedroom (fig. 5). In this intimate setting, before a bed, canopied and curtained with luxurious textiles, Mary is welcomed by her pregnant cousin Elizabeth, who reaches out to embrace her. One of Elizabeth's hands is placed on the Virgin's abdomen, modestly concealed by the folds of her blue mantle. Elizabeth is wimpled, veiled, and wears a red gown under a blue vair-lined mantle. Upon the bed is an open book, which Elizabeth has put down.

Mary's gesture, left hand raised, right hand held parallel to her chest, indicates that she is speaking, probably greeting her cousin (Luke 1:40). Elizabeth's hand placed on the Virgin's abdomen draws the viewer's attention to the subject of Elizabeth's address (Luke 1:42), the child Mary carries but which the mantle folds hide. The difference in age between the two cousins (Luke 1:36) is conveyed by the women's clothes and physical appearance. Elizabeth's face and figure are fuller than Mary's. Unlike her young cousin, the older woman's neck and hair are covered.

Although the Gospel of Luke relates that the Visitation took place in Zachary's house, visual representations of the event do not usually show the women meeting in Elizabeth's bedroom.[49] The scene is often depicted in an unspecific location, set against a neutral background, with no household furnishings, or outdoors. Here the Visitation is set in a contemporary bedroom outfitted with fine textiles, a place where women of means would have received female friends and kin. The holy women appear to share the customs, tastes, and economic standing of contemporary upper class women. These similarities might have led the female viewer to see other links between herself and Elizabeth and Mary.[50]

Usually in scenes of the Visitation depicted in English Gothic manuscripts, Elizabeth and Mary are shown embracing each other.[51] However, in this manuscript Elizabeth's placement of her hand on the Virgin's abdomen draws attention to her recognition of Christ as her Lord and Mary as his mother. Because Elizabeth was the first person to do so, the image could serve as a reminder of the favor God accorded some women. The inclusion of the book in Elizabeth's room is another positive attribute, suggesting her devotion and occupation with prayer and holy reading. In contrast to the representation of the relationship of the abbess and her envious and disloyal nuns accompanying the Hour of Matins, the illustration in the historiated initial at Lauds shows an affectionate relationship between women and Elizabeth's devotion to her cousin, Mary.

Armorials

In the square background of the initial "D" are the arms of England, quartered with the *fleur-de-lis* of France (the post-1340 arms of the Kingdom), (fig. 5). In the left border, in the extensions of the historiated initial, are two shields. The top one displays the post-1340 arms of England while the one below has quarterly France and England, with a label argent. These arms, have been identified by Sandler as those of the heir apparent.[52] Three lines below the depiction of the Visitation is a two-line initial "D,"containing a shield with the Bohun arms at the opening of Psalm 92.

Which heir apparent is made reference to on this folio is open to conjecture. As Sandler has suggested, the arms of the heir apparent, paired with the sovereign, might be retrospective, referring to the succession from Edward III to his son Edward, the Black Prince (heir apparent until his death in 1376), or from Edward III to his grandson Richard of Bordeaux (heir apparent 1376–1377).[53] Alternatively, the arms might be a forward-looking dynastic statement, referring to Richard II and to his yet unborn son.[54]

The arms of England quartered with France and those of the heir apparent in Thott 547, 4° refer to nobles who were kinsmen of the Bohuns, and their devices would have been included in the manuscript to remind the reader to pray for her deceased relations. Additionally, as in the imagery on tombs, such as the one made for Philippa of Hainault, the presence of these shields testifies to the importance that alliances with families of greater status had.[55] The coats of arms on the page could have been understood as recording and celebrating the prestige of the family line as well as mirroring the eternally established social order. It is also not impossible that arms of the heir apparent above those of Bohun would have drawn the reader's attention to the importance of heirs and heiresses for their families.

Bas-de-Page: Legend of Theophilus

The core of this narrative as it appears in many collections, including the *Speculum historiale* and the *Golden Legend*, can be summarized as follows:

> An archdeacon named Theophilus was chosen by the people to be their bishop. However, another cleric was consecrated instead of him. In anger, Theophilus approached a Jew who brought him to the devil. In exchange for restoration to his former office, Theophilus first renounced his religion, and then signed a pact with the devil and sealed the wax with his ring. Thereafter he was restored to his position. A short time later, he regretted what he had done and prayed fervently for the Virgin's intercession on his

behalf. In a vision, the Virgin appeared to Theophilus, and returned the document with his seal. When Theophilus awoke and found the document he was filled with remorse for what he had done. He went to church, found the bishop and confessed his sin before all the people. The bishop instructed him to burn the document and three days later he died.

In the lower border, in the first of four scenes, stands a bishop in a rose cope with a gold border and a gold miter attended by two clerks (fig. 6). He points to the ground and faces the bearded and tonsured Theophilus in clerical garb, a rose-colored cape and robe. Theophilus's left hand is in his pocket while his right arm is bent at the elbow and held parallel to his chest. His hand gesture directs the viewer's attention to the following scene. In it Theophilus sits on the ground writing on a parchment with an attached a seal. Over him stands a black, horned devil, who is holding onto the document with his left paw while laying his right paw on Theophilus's head. Standing directly behind the cleric is a bearded man in a tall, soft, conical cap. His headgear identifies him as a Jew. In the following scene, Theophilus kneels in prayer before a polychromed sculpture of the crowned Virgin and Child on a canopied altar. On either side of the altar are riddle posts of wrought iron supporting a fabric. In the fourth and final scene, the crowned Virgin birches the crouching devil and returns the document to Theophilus, who is kneeling on the right.

The story of Theophilus was one of the oldest and most common Marian legends in circulation in England as well as western Europe in the Middle Ages.[56] It appears in some of the most widely disseminated works such as Vincent de Beauvais's *Speculum historiale*, Gautier de Coinci's *Miracles de Nostre Dame*, and Jacobus de Voragine's *Golden Legend*.[57] It was also the most popular Marian miracle chosen for representation in personal devotional books.[58]

In textual versions of this legend, such as *Le Gracial* and the *Golden Legend*, Mary takes the charter signed by Theophilus from the Devil and places it on the archdeacon's chest while he sleeps. In Thott 547, 4°, as in some earlier English miniatures, the recovery of the charter is much more dramatic.[59] In the *bas-de-page* Mary chastises and humiliates her enemy, asserting her power over him. The representation of Mary birching the devil thus visualizes her triumph over Satan's dark forces.

The image also demonstrates the Virgin's power over apostasy.[60] In the legend Theophilus's ambition turns him against Christ and the Virgin as well as his Christian brothers, renouncing them for the Jew and the devil. Theophilus's behavior in the *bas-de-page* is in direct contrast to that of Elizabeth in the historiated initial in the upper portion of the page. While Elizabeth recognizes Christ as her Lord, Theophilus acknowledges the devil as his.

Three episodes from the legend of Theophilus were depicted in the Bodleian Psalter Hours at Matins, f. 182: Theophilus, in supplication before the devil, Theophilus signing the charter while the devil pulls on his hair and Theophilus in payer before the Virgin and Child as the devil flees. Two similar scenes from the legend are also represented in the Egerton Psalter-Hours in the border accompanying the historiated initial "D" at Vesper illustrated with scenes from Christ's ministry (Luke 14:21, 15:1–7 and 15:11–12), f.126v. They are: Theophilus signing the charter in the devil's presence and Theophilus praying to the Virgin holding the Child, document and birch in right hand as the devil runs away. The Bohun manuscripts in London and Oxford do not depict the Jew in the Theophilus scenes.

Plate 3. Folio 14v. Prime.
Haut-de-Page: Annunciation to the Shepherds (Luke 2:8–14)

> Luke 2:8 And there were in the same country shepherds watching, and keeping the night watches over their flock. 9 And behold an angel of the Lord stood by them, and the brightness of God shone round about them; and they feared with a great fear. 10 And the angel said to them: Fear not; for, behold, I bring you good tidings of great joy, that shall be to all the people: 11 For, this day, is born to you a Saviour, who is Christ the Lord, in the city of David. 12 And this shall be a sign unto you. You shall find the infant wrapped in swaddling clothes, and laid in a manger. 13 And suddenly there was with the angel a multitude of the heavenly army, praising God, and saying: 14 Glory to God in the highest; and on earth peace to men of good will.

At the top of the page are two scenes in a continuous verdant landscape, each flanked on one side by a medallion with an angel musician (fig. 7). In the first scene there is a pair of shepherds, one standing, the other seated, with their dog and flock. The men, like the angels in the seven medallions on this folio, play musical instruments. In the second scene, a shepherd in three-quarter back view and holding a crook, shields his eyes from the rays of light emanating from an angel with green, pink, white, and light blue wings. Beneath the angel is a howling dog and a grazing sheep. The scroll the angel holds has a pseudo-inscription.

The Annunciation to the Shepherds usually was the prime illustration for the Hour of Terce. Here it is placed in the *haut-de-page* of the folio with the opening text of the Hour of Prime and the historiated initial of the Nativity.[61] The humble pastoral concert, although not mentioned in the Gospel, was usually part of depictions of the Annunciation of the Shepherds. Their music-making heralds the celestial music to come, suggested by the passages in the Gospel describing the heavenly army praising God (Luke 2:13–14) and represented by the angel musicians in the borders. The fear the angel's arrival arouses (Luke 2:9–10) is expressed by the howling dog. Although the scroll the angel holds does not bear an actual text, it would have been viewed as conveying a Biblical passage. In some miniatures depicting the Annunciation to the Shepherds, the text of the scroll is written out and, commonly, is inscribed with some of the words the angel utters (Luke 2:10–11: annuncio vobis gaudium magnum) or an Old Testament prophecy foretelling the birth of Christ, most often Isaiah 9:6 "puer natus est."

Five lines from the top of the folio, inside of the three-line initial "D" introducing the prayer "Deus a quo sancta desideria," is a shield with the Bohun arms.

Historiated Initial "D": Nativity (Luke 2:7)

> Luke 2:6 And it came to pass, that when they were there, her days were accomplished, that she should be delivered. 7 And she brought forth her firstborn son, and wrapped him up in swaddling clothes, and laid him in a manger; because there was no room for them in the inn.
>
> Isaiah 1:3 The ox knoweth his owner, and the ass his master's crib: but Israel hath not known me, and my people hath not understood.
>
> Isaiah 1: 6 For a CHILD IS BORN to us, and a son is given to us, and the government is upon his shoulder: and his name shall be called, Wonderful, Counsellor, God the Mighty, the Father of the world to come, the Prince of Peace.

Inside the initial "D," the crowned Virgin, attended by a nimbed censing angel, sits up in bed and nurses the newborn Child, cradling him in her arm. Although her breast is exposed, the rest of her body is concealed. Mary's head is demurely inclined and her breast is seen in profile and placed unnaturally high on her torso. She modestly avoids the viewer's gaze as well as that of the angel in the center of the initial, focusing her attention on the vulnerable infant. Joseph, wearing a skullcap and holding a staff, sits in a curtained wooden chair. In contrast to the youthfulness of the Virgin, Joseph is depicted with white hair, mustache, and beard and a wrinkled brow. In the foreground, an ox and ass (Isaiah 1:3, Pseudo-Matthew, XIV) feed out of a wicker manger.

As was common, the Hour of Prime is illuminated with a scene depicting the Nativity. The Virgin nursing her infant at the Nativity appears with some regularity in English Psalters from the late thirteenth century on.[62] The Virgin's lactating breast draws attention to Christ's humanity, namely that he, like all babies, needed to feed. The potential eroticism of the Virgin's bare breast is downplayed in this miniature.[63] Mary's demeanor is pious and most of her body, except for her bosom, neck, face, and hands, is concealed. The displayed female breast and baby's body draw the viewer's attention to the Mother and Child's flesh and could be understood as illustrating beliefs like the one in the text of the hymn on the opposite page, f. 15: "That thou sometime didst take on thee, Of a pure virgin being born, The form of our humanity." The antithesis of this representation is the one depicted in the *bas-de-page* of the first Hour, namely of the abbess with both breasts exposed. These breasts, which are supple in appearance and have areolæ painted a different color than the flesh, are more fully visible and more naturalistically depicted than the Virgin's abstracted monochrome breast. In contrast to the image of the nursing Virgin, the abbess's dry breasts squeezed by the bishop are metonyms for her sexual sin and relinquished maternity.

In the visual arts, Joseph was traditionally represented as an old man and often situated in a peripheral position to the Mother and Child, alluding to his chaste relationship with Mary and his tangential role in the virgin birth of Jesus. The elaborate architectural band above the scene as well as the furnishings, the bed covering and pillow, the curtain and carved wooden chair, are in stark contrast with the other elements of the setting, such as the animals and the manger from which they feed. The placement of these types of contemporary objects in the scene of the Nativity might have lent an air of familiarity to the event and might have conveyed the impression that aspects of caring for an infant were part of a shared feminine experience.

Bas-de-Page: Legend of the Jew of Bourges

In the lower border three scenes show episodes from the Legend of the Jew of Bourges, one of the oldest and most popular Marian legends in circulation in Western Europe (fig. 8).[64] The core of the legend can be broadly summarized as follows:

> A Jewish boy takes communion with his Christian friends in a church in which there is an image of the Virgin above the altar. When the child's father finds out what had transpired, he pushes his son into his furnace for glass. The cries of the mother, who had run into the street, attract a crowd. The child is protected from the fire by Our Lady, whose image he saw in church.[65]

In front of an altar, supporting a gold chalice and retable of the Crucifixion with Mary and St. John, the crowned Virgin in a blue mantle and pink gown and a tonsured priest in rich vestments face a row of seven kneeling children waiting to receive the Eucharist. The priest holds a gold paten, and above it, in his other hand, the host. The Virgin points to a boy at the nearer end of the row, while laying her left hand on the head of the last of the waiting children. The hands of all the children are covered by a houseling cloth. In the second scene, a bearded man wearing a rose-colored turban pushes a naked boy into a fiery furnace. Flames engulf the child's head. On the other side of the oven is a group of people. In the foreground a woman wearing a veil, knotted at one side, and a turbaned man point at the culprit of the crime committed in front of their eyes. Their brows are furrowed and they appear distressed. The woman places one of her hands on her companion's body. The man is similar in appearance and dress to the one pushing the child into the oven except that his clothes are shorter in length and he wears rose-colored stockings instead of blue ones. Both the Jewish father and the woman's companion have much larger heads than, for example, the priest. The head coverings worn by the woman, her husband, and her companion, as well as the stereotyped Semitic features of the men, denote that they are Jews. In the third scene, the crowned Virgin, who has placed a portion of her mantle under the legs of the naked but unscathed boy, reaches into the furnace to rescue the unperturbed child.

Although many of the events and details described in written accounts are not represented in the *bas-de-page* of f. 14v, the episodes narrated in the Copenhagen manuscript find textual parallels among others in Vincent de Beauvais's *Speculum historiale*, Gautier de Coinci's *Miracles* and Jacobus de Voragine's *Golden Legend*.[66] More specifically, the version depicted in the Copenhagen manuscripts draws on the variant of the tale in which Mary uses her cloak to protect the child.[67] The retable of the Crucifixion with Mary and John on the altar in the *bas-de-page* probably represents the image of the Virgin the Jewish child in the textual accounts had seen in church.[68] In some written accounts of this tale, the boy survives thanks to the intervention of Mary prompted by the Jewish mother petitioning the Virgin for help. In the aftermath of a number of versions, including Vincent's, Adgar's, and Gautier's, the boy and his mother are baptized. In the Copenhagen Bohun Hours, however, the Jewish mother is not presented in a particularly positive light.[69] She stands side by side with a Jewish man who greatly resembles her husband. Although she appears to be distraught about the fate of her child, her passivity and her turning to the Jewish man for comfort might also imply a degree of culpability. Her conversion is not shown in the *bas-de-page* scenes.

The pose of the Jew in the second scene and the position of the Virgin's body in the third are similar and invite comparison between their actions, the pushing into the flames of the child seen from the back and the removal of the child from the furnace in frontal view. The conclusion that may be drawn from these compositional similarities is that the viewer is meant to compare the cruel behavior of the Jew towards his own son with the compassionate reaction of Mary. Also, it can be seen that the Virgin extends to the boy the same expression of maternal love she shows her own Son in the historiated initial of the Nativity. Mary's action could also be understood as a response to the petition for help at the opening of Prime, directly above the *bas-de-page*: "Deus in adiutorium meum intende. Domine ad adiuvandum me festina. Gloria patri et filio et spiritui sancto. Sicut" (O God, incline unto my aid. O Lord make haste to help me) and the lines of text on the facing folio, f. 15, in which Mary, mother of mercy, is asked for assistance: "Maria plena gracie, mater misericordie, tu nos ab hoste protege, et in hora mortis suscipe." (Mary full of grace, Of mercy mother also art, Save and defend us from our foe, Receive us when we hence depart). Mary's placing of her cloak around the boy to protect him is reminiscent of the gesture she makes in the Last Judgment scene where she wraps souls in her cloak (fig. 17).

In the Copenhagen Bohun Hours, the fact that the two primary areas of illumination, the initial and *bas-de-page*, depict two families also invites comparison. The close and affectionate relationship between the Mother and Child and the protective air of Joseph, their guardian, in the large historiated initial seem to be juxtaposed to the seriously flawed Jewish parents depicted on the bottom of the page. Rather than protecting his son, the Jewish father attacks him. In contrast, Joseph, at the side of the bed of the mother and child, is ready to serve and aid them. His imposing size also appears to be a positive and protective attribute.[70]

Directly below the initial depicting Mary nursing her infant in the *bas-de-page*, children wait to receive the Host and wine, the body and blood of Christ. Since in medieval times breast milk was believed to be transmuted blood, an analogy was probably intended between the Virgin whose blood becomes food for her Child, and God who feeds humankind with his blood in the Eucharist.[71] There was a long tradition of connecting the body of the newborn Child and the bread of the Eucharist. The association between Christ and bread was grounded on the words of Christ (John 6:51) "I am the living bread which came down from heaven. If any man eat of this bread, he shall live for ever; and the bread that I will give, is my flesh, for the life of the world." At least as early as the Christmas homily of St. Gregory, the Nativity scene was interpreted in Eucharistic terms.[72] The placement of the image of the beasts feeding on hay above man "eating" the flesh of Christ also suggests that the former has Eucharist implications.[73] Although the ass and the ox were commonplace in representations of the Nativity, they were not always shown feeding. Numerous medieval sermons connect altar and manger and in some the beasts are likened to the communicants and the fodder to the body of Christ.[74] The Crucifixion retable depicted in the communion scene underlines Christ's sacrifice reenacted in the Mass. The imagery on this page thus appears to have been designed to expand on the Eucharistic connotations traditionally associated with the legend of the Jew of Bourges.[75]

The way in which the glowing fire in the oven is painted, as gold and red lines emanating from the child's unscathed body, in a manner analogous to the light emanating from angels (e.g. fig. 1), suggests that we are to understand it as supernatural. The child the Virgin protects with her spread cloak does not look like the boy represented in the first and second *bas-de-page* scenes. Rather, he resembles the Child she holds and suckles in the historiated initial. While the image could be read as the child reborn in the flames, it could allude also to Christ's death at the hands of the Jews and to his Resurrection.

Other negative associations with the Jews can also be found on this folio. In the Copenhagen Hours the Jewish man, who is enraged by his son's partaking of the Eucharist, can be understood as the embodiment of the disbelieving Jews and is juxtaposed to the Christians who accept the miracle of the Host. The central motif of the child being pushed into the oven could have conceivably reinforced the belief that Jews murdered (Christian) children.[76] Several Marian miracle tales, albeit none represented in the *bas-de-page* of this manuscript, relate how Jews abused and killed innocent children.[77] This Marian legend in which the Jewish boy embraces Christianity follows the tale of Theophilus, in which the protagonist renounces Christ and Mary and embraces the devil. Both narratives contain elements that spawn anxieties about the activities of those members of society who do not accept Christ as their savior.

The legend of the Jew of Bourges was represented in the Bodleian Psalter Hours at Terce, f. 203v.[78] In the miniature, the Virgin, with her back to an altar on which there is a chalice and an image of the Mother and Child, raises two fingers to bless seven children whose hands are covered by a houseling cloth. Next to her a priest holds the host. Both Virgin and priest gaze in the direction of the Jewish father peering in. In the second scene, the Jew pushes his son into the oven with a three-pronged fork. Next to the oven, stands the Virgin who appears to be ready to take hold of the boy. Glover suggested that the image of Mary saving the Jewish boy from the flames of the furnace in the Bodleian manuscript might be associated with the Virgin saving her devotees from purgatorial fire.[79] But, as in the Copenhagen manuscript, it might also allude to Christ's death at the hands of the Jews.

Plate 4. Folio 17v. End of Prime. Three-line initial "C": Shield with the arms of St. George (*argent a cross gules*)

> Concede nos famulos tuos quesumus domine deus perpetua mentis et corporis salute gaudere, et gloriosa beate marie semper virginis intercessione a presenti liberari tristicia et eterna perfrui leticia. Per dominum nostrum ihesum xpm filium tuum qui tecum vivit et regnat in unitate spiritus sancti per omnia secula seculorum. Amen. Benedicamus domino. Deo gracias. (Grant to your servants, we beseech you O Lord God, the joy of continual health in mind and body. And with the prayers of the Virgin Mary to help us, guide us through the sorrows of this life to eternal happiness in the life to come. Through our Lord Jesus Christ, your Son, who lives and reigns

with you and reigns in unity with the Holy Spirit, for ever and ever. Amen. Let us give praise unto the Lord. Give thanks to God.)

The three-line initial containing the shield with the banner of St. George introduces the collect "Concede nos famulos tuos." It is placed on the folio facing one with a historiated initial depicting the Adoration of the Magi, f. 18, at Terce (Plate 5). There are no armorials on folio 18.

The decision to decorate the interior of the initial "C" with a shield bearing the arms of St. George was probably not arbitrary.[80] St. George, a soldier of noble birth in Emperor Diocletian's army, was believed to have a special relationship to the Virgin, who, according to legend, miraculously resuscitated him after his martyrdom.[81] The reader of the Copenhagen Hours could have understood the line of the collect that describes the Virgin's intercessory prayers as also referring to Mary's role in assisting St. George.

St. George was significant in other ways. He was associated with the Crusade and was chosen and promoted by Edward III as the protector of England and patron of the king's new order of the Garter.[82] The saint was also the spiritual patron of Edward III and was given a prominent role in the imagery of works made for the king.[83] For example, in the now lost paintings for the king's household and family chapel of St. Stephen, Westminster, on the north side of the altar wall, St. George in contemporary dress beckoned in a comradely manner the kneeling Edward III as well as his sons to contemplate the Virgin and Child adored by the Magi, to whom the king had special devotions.[84] Another monarch who advertised his devotions to both St. George and the Magi was Richard II. The red cross of St. George was added to the label on the arms of Richard of Bordeaux before he became king. Associations between Richard, who was born on the day of the feast of the Epiphany, and the Magi were drawn in art and celebrations.[85] The shield of St. George paired with the Adoration of the Magi on the facing folio in Thott 547, 4° might, therefore, allude to Edward's devotion to St. George and the Magi, or perhaps to Richard II's.

Although St. George had importance for the monarchy, there might have been more personal reasons for the inclusion of the saint's arms in the Copenhagen Hours. A number of members of the Bohun family as well as their close relatives were made knights of the garter on St. George's day. Humphrey de Bohun, the seventh earl, was a garter knight from c. 1365, as was his father, William de Bohun, Earl of Northampton, and his uncle, Hugh de Courtenay, husband of Margaret de Bohun. In 1377, Henry of Bolingbroke, along with Richard of Bordeaux, was made a knight of the Garter. During the reign of Richard II, in 1380 or 1381, Thomas of Woodstock also became a garter knight. The Bohun heiresses, Eleanor and Mary were invested as Lady Companions, Order of the Garter, in 1384 and 1388, respectively.

The shield with the banner of St. George depicted at the end of Prime in the Copenhagen Hours, is also shown in other Bohun manuscripts. It appears in the borders on f. 4v of the Pommersfelden manuscript. It is held by the saint himself in the pictorial tables of saints in the Bodleian Hours, f. 236v, and the fragment in Pommersfelden, f. 10 as well as by a composite figure in the border of f. 114v in the Egerton Psalter-Hours. St. George was included in the Litany of the Copenhagen Hours.[86]

The inclusion of the shield with the arms of St. George in this manuscript may not have had one significance but several. It might have been an allusion to yet another miracle of the Virgin's, to the Bohun's connections to the royal family, as well as/or a reference to the monarchy, the Order of the Garter, and royal devotion to the saint and the Magi.

Plate 5. Folio 18. Terce.
Historiated Initial "D": Adoration of the Magi (Matthew 2:9–11)

> Matthew 2:9 Who having heard the king, went their way; and behold the star which they had seen in the east, went before them, until it came and stood over where the child was. 10 And seeing the star they rejoiced with exceeding great joy. 11 And entering into the house, they found the child with Mary his mother, and falling down they adored him; and opening their treasures, they offered him gifts; gold, frankincense, and myrrh.

Under an arcade topped by architectural elements, a battlement, turret, and gables, are the three Magi offering their gifts to the Child held by his Mother. The Virgin is regally depicted, crowned, and wearing a blue mantle patterned with gold stars and stylized leaves and seated on a gold throne, backed by an ornate cloth of honor. The cross-nimbed Child, standing on the Virgin's knee, holds his hands above the gold cup presented to him by the elderly, kneeling, bareheaded Magus. The cup's cover is held in the king's left hand and his crown hangs from his wrist. The Magus standing behind him looks over his shoulder at the third king, drawing his attention by pointing to the star, which emanates red and golden rays.

The depiction of the Adoration of the Magi often accompanied one of the Hours of the Virgin. As was common, the image depicts three events described in the Gospels, the Magi finding the Child beneath the star (Matthew 2:9), worshiping the Child (Matthew 2:11), and opening their treasures and offering Him gifts (Matthew 2:11). The regal precedence of the Mother and Child over the Magi is connoted by their position on the throne, backed by an ornate cloth of honor. The king has removed his crown and kneels before the Virgin and Christ, in acknowledgement that he is a subject of their higher authority.[87] More generally, the Magus could be understood as a model of devotion for the viewer.

Bas-de-Page: Legend of the Child Image taken Hostage

Jacobus de Voragine, *The Golden Legend*

> A woman who had lost her husband had her only son, whom she loved tenderly, for consolation. It happened, however, that the son was captured by enemies and imprisoned in chains. When she heard this, she wept inconsolably, and prayed incessantly to the blessed Virgin, to whom she was much devoted, to obtain her son's liberation. Then, seeing that her prayers were not answered, she went alone into a church where there was a sculptured image of blessed Mary, and, standing in front of the image, she addressed it in these terms: "O Virgin blessed, I have often asked you for the liberation of my son, and so far you have not come to the aid of this pitiable mother; I have sought your patronage for my son and see no return for my prayers. Therefore, as my son has been taken away from me, I will take your Son away from you and hold him in custody as a hostage for mine." She then went up and took the image of the Child from the Virgin's lap, went home with it, wrapped it in spotless cloths, and hid it in a cupboard, which she locked carefully. Thus she could rejoice at having a good hostage for her son and guarded it closely.
>
> The following night the blessed Virgin appeared to the young man and opened the door of the prison. She told him to get up and leave, and said: "Son, you will tell your mother to give my Son back to me as I have given hers back to her." The youth walked out, went to his mother, and told to her how the Virgin had set him free. Overjoyed, she took the image of the

> Child, went to the church, and returned her Son to Mary, saying: "I thank you, my lady, for restoring my only son to me, and now I return your Son to you because I acknowledge that I have received my own."[88]

In the foreground of the first scene a wimpled and veiled woman places the image of the Christ-Child into an open chest before a house (fig. 10). The woman has turned her head to look behind her at the canopied, polychromed sculpture of the crowned Virgin on a draped altar. On the right side of the altar is a riddle, from which is suspended a fabric, and on the left side is a stone buttress. In the middleground of the center scene is a square building with four round turrets and two barred windows. On the left and in front of the building is the crowned Virgin holding the bars of one window and looking inside at the prisoner. His eyes are downcast and he seems unaware of the Virgin's presence. The third scene takes place in a vaulted space inside a building with battlements. The crowned Virgin, a boy, and a woman stand around an open chest. The boy gestures and the Virgin points at the woman at whom they both stare. The woman is slightly bent over the chest and ready to grasp the image of the Child, whose arm is raised and extended towards his mother's hands.

The Legend of the Christ-Child as Hostage, illustrated in the lower border, was not disseminated as widely as some of the other miracle tales represented in this manuscript.[89] Nevertheless, the story would have been known through its diffusion in the *Golden Legend*. The events depicted in the Thott 547, 4° closely follow the key narrative moments of Jacobus de Voragine's work.

The decision to illuminate the lower border with this rarely depicted tale might have been thought appropriate to compliment the image of the Adoration of the Magi, f. 18, and some of the lines of two Hymns on folio 18. Both the historiated initial and the scenes in the *bas-de-page* deal with maternity, as do the two Hymns on folio 18: "Memento salutis auctor" and "Maria mater gracie" (Remember, author of our salvation, that you once took upon yourself the form of our body by being born of the unsullied Virgin. Mary that mother art of grace, Of mercy mother also art). The placement of Mary's hands in the Adoration, tenderly supporting her infant, and the first scene in the *bas-de-page* encircling a void and emphasizing the absence of her Child, are used to bring attention to her maternity and her loss of her Son who will later be taken from her by His death on the cross. The placement of the Child in the chest is evocative of Christ's Entombment. The woman's desperate act also draws attention to her maternity.

The imagery in the lower marginal illuminates other aspects of the texts on this folio, for example the necessity to actively ask for help announced in the incipit "Deus in adiutorium meum intende. Domine ad adiuvandum me festina" (O God, incline unto my aid. O Lord make haste to help me) and for mercy, expressed in the Hymn (Mary that mother art of grace, Of mercy mother also art). Even though the woman behaves in a vindictive manner, Mary does not punish her. Instead she is merciful and assists her, revealing that the Virgin could understand her maternal plight.

This legend, which was rarely represented in the visual arts, is illustrated in two other Bohun manuscripts, the Bodleian's Psalter-Hours at None, f. 209, and in the Egerton Psalter and Hours, f. 123, where it also accompanies Terce.[90] Besides allusions to the already discussed Christological events, the legend might have had other meanings for its audience. In this period, in which war and rebellions were commonplace and terrestrial justice was viewed as imperfect, the scenes from the legend could be interpreted as reassuring their audience that justice was dispensed from heaven. Additionally, the legend may have allusions to Mary's power to deliver prisoners from captivity, one of the most common types of miracles associated with the cult of saints.[91]

Plate 6. Folio 20. Sext.
Historiated Initial "D": Presentation of the Child in the Temple and the Purification of the Virgin (Luke 2:22–34)

> Luke 2:22 And after the days of her purification, according to the law of Moses, were accomplished, they carried him to Jerusalem, to present him to the Lord: 23 As it is written in the law of the Lord: Every male opening the womb shall be called holy to the Lord: 24 And to offer a sacrifice, according as it is written in the law of the Lord, a pair of turtledoves, or two young pigeons: 25 And behold there was a man in Jerusalem named Simeon, and this man was just and devout, waiting for the consolation of Israel; and the Holy Ghost was in him. 26 And he had received an answer from the Holy Ghost, that he should not see death, before he had seen the Christ of the Lord. 27 And he came by the Spirit into the temple. And when his parents brought in the child Jesus, to do for him according to the custom of the law, 28 He also took him into his arms, and blessed God, and said: 29 Now thou dost dismiss thy servant, O Lord, according to thy word in

peace; 30 Because my eyes have seen thy salvation, 31 Which thou hast prepared before the face of all peoples: 32 A light to the revelation of the Gentiles, and the glory of thy people Israel.

Leviticus 12:1 And the Lord spoke to Moses, saying: 2 Speak to the children of Israel, and thou shalt say to them: If a woman having received seed shall bear a man child, she shall be unclean seven days, according to the days of the separation of her flowers. 3 And on the eighth day the infant shall be circumcised: 4 But she shall remain three and thirty days in the blood of her purification. She shall touch no holy thing, neither shall she enter into the sanctuary, until the days of her purification be fulfilled. 5 But if she shall bear a maid child, she shall be unclean two weeks, according to the custom of her monthly courses, and she shall remain in the blood of her purification sixty-six days. 6 And when the days of her purification are expired, for a son, or for a daughter, she shall bring to the door of the tabernacle of the testimony, a lamb of a year old for a holocaust, and a young pigeon or a turtle for sin, and shall deliver them to the priest: 7 Who shall offer them before the Lord, and shall pray for her, and so she shall be cleansed from the issue of her blood. This is the law for her that beareth a man child or a maid child. 8 And if her hand find not sufficiency, and she is not able to offer a lamb, she shall take two turtles, or two young pigeons, one for a holocaust, and another for sin: and the priest shall pray for her, and so she shall be cleansed.

In the center of a vaulted interior space stands the crowned Virgin in three-quarter view, with loose golden hair. She is turned towards a draped altar over which she and Simeon, coped and in a skull-cap, hold the naked infant Christ. The Child has placed his right hand inside the front of his mother's gown, anchoring himself to her. Behind Simeon is a wimpled and veiled female, less visible than the other figures. To the left of the Virgin is a wimpled and veiled woman holding a candle, probably the prophetess Anna (Luke 2:36–38), as well as Joseph, in a skull-cap, with a basket with three doves (Luke 2:24).

The opening of Sext of the Hours of the Virgin is illuminated with a scene of the Presentation of the Child in the Temple and Purification of the Virgin. These events usually, but not always, accompanied the Hour of None. Mosaic Law required that a first-born male child after birth be brought to the temple to be dedicated to God. Forty days after the birth, the mother had to present herself for ritual cleaning and bring a sacrifice

(Leviticus 12:4, 6–8). In St. Luke's Gospel the presentation of the baby Jesus and the purification of the Virgin are described as occurring on the same day. Simeon, who wears rich vestments, is depicted in the miniature as high priest of the temple (Protoevangelium XXIV). As was common in works of art of this period, the Virgin and Child are accompanied by Joseph, who brings an offering, and an attendant figure, who in some representations holds a candle. The latter item is an allusion to Simeon calling Christ "a light to enlighten the Gentiles, and the glory of Thy people Israel" (Luke 2:32), and to the custom of celebrating the feast with a procession of candles.[92] The source for the representation of the Child holding on to Mary might derive from the *Meditations on the Life of Christ* (XI), or from pictorial sources.[93]

Bas-de-Page: Legend of the Monk and the Roses

Jean Miélot, *Miracles de Nostre Dame*

> A young monk […] placed daily a wreath of roses on the Virgin's image all through the rose season. […]Whenever he did so the image bowed to him. […]When the season was over he was sad and distressed. […] When the abbot […] asked the reason why he was so sad, the monk told him the truth […]. To console him the abbot said "instead of making the wreath for Our Lady I order you to say twenty-five *Aves* daily before her image." The monk did as the abbot commanded and […] at each *Ave* the image of the Virgin produced a fresh red rose, […] until she had completed the chaplet for herself. He was greatly consoled […] and his devotion to the Virgin grew. This monk had a mother and father […] and was granted permission by the abbot to travel to see them with a companion […]. When he realized that he had forgotten to salute the image before leaving the abbey […] he sent his companion on ahead […]. When he was alone […] he said his twenty-five *Aves* behind a hedge […]. Looking for his companion, the other monk returned to the place they had parted ways and saw the crowned Virgin in the air, attended by angels and noble virgins. It seemed to him that the lady was making a wreath of very beautiful roses. […] They returned to their abbey to always serve the Virgin Mary devotedly and finished their lives happily with our Lord.[94]

Dominic of Prussia, *How the Rosary Came to be*

> [...] Then one day he was sent on an errand that required him to ride through a forest that harbored thieves. In the forest he tied his horse to a tree, knelt down, and was reciting his fifty *Ave Marias* when thieves saw him and decided to rob him and steal his horse. But as they approached him, they saw from a distance a wonderfully beautiful maiden standing by him who, every little while, took from his mouth a beautiful rose and added it to a chaplet she was making. When the rose chaplet was complete, she placed it on her head and flew off to heaven. The robbers were thoroughly amazed and ran to the brother asking him who the beautiful maiden was that they had seen beside him. The lay brother replied: "I did not have any maiden with me. I have only been reciting fifty *Ave Marias* as a chaplet for Queen Mary, as I was instructed. And that is all I know." When the robbers told him what they had seen, the lay brother, and the robbers, too, realized that it was the most revered Mother of God who, in person, had accepted the rose chaplet that we are accustomed to send to her daily through our angel.
>
> Then the brother rejoiced from the depths of his heart, and, from that day forward, made a spiritual rose chaplet of fifty *Ave Marias* for Queen Mary daily and instructed other good people in the practice. In this manner, the rosary was created and made known to us. And one may believe that the robbers bettered their lives as a result, because God's grace had permitted them to behold the Mother of Mercy.[95]

In the lower border are three scenes of the Legend of the Monk and Roses (fig. 11). In the first, a monk wearing a black habit kneels upon a draped altar and with both hands puts a wreath of flowers on the head of a seated polychromed image of the Virgin holding her Child. Behind the sculpture and atop of the altar is a large flat panel with a trefoil arch. On either side of the altar are riddle posts of wrought iron supporting a rose-colored fabric. The next scene takes place beneath an arch of a building with traceried windows and in front of a lavender curtain. A hooded monk in profile, gesticulating with his left hand and holding a golden hoop in his right, is turned toward another hooded monk, seated on a bench with bent head, holding one of his knees. In the foreground of the final scene a monk kneels to the crowned Virgin standing in a clearing between trees. She holds a wreath of flowers in her left hand and a single flower between the thumb and index finger of her right one. Behind the monk are two horses, and two men, one holding a round object in his right hand and pointing at the Virgin with his left. To the right of the Virgin, there are five men hiding behind trees, two of whom are pointing at the central group.

With the exception of the concluding episode, the miracle of the monk and the roses depicted in the Copenhagen Bohun Hours illustrates, as pointed out by James, the tale told by Jean Miélot in the collection of Marian miracles for Philip the Good of c. 1456, and might, therefore, illustrate an earlier version of this legend.[96] As in Miélot's narrative, in the *bas-de-page* of Thott 517, 4° the monk places a garland of roses on the image of the Virgin. Explanations for details found in the second scene can be located in Miélot's account: the sadness of the monk can be attributed to the season of roses being over, and the exchange between the monk and another member of his order represent the monk being told by the abbot to say twenty-five *Aves*. The third scene, which takes place outside the monastery, probably illustrates the monk reciting his *Aves* during a journey, and the Virgin completing the wreath with the flower that she holds in her hand. However, the concluding episode in the Copenhagen manuscript includes a number of details not present in Miélot's account, such as the men hiding behind the trees and witnessing the miracle.[97] Some variants of this legend entail a member of a religious order, the recitation of *Ave Marias*, and the undertaking of a journey, and conclude with an episode involving thieves or brigands. For example, in an early fourteenth-century manuscript (Munich, Bayerische Staatsbibliothek, Cod. lat. 5927, f. 195), a brigand who is lying in wait sees a maiden carrying a golden hoop and gathering roses that are falling from the lips of the main protagonist, a cellarer of a Cistercian abbey, at each *Ave* and weaving them into a garland.[98] Dominic of Prussia's (1382–1461) version of the legend, although later than the Copenhagen Bohun Hours, gives an account of the events in the forest that conforms with greater fidelity to those depicted in the third scene in the *bas-de-page*.

As in all the *bas-de-page* illustrations studied thus far in Thott 547, 4°, the supplicant's devotion to Mary can be directly connected to the Virgin offering her petitioner assistance. This particular legend additionally contains the reassuring motif of Mary protecting her devotee from danger on a journey, which might have had significance for the reader and her family. In Medieval England members of the upper classes would have travelled for various reasons, to their different residences as well as those of relatives, to sanctuaries, etc. Attesting to the anxieties travelers experienced before undertaking a journey is the inclusion in Books of Hours of prayers for safe travel. For example, in the fragmentary Bohun manuscript (Private Collection), f. 121, there is prayer preceded by a rubric explaining its use before going on a journey.[99]

The Presentation in the Temple is the last scene in the manuscript's Infancy cycle. The imagery on this folio may announce Christ's Passion, represented at the opening of None, the next canonical hour, f. 22v. The connection between the presentation and the Passion is found in the words spoken by Simeon (Luke 2:34), who during the presentation of the infant Jesus in the temple, prophesied the purpose of Christ's sacrifice: "Behold this child is set for the fall, and for the resurrection of many in Israel, and for a sign which shall be contradicted." Further allusions to Christ's suffering as recorded in the Gospels may be intended by the placement of the rose miracle in the *bas-de-page* on the same folio as the Presentation. Both St. Bernard of Clairvaux and St. Bonaventure associated the rose with the Passion.[100]

The rose imagery in the *bas-de-page* may have had other meanings as well. By the thirteenth century there was a general acceptance of the identification of Mary with roses.[101] In the Middle Ages the flower was also associated with love and passion. The motif of the lover placing a chaplet of roses on the head of the beloved, described in poetry and represented on secular ivories, symbolized his ardor.[102] Here the imagery is used probably to denote the monk's ardent devotion to Mary.[103]

The Virgin's submission to the rites of purification, which it was generally believed she did not need to undergo since she contracted no trace of sin in giving birth to Christ, visualizes how Mary is virtuous above all other women.[104] Additionally, the representation of her compliance was considered to provide others with an exemplum of purification and humility.[105] Mary's exceptional nature might also be suggested by the *bas-de-page* image of her being crowned, in all likelihood an allusion to her Coronation.[106] The proximity of the representation of the Virgin handing over her Child in the Temple in the historiated initial to the one in the lower border of her likeness on an altar receiving a garland might have invited the viewer to see a causal connection between Mary submitting to the will of God and the favors bestowed on her. A female audience might have perceived the imagery as implying that the fulfillment of duty had its rewards.

The legend, which was rarely depicted in the visual arts of this period, was not represented in either the British Library's or the Bodleian Library's Bohun manuscript.[107]

Plate 7. Folio 22v. None.
Historiated Initial "D": Crucifixion (Matthew 27:33–55, Mark 15:22–41, Luke 23:26–49, John 19:16–37)

> Luke 23:44 And it was almost the sixth hour; and there was darkness over
> all the earth until the ninth hour. 45 And the sun was darkened, and the
> veil of the temple was rent in the midst. 46 And Jesus crying out with a loud
> voice, said: Father, into thy hands I commend my spirit. And saying this, he
> gave up the ghost. 47 Now the centurion, seeing what was done, glorified
> God, saying: Indeed this was a just man. 48 And all the multitude of them
> that were come together to that sight, and saw the things that were done,
> returned striking their breasts. 49 And all his acquaintance, and the women
> that had followed him from Galilee, stood afar off, beholding these things.

> Mark 15:33 And when the sixth hour was come, there was darkness over
> the whole earth until the ninth hour. 34 And at the ninth hour, Jesus cried
> out with a loud voice, saying: Eloi, Eloi, lamma sabacthani? Which is, being
> interpreted, My God, my God, why hast thou forsaken me? 35 And some of
> the standers by hearing, said: Behold he calleth Elias. 36 And one running
> and filling a sponge with vinegar, and putting it upon a reed, gave him to
> drink, saying: Stay, let us see if Elias come to take him down. 37 And Jesus
> having cried out with a loud voice, gave up the ghost. 38 And the veil of the
> temple was rent in two, from the top to the bottom. 39 And the centurion
> who stood over against him, seeing that crying out in this manner he had
> given up the ghost, said: Indeed this man was the son of God. 40 And there
> were also women looking on afar off: among whom was Mary Magdalen,
> and Mary the mother of James the less and of Joseph, and Salome: 41 Who
> also when he was in Galilee followed him, and ministered to him, and many
> other women that came up with him to Jerusalem.

In the center of the historiated initial is the crucified Christ, head bowed, eyes shut, and blood flowing from his hands, side, and feet. He wears the crown of thorns and a loin cloth. The dove of the Holy Spirit, leaving behind white streaks trailing back to the head of Christ, ascends towards God the Father in the spandrel in the upper left corner. To the left of the vertical stem of the letter "D" stands the bearded Longinus wearing a round cap-shaped hat and red orange tunic, pointing to his one opened eye while piercing Christ's side with a lance. Above and below him, in the circular projections of the letter "D", are two angels. To the left of the Crucified Christ, the Virgin swoons at her Son's death and is supported by her female companions. At the foot of the cross Mary Magdalene kneels in grief while to her right St. John prays, looking up at Christ. A group of three witnesses, in contemporary dress and round cap-shaped hats, stand to the right of the apostle. The bearded one, in the foreground, has raised his left hand toward Christ and with his right points at St. John. Outside of the initial to the right, the sun is obscured by a black cloud.

The opening of the Hour of None of the Office of the Virgin was frequently illuminated with the Circumcision or the Presentation in the Temple. However, like many English Books of Hours of the late thirteenth and fourteenth centuries, in Thott 547, 4°, Infancy imagery does not accompany all the Hours.[108] The place where the Infancy cycle was interrupted varied. In the Copenhagen Bohun Hours, None, the Hour of Christ's death is the Hour with which the Passion cycle starts.[109]

In accordance with descriptions of the Crucifixion in the Gospels, there are many witnesses to Christ's death represented on this folio. Mary and John, as was common in the visual arts, are present (John 19:26–27), as is Mary Magdalene (John 19:25). The man piercing Christ's side (John 19:34–35) and touching his eye is a figure who was associated by tradition with Longinus. According to legend he was blind in one eye until the blood from Jesus' side spattered on his face. After being healed he became a Christian. The figure sometimes displays Jewish characteristics, to emphasize the theme of conversion.[110] In the Copenhagen Bohun Hours he wears a round cap-shaped hat and red tunic, the latter is very similar in color and cut to the one worn by the Jewish father on f. 14v (fig. 7).[111] The man pointing may be the centurion who, after Christ had given up the ghost, said: "Indeed this was the Son of God" (Mark 15:39, Luke 23:46–47).[112]

The suffering of the crucified Jesus is reflected in the mournful attitudes of St. John, the Magdalene, some of the accompanying figures, and especially his mother. The pose of the Virgin, head held to one side and collapsing in the arms of her companions, echoes the pose of Christ expiring. It was believed that the Virgin's motherhood and her suffering with her Son at the Crucifixion, gave her the authority and capacity to intercede with Christ, to ask for mercy on the behalf of her devotees, and to bring the individual to salvation.[113]

Bas-de-Page: The Soul Saved

In the lower border, there are three scenes in a room with a curtained bed in which lies a bearded man (fig. 13). In the first scene the man is turbaned and his eyes are closed. On the near side of the bed is an angel, on the far side a black, horned devil. In the following scene the figures at the bedside have been replaced by the crowned, nimbed Virgin kneeling on the near side and the bare-chested Christ surrounded by rays on the far side. Both Mary, who holds her bared breast with her right hand and raises her left, and Christ, who exposes his wounds, look upward at the head of the nimbed Lord, emanating rays of light. In the third scene the man in the bed, bare-headed and awake, lifts his hands towards an angel standing near his feet.

This legend involves an angel and a devil contending for the soul of a man on his deathbed and the intervention of the Virgin and her Son on the man's behalf. M. R. James proposed, albeit with reservations, that the subject depicted in the *bas-de-page* was the miracle of the usurer's soul.[114] The scenes in the Copenhagen Hours do not illustrate events described either in the legend recounted by Caesarius of Heisterbach 2:31 or in a similar one in *La Vie des Pères*.[115] The *bas-de-pages* scenes have some elements in common with two miniatures in the *Taymouth Hours* (London, British Library, MS Yates Thompson 13). On f. 150v of the London manuscript the dying man, identified in the inscription below as a merchant, lies in a bed, with a devil at his head and a priest, holding a pix, containing the host, at his side.[116] Like the Copenhagen *bas-de-pages* scenes, the miniature in the *Taymouth Hours* is connected with mercy. Another scene from the legend is represented in the London manuscript on f. 151 in which the same man in a bed is attended by the Virgin, the Holy Spirit, and St. Michael who is weighing souls as well as two devils.[117]

The legend in the *bas-de-page* reflects the generally held belief that there was always a dispute between devils and angels for each man's soul when he died, and it is the first of two legends in this manuscript depicting this struggle.[118] Additionally, it incorporates the image of the interceding Mary, perhaps at the sickbed of the mortally ill and, as in a number of legends described in collections, restoring health.[119] In the Copenhagen Bohun Hours, the turban the man initially wears probably signifies that he is ill. In the third episode he is bareheaded, awake, and propped up on his pillow, lifts his hands towards an angel and is more active than in the first two scenes, suggesting that he is well again. These particular scenes might have been chosen to illustrate the three lines of the hymn above the *bas-de-*

page on folio: "Memento salutis auctor quod nostri quondam corporis, ex illibata virgine nascentdo, formam sumpseris. Maria plena gracie, Mater misericordie, tu nos ab hoste" (Be mindful author of our health/salvation, That thou sometime didst take on thee, Of a pure virgin being born, The form of our humanity. Mary full of grace, Of mercy mother also art, Save and defend us from our foe).[120] The text/image juxtaposition suggests that the man is saved from being taken by the devil due to the Lord's and the Virgin's intervention. These types of ideas may also have been implied by the text image juxtaposition in the Egerton manuscript, f. 129, where two scenes of the soul saved in the margins, and alongside the historiated letter "D" are close to the text "Converte nos deus salutaris noster. Et averte iram tuam a nobis" (Convert thou us, O God our Savior: and turn away thine anger from us.)

Directly below the line of text describing Mary as "our mother of mercy" is the image of the Virgin baring one of her breasts with which she nourished her Son, and, in this attitude of supplication, asking Him to intercede with God the Father. Mary showing her naked breast and Christ exposing his wounds symbolize the offer of mercy to the dying man.[121] A wider significance is given to the *bas-de-page* scene when it is contemplated in relationship to the historiated initial on this folio. The two scenes can be understood as reinforcing the belief that Christ's sacrifice, symbolized by the representation of the Crucifixion, makes not just the dying man's but all of humanity's salvation possible.

The displaying of the Virgin's naked bosom and Christ's torso are visual reminders that the Lord took on flesh from Mary. This aspect of the relationship between the Mother and Son is also stressed in the text of the hymn on the facing folio, 23: "That thou sometime didst take on thee, Of a pure virgin being born, The form of our humanity." The image of the Virgin exposing her bosom might also remind audiences of miracles in which the Virgin offers her breast to a gravely ill man and her milk cures him. In Gautier de Coinci's version of the legend, the poet describes the Virgin as a healer: "Highest lady, highest queen, are you not the physician and medicine who heals and cures all illnesses?"[122]

Two scenes depicting this miracle were represented at Compline in the Egerton Psalter-Hours, f. 129, in the circular projections of the historiated initial. In the upper one, a man with longhair and closed eyes lies in bed. Over his body, an angel contends with a black, horned devil. In the lower scene, on one side of the bed, the Virgin holds her exposed breast attended by a kneeling and praying angel. On the other side of the bed is the cross, nimbed bare-chested resurrected Christ, blessing with one hand and holding a cross staff in his other hand. The man's appearance, long-haired and bearded, suggests he has been confined to his bed for some time. The legend was not represented in the Bodleian Library's manuscript.

Plate 8. Folio 24. Vespers. Historiated Initial "D": Resurrection (Matthew 27:62–66)

> Matthew 27:62 And the next day, which followed the day of preparation,
> the chief priests and the Pharisees came together to Pilate, 63 Saying: Sir,
> we have remembered, that that seducer said, while he was yet alive: After
> three days I will rise again. 64 Command therefore the sepulchre to be
> guarded until the third day: lest perhaps his disciples come and steal him
> away, and say to the people: He is risen from the dead; and the last error
> shall be worse than the first. 65 Pilate saith to them: You have a guard;
> go, guard it as you know. 66 And they departing, made the sepulchre sure,
> sealing the stone, and setting guards.

In the center of the initial, the nimbed and crowned Christ, partly draped in a blue mantle, steps out of the tomb amid red and gold rays. He holds a cross staff in his left hand and raises his right in a gesture of blessing. Three soldiers sleep in front of the elaborate tomb. Armed with a spear and a sword, a fourth soldier is placed to the left of the stem of the letter "D," and a fifth one crouches in the lower right corner of the background of the initial. In the upper left and right spandrels, over the historiated letter, is a pair of angels swinging chains attached to censers above two other praying angels who kneel at either end of the tomb.

The historiated initial "D" for Vespers is illuminated with the Resurrection, a scene that continues the Christological narrative represented in the previous Hour. According to the Gospels, after Christ had been crucified he was entombed (Matthew 27:62–66) and remained in the guarded sepulcher. In the Gospels, confirmation of His resurrection was first borne out by the discovery of the empty tomb by the three women and was related to them by an angel (Matthew 28:5–6, Mark 16:5–6, Luke 24:1–6). The scene shown in the historiated initial of Christ leaving the tomb was not described in the New Testament but is based, rather, on pictorial tradition. In the representation of the Resurrection, as was common in the visual arts,

Christ is shown leaving the guarded tomb, raising his right hand in blessing and carrying a cross staff, a symbol of his triumph over death.

Bas-de-Page: Legend of the Drowned Sacristan

Jacobus de Voragine, *The Golden Legend*

> There was a monk much given to lechery but very devoted to Blessed Mary. One night, on his way to commit the usual mischief, he passed before the altar and greeted the Blessed Virgin, then left the church. He had to cross a river but fell in and drowned. When the devils came and took away his soul, angels were there to keep it free. The devils said to them: "What are you doing here? you have no claim to this soul!" Instantly blessed Mary was present and reproached the evil spirits for presuming to lay hands on the monk's soul; but they said that they had found him about to die and bent on wrongdoings. Mary retorted: "Your accusations are false! I know that whenever he was going somewhere he first greeted me, and did the same on his way back. But if you say that you are being treated unjustly, we will submit the case to the judgment of the King of kings." When the question was argued befor God, it pleased him to have the soul return to the sinner's body and there do penance for his actions. Meanwhile his brother monks noticed that matins had not been rung, so they looked for the sacristan and found him drowned in the river. They pulled the body out and wondered what had happened, when he suddenly came to life and told the whole story. Thereafter he lived out his life in good works.[123]

In the *bas-de-page* are three scenes from the Legend of the Drowned Sacristan, found in several medieval English Marian collections (fig. 14). The legend was also popular on the continent, and was included both in the Pez collection and in the widely disseminated *Golden Legend*.[124]

Under a canopy and on a draped altar is the seated polychromed sculpture of the crowned Virgin and Child. To the left of the altar is a riddle post of wrought iron supporting a fabric. A tonsured monk in a black habit, his hands joined, bows to the image. Behind him is an entrance to a turreted square building. On the opposite side of the structure a doorway leads to a bridge on which a hooded monk stands, bending slightly forward. Two devils, one whose head is seen over the bridge and another in the water below, attempt to pull the monk into the water with hooks or grapnels they have fastened onto his habit. In the third scene the standing crowned Virgin, attended by an angel, takes the hands of the drowned monk, who is lying on his stomach in the water, while she looks up at the rayed head of God. A small naked figure, the monk's soul, stands on the bridge and gazes up and over his shoulder at the Lord. At the end of the bridge, there is a gateway in which there are three monks, two standing, the third kneeling in prayer. In between the representation of the soul and the praying monk are three brown devils.

In the first scene in the Copenhagen manuscript, the sacristan, as in the literary works, salutes the Virgin. The turreted square building in the following scene probably represents the walls and gateway of the monastery through which the monk passes on his way to meet his lover.[125] In Thott 547, 4° he is attacked by devils on a bridge, an allusion to the sinful activity which leads the monk to leave the monastery and to his plunging to his death.[126] The events in the third scene illustrate ones narrated in the textual accounts. Here, the dispute over the deceased man's fate between the Virgin, attended by an angel, and the demons on a bridge is resolved by the Lord.[127] The episode on the right might show the resurrected monk with his brethren, or the brothers leaving the monastery to search for the missing monk.[128]

The *bas-de-page,* which appears directly below the opening lines of Vespers, "Deus in adiutorium meum intende. Domine ad adiuvandum me festina. Gloria patri et filio et spiritui sancto. Sicut erat in principio et nunc et semper et" (O God, incline unto my aid. O Lord make haste to help me. Glory be to the Father, and to the Son: and to the Holy Ghost. As it was in the beginning, and now, and ever: and), could be interpreted as illustrating these lines of text. The representation of the naked soul looking upward at God calls to mind the naked souls gazing towards the Lord while awaiting Judgment and sheltered by the Virgin under her cloak (fig. 17). The image of Mary intervening to save the monk's soul from damnation could be read as a more general promise of the Virgin's intercession for those who honor and pray to her. The proximity of the image of the soul, which has risen from the body in the narrative at the bottom of the page, to the depiction of the resurrected Christ may be understood as alluding to the belief that the reward of the faithful will be resurrection and the ultimate defeat of death.

In the Bodleian Library's Psalter-Hours, the miniature marking Compline, f. 219, like the *bas-de-page* on f. 24v in the Copenhagen Hours, shows a tale involving a drowned member of a religious order.[129] In a spired church, in front of an altar with an image of the crowned Virgin and Child, is a flower-strewn bank and a stream in which there is a submerged, reclining, habited figure.[130] The figure's eyes are closed and from his/her mouth rises a scroll inscribed "salve regina miseri(cordie)." To the right, on a bank between two trees, sits a black-habited figure with joined hands looking into the water. Since the inscribed scroll rises from the figure's mouth up towards the statue of the Virgin, the words can be understood as an appeal for help to the Virgin from the drowning figure.

Plate 9. Folio 28v. Compline. Historated Initial "C": Coronation of the Virgin

> Song of Songs 4:8: Come from Libanus, my spouse, come from Libanus, come: thou shalt be crowned

> Psalm 44:10: The queen stood on thy right hand, in gilded clothing; surrounded with variety.

In the center of an elaborate architectural structure with turrets, battlements, and balconies are the seated Virgin and Christ, flanked by censing angels. Rays of light radiate from behind Christ's side of the bench. Mary and her Son are blond, have similar facial features and are clad in clothing made of the same fabric. The Virgin wears a patterned, rose-colored cloak while Christ wears a tunic made of this same material under his blue and gold mantle. Christ places a crown, resembling the one he wears, atop of the Virgin's head, and with his right hand he blesses her. The Virgin holds out her hands in prayer and bows her head, humbly accepting her crown. Exiting from a doorway outside the letter "C" is a standing female figure whose hands are held together in prayer. A shield with the Bohun arms is placed to the right of the Virgin and within the outline of the initial "C". To the left of the structure and on its upper parts are angels playing musical instruments.

The final Hour of Compline was often illustrated with the Coronation of the Virgin. In this manuscript, the Coronation is situated inside the gilded palace of heaven in the presence of angels. The manner in which Christ and Mary are depicted emphasizes that they are related and that He was "made of a woman" (Galatians 4:4). Although they are both depicted as rulers of heaven, the image does not gloss over her submission to the will of the Lord. The miniature in Thott 547, 4°, as was common in the visual arts, combines two motifs: Christ crowning Mary, and the "Triumph of the Virgin," the holy mother, regally clad and seated beside her Son.[131] The Coronation of the Virgin was not described in the Gospels. The texts upon which the image depends are the Song of Songs 4:8 and Psalm 44:10. The first text was also the source for the understanding of the Virgin as Christ's bride.[132] Because Mary was allegorically thought of as Ecclesia, the image could also symbolize Christ's loving relationship to the Church as well as the Church Triumphant.

At the level of the head of the praying women in one of the niches of Paradise is the part of the text "Et averte iram tuam a nobis," imploring God "to turn off [his] anger from us."[133] At about the same height on the page, on the opposite side of the structure, are the arms of the Bohun family. The image-text juxtaposition might have led the book owner to understand the image as herself at the gates of Paradise, uttering the words of the Psalm, which are written at the same height as the figure's mouth. The pairing of the Marian subject with a praying figure at the gates of Paradise on a folio with the antiphon: "Cum iocunditate" (With joy let us celebrate the memorial of holy Mary, that she may intercede for us to the Lord, Jesus Christ) evokes once again the Virgin's role as intercessor.

Bas-de-Page: Legend of the Jew and the Merchant

The legend, as told by Adgar in *Le Gracial*, can be broadly summarized as follows:

> A Christian merchant of Constantinople named Theodore loses his fortune and asks a Jew, Abraham, for a loan. He has no guarantor, but tells the Jew he will ask the Virgin to be the witness to his loan. The two go before the image of the Virgin in the Hagia Sophia, where Theodore swears an oath of fidelity to the loan. The Jew lends him the money and sets a date for repayment. Theodore then sails to Alexandria or to 'barbarian regions' and either forgets the date of repayment or is unable to sail back due to a storm. In an attempt to be faithful to his promise, Theodore encloses the money in a chest along with a note of explanation to Abraham, and casts it onto the sea with a prayer to the Virgin. Miraculously, the chest washes up on the shore and the Jew receives the payment. Abraham, however, puts

> the empty chest under his bed to hide the evidence and demands payment from the Christian upon his return. Theodore calls upon his witness to prove he has already been made reparation for his debt. The image declares that the debt has been paid, and the Jew admits his error, declares the greatness of the Virgin, and converts to Christianity.[134]

Beneath a broad arch in the first *bas-de-page* scene is a vaulted and fenestrated interior in which a hooded man wearing a rose-colored mantle, a short belted tunic, and a chain around his neck, holds a polychromed sculpture of the crowned Virgin with a downturned mouth (fig. 16). Another man, who has a long beard and wears a loose pointed cap and red caped robe, reaches for the sculpture with his right hand and with his left points to a pile of gold coins on a four-legged table. In the background of the second scene is a ship with a broken mast on a stormy sea; above it, hailstones and rain fall from a cloud. On either side of the water there is a tree and a shore, the left one green, the other, rocky. On the right shore a kneeling man, his hood pulled off his head, places a boat in the water. On the left shore, the man with the long beard holds a parchment with a pseudo-inscription, while with his right he touches a small boat. In the third scene, the man with the long beard and the man in the rose-colored mantle stand on either side of a judge in a high-backed chair. In his outstretched arms, the man on the left holds the sculpture of the Virgin. The other man and the judge point to the man with the long beard, and he, in turn, points with his left hand to the sculpture of the Virgin. Nine men, one with a staff, stand behind them.

The legend of the Image as Pledge was very popular with medieval authors and it had a number of redactions.[135] However, it did not enjoy the same degree of dissemination in the visual arts as in literary works.[136] The version in the Copenhagen manuscript shares some common threads with the events narrated in *Le Gracial*, suggesting that the designer of Thott 547, 4° might have been familiar with Adgar's poem. However, as will become apparent from the analysis below, the designer could also have been influenced by other texts and visual sources.

The first episode on f. 28v does not appear to show the merchant making a pledge before the image of Mary as described in *Le Gracial* and in most other textual versions of this legend. Rather, it depicts him delivering a sculpture of the Virgin whose expression denotes her displeasure at being given to the Jew in exchange for money. The events depicted in the second and third scenes, for the most part, correspond to ones in Adgar's narrative. In the second *bas-de-page* scene the merchant, who had travelled abroad and has to pay back his debt on time, commits the money he owes the Jew to the sea. Adgar and most other textual sources state that the merchant placed the money in a chest, but in the lower margin of Thott 547, 4° he launches a small boat, presumably containing the money he owes. The ship with the broken mast depicted in the background of the second *bas-de-page* scene may illustrate the episode noted in Adgar's poem and in some other versions, mostly English, of the merchant delayed by storms and forced to entrust his payment to the waves.[137] The money and an accompanying letter, as described in *Le Gracial* as well as in some of the English sources, fall into the hands of the Jew on another shore.[138]

In most versions of the tale, the moneylender denies ever being repaid by the merchant and his lie is later revealed. However, the intervention of a judge, as shown in the Copenhagen manuscript, does not figure in most versions. In Adgar's *Le Gracial*, the two protagonists, Theodore, the merchant, and Abraham, the Jew, accompanied by a crowd, appear in front of a judge before whom the Jew perjures himself:

... il uint auant a iugement,
Deuant iustice e deuant gent
Li jueu ne tint nul desrei,
De parjurer la nostre lei.[139]

(... he went to judgement, Before the justice and before the people, The Jew had no anxiety To perjure our law.)

In a number of the textual sources, this tale closes with the Jew's acceptance of Christianity. For example, in Adgar's *Le Gracial*, after the encounter with the judge, the two men make their way to Our Lady's image in Hagia Sophia where the Virgin exposes the Jew as a liar, relating to all those assembled that he was repaid but that he hid the money.[140]After the Virgin's revelations, the moneylender, in awe, admits his error and converts to Christianity. But in the Copenhagen *bas-de-page* scenes, the narrative concludes with the return of the image of the Virgin to its rightful Christian owner in court.[141] The imagery of terrestrial justice may be understood as acting as a prelude to the scenes of divine justice, the subject of the next fully decorated folio of this manuscript, accompanying the Seven Penitential Psalms.[142]

As in the *bas-de-page* scenes of the miracle of the Jew of Bourges, the conversion of the Jewish moneylender is not depicted. Thus, rather than functioning as a conversion miracle, the legend could be interpreted in other ways. For example, it could be read as the Virgin's triumph over the Jew and thus would reinforce the imagery of the triumphant Virgin in the historiated initial and allude to the triumph of the Church over the Synagogue.

The legend was not represented in either the British Library's or the Bodleian Library's manuscript.

Plate 10. Folio 32. Seven Penitential Psalms. *Haut-de-Page*: The Just in the New Jerusalem (Revelation 21) Historated Initial "D": Last Judgement (Psalm 9:8–9, Matthew 19:28; 22:31–46, 24:30–31, 25:31–46, Mark 13:24–37, John 5:21–30; Acts 17:30–31; 2 Corinthians 5:10, Revelation 20:11–15) *Bas-de-Page*: The Dead are Raised, Separation of Souls

> Psalm 9:8 But the Lord remaineth for ever. He hath prepared his throne in judgment: 9 And he shall judge the world in equity, he shall judge the people in justice.
>
> John 5:21 For as the Father raiseth up the dead, and giveth life: so the Son also giveth life to whom he will. 22 For neither doth the Father judge any man, but hath given all judgment to the Son. 23 That all men may honour the Son, as they honour the Father. He who honoureth not the Son, honoureth not the Father, who hath sent him. 24 Amen, amen I say unto you, that he who heareth my word, and believeth him that sent me, hath life everlasting; and cometh not into judgment, but is passed from death to life. 25 Amen, amen I say unto you, that the hour cometh, and now is, when the dead shall hear the voice of the Son of God, and they that hear shall live. 26 For as the Father hath life in himself, so he hath given the Son also to have life in himself: 27 And he hath given him power to do judgment, because he is the Son of man. 28 Wonder not at this; for the hour cometh, wherein all that are in the graves shall hear the voice of the Son of God. 29 And they that have done good things, shall come forth unto the resurrection of life; but they that have done evil, unto the resurrection of judgment.
>
> Matthew 19:28 And Jesus said to them: Amen, I say to you, that you, who have followed me, in the regeneration, when the Son of man shall sit on

the seat of his majesty, you also shall sit on twelve seats judging the twelve tribes of Israel.

Matthew 24:29 And immediately after the tribulation of those days, the sun shall be darkened and the moon shall not give her light, and the stars shall fall from heaven, and the powers of heaven shall be moved: 30 And then shall appear the sign of the Son of man in heaven: and then shall all tribes of the earth mourn: and they shall see the Son of man coming in the clouds of heaven with much power and majesty. 31 And he shall send his angels with a trumpet, and a great voice: and they shall gather together his elect from the four winds, from the farthest parts of the heavens to the utmost bounds of them.

Matthew 25:31 And when the Son of man shall come in his majesty, and all the angels with him, then shall he sit upon the seat of his majesty. 32 And all nations shall be gathered together before him, and he shall separate them one from another, as the shepherd separateth the sheep from the goats: 33 And he shall set the sheep on his right hand, but the goats on his left. 34 Then shall the king say to them that shall be on his right hand: Come, ye blessed of my Father, possess you the kingdom prepared for you from the foundation of the world. 35 For I was hungry, and you gave me to eat; I was thirsty, and you gave me to drink; I was a stranger, and you took me in: 36 Naked, and you covered me: sick, and you visited me: I was in prison, and you came to me. 37 Then shall the just answer him, saying: Lord, when did we see thee hungry, and fed thee; thirsty, and gave thee drink? 38 And when did we see thee a stranger, and took thee in? or naked, and covered thee? 39 Or when did we see thee sick or in prison, and came to thee? 40 And the king answering, shall say to them: Amen I say to you, as long as you did it to one of these my least brethren, you did it to me. 41 Then he shall say to them also that shall be on his left hand: Depart from me, you cursed, into everlasting fire which was prepared for the devil and his angels. 42 For I was hungry, and you gave me not to eat: I was thirsty, and you gave me not to drink. 43 I was a stranger, and you took me not in: naked, and you covered me not: sick and in prison, and you did not visit me. 44 Then they also shall answer him, saying: Lord, when did we see thee hungry, or thirsty, or a stranger, or naked, or sick, or in prison, and did not minister to thee? 45 Then he shall answer them, saying: Amen I say to you, as long as you did it not to one of these least, neither did you do it to me. 46 And these shall go into everlasting punishment: but the just, into life everlasting.

> 2 Corinthians 5:10 For we must all be manifested before the judgement seat of Christ, that every one may receive the proper things of the body, according as he hath done, whether it be good or evil.

> Revelation 21:8 But the fearful, and unbelieving, and the abominable, and murderers, and whoremongers, and sorcerers, and idolaters, and all liars, they shall have their portion in the pool burning with fire and brimstone, which is the second death.

> Revelation 21:23 And the city hath no need of the sun, nor of the moon, to shine in it. For the glory of God hath enlightened it, and the Lamb is the lamp thereof. 24 And the nations shall walk in the light of it: and the kings of the earth shall bring their glory and honour into it.

> Revelation 22:5 And night shall be no more: and they shall not need the light of the lamp, nor the light of the sun, because the Lord God shall enlighten them, and they shall reign for ever and ever.

The central image of the upper border is a golden throne, emitting a cluster of rays. It is flanked on the left by an angel with a psaltery and on the right by an angel with a harp. On either side of the angels are a group of men and women, naked except for their crowns, surrounded by bunches of rays. At the far left end of the upper border are two angels with musical instruments atop of a gate, while on the far right end is an angel with a tambourine.

Different events connected to the Last Judgment are represented in all four borders and in the initial. The subject of the *haut-de-page* is the salvation promised to the just, who are depicted as crowned male and female figures. The place in which they are rewarded is the New Jerusalem, the celestial city which was often represented in portals of churches in connection with the Last Judgment.[143] The balanced composition of the *haut-de-page* visualizes the harmonic perfect proportions of the celestial city, described in Revelation 21:12–16. Also mentioned in Revelation 21:12 are the angels in the tower gates. In the center of the *haut-de-page* and of the heavenly domain is the throne of God, emanating eternal light (Revelation 21:23–24, Revelation 22:5).

In the center of the initial "D", the enthroned, nimbed, bearded Christ, partially draped in a blue mantle, displays his wounds and raises his right hand in blessing. He is flanked on either side by six of his twelve apostles.

Above them, in the sky, is the sun on the left and the moon on the right (Matthew 24:29). In the foreground, on the left, the crowned nimbed Virgin shelters naked souls under her blue cloak and draws the head of one to her bosom. Her cloak, spread over the souls, is held up by two kneeling angels. In attendance is a third angel with a cross. In the upper right spandrel an angel holds scourges, and below, in the lower right, another angel clutches nails. In the left margin, more angels hold other instruments of the Passion, the crown of thorns, the spear, reed, sponge, and bucket.

In a medallion in the outer border, to the left of the decorated letter "E", is an angel next to a soul in a gateway, towards which four souls make their way, climbing a ladder positioned above a square tower of a turreted, crenelated building in the *bas-de-page*. At the foot of the ladder above the tower is a fifth soul. The text of Psalm 6:4, introduced by the decorated letter "E:" "et anima mea turbata est valde et tu Domine usquequo (4 And my soul is troubled exceedingly: but thou, O Lord, how long?) and of Psalm 6:5 opening with the initial "C": Convertere Domine et eripe animam meam salvum me fac propter misericordiam tuam" (Turn to me, O Lord, and deliver my soul: O save me for thy mercy's sake), containing references to the soul, is probably the reason the souls are represented near these lines.

The *bas-de-page* shows scenes with the saved on the right, and on the left with the damned. In the lower border, in the center of the building, the heads of souls are visible above the round tower. In the gateway, a naked soul is admitted. In each of the turrets there are two angels with long trumpets (Matthew 24:31), and next to them, six monks in black habits. Below them a group of figures make their way towards the gateway, including a pope, two crowned women, and a crowned man. In the foreground, a king in a coffin holds open the lid with his hands. The damned rise up from the coffins and graves; while lost souls make their way into the flames and the mouth of Hell (Revelation 21:8). Above them are five devils, one beating a drum. In the right margin, two winged devils each carry off a soul. Above them, in a medallion, an angel holds a sword.

As was common in devotional manuscripts produced during the thirteenth and fourteenth centuries, the illumination for the opening of the Seven Penitential Psalms shows Judgment Day. The Seven Penitential Psalms (Psalms 6, 31, 37, 50, 101, 129, and 142) were believed to have been composed by King David as penance for his grievous sins and were associated with atonement.[144] Because in these Psalms the Psalmist fears the punitive anger of God and begs for mercy and salvation, they were associated with the Last Judgment, when, it was held, each individual had to account for his or her life, especially for the sins he or she had committed.[145]

The essential elements for the pictorialization of the Last Judgment were established earlier on and appeared in portal sculpture. As was customary, the imagery combines events described in the Gospels, primarily from Matthew, with Apocalyptical ones from the Book of Revelation. Many of the iconographic motives included on this page were common: the twelve apostles seated on either side of Christ to assist at the Judgment; the Virgin Mary appearing as intercessor; instruments of the Passion, trumpeting angels, the dead rising from their graves; the separation of the elect from the damned and their processions either to Heaven or to Hell, etc.[146] The theme of the Virgin of Mercy sheltering naked souls under her cloak as they await Judgment had its origins in Italy and was taken up in England.[147] It appears in a manuscript of St. Augustine's *De Civitate Dei*, then in the Vienna Bohun Psalter and later in the Copenhagen Hours.[148] The importance of the Virgin in the heavenly hierarchy is symbolized by her size and her resemblance to her son. The different representations of the soul making its way up to the Deity and gathered together with other souls witnessing a vision of the divine before the Last Judgment may have been influenced by devotional literature of this period.[149]

Three earlier Bohun manuscripts, the Vienna Bohun Psalter, f. 141, the Bodleian's Psalter-Hours, f. 169, and the Fitzwilliam Psalter, contain large initials placed at the opening of the Penitential Psalms illuminated with the Second Coming.[150] These depictions show, in the center of the miniature, Christ partially naked, his hands raised, and his mantle open to show his wounds. In attendance are angels carrying instruments of the Passion. Below Him, the Dead, including ecclesiasts and a king, emerge from their coffins. Outside of the main miniatures, the damned are portrayed in the mouth of hell. While the essentials of the compositions are similar to the representation of the Last Judgment in the Copenhagen Hours, there are a number of differences. The imagery in the Copenhagen Bohun Hours is expanded even though the dimensions of its pages are smaller than those of the Vienna, Oxford, and Cambridge books. The design of the page of Thott 547, 4° is also quite different. The tiny compositions are crammed with details and contain many elements not found in the earlier manuscripts. None of the earlier Bohun devotional books show the apostles and the Virgin is shown as intercessor only in the Vienna Psalter. The four-sided border with *bas-de-page* and *haut-de-page* scenes is unique to the Copenhagen Hours. The closest manuscript in this format is the *Lichtenthal Psalter*, particularly

f. 1, which has, like Thott 547, 4°, scenes represented in all four borders. A significant difference between the illumination at the Seven Penitential Psalms in the Copenhagen manuscript and the Bohun books in Vienna, Oxford, and Cambridge is that in Thott 547, 4° no armorials are depicted.

Plate 11. Folio 43. Office of the Dead. Historiated Initial "D": Job and Satan before God (Job 1:6–8)

> Job 1:6 Now on a certain day when the sons of God came to stand before the Lord, Satan also was present among them. 7 And the Lord said to him: Whence comest thou? And he answered and said: I have gone round about the earth, and walked through it. 8 And the Lord said to him: Hast thou considered my servant Job, that there is none like him in the earth, a simple and upright man, and fearing God, and avoiding evil? 9 And Satan answering, said: Doth Job fear God in vain? 10 Hast not thou made a fence for him, and his house, and all his substance round about, blessed the works of his hands, and his possession hath increased on the earth? 11 But stretch forth thy hand a little, and touch all that he hath, and see if he blesseth thee not to thy face. 12 Then the Lord said to Satan: Behold, all that he hath is in thy hand: only put not forth thy hand upon his person. And Satan went forth from the presence of the Lord.

In the central and tallest arch sits the nimbed, bearded, blond Lord. He is flanked on either side of his throne by an angel, standing beneath one of the side arches. God's right arm is bent at the elbow and with his index finger he points at the praying, white-haired, bearded man dressed in a short tunic and mantle. The Lord lays his left hand on the head of a standing black demon.

The scene within the historiated initial shows the day when Satan and the sons of God, symbolized by the angels, came to stand before the Lord (Job 1:6), and Job, denoted by the Lord's gesture, was singled out (Job 1:8). Scenes from this Old Testament Book were chosen to accompany the Office of the Dead in devotional manuscripts because the nine lessons from Matins were extrapolated from the Book of Job.[151] As was common in manuscripts illuminated with this subject matter, the initial does not illustrate the texts in the Office of the Dead drawn from Job, ff. 49–59 (first nocturne, Reading

I, Job 7:16–21, Reading II, Job 10:1–7, Reading III, Job 10:8–12, second nocturnes Reading IV, Job 13:23–28, Reading V, Job 14:1–6, Reading VI, Job 14:13–16, third nocturnes, Reading VII, Job 17:1–3 and 11–15, Reading VIII, Job 19:20–27 and Reading IX, Job 10:18–22).

Bas-de-Page: The Misfortunes that befall Job, Job rends his Garments (Job 1:15–21, 2:9)

Job 1:13 Now upon a certain day when his sons and daughters were eating and drinking wine in the house of their eldest brother, 14 There came a messenger to Job, and said: The oxen were ploughing, and the asses feeding beside them, 15 And the Sabeans rushed in, and took all away, and slew the servants with the sword, and I alone have escaped to tell thee. 16 And while he was yet speaking, another came, and said: The fire of God fell from heaven, and striking the sheep and the servants, hath consumed them, and I alone have escaped to tell thee. 17 And while he also was yet speaking, there came another, and said: The Chaldeans made three troops, and have fallen upon the camels, and taken them, moreover they have slain the servants with the sword, and I alone have escaped to tell thee. 18 He was yet speaking, and behold another came in, and said: Thy sons and daughters were eating and drinking wine in the house of their elder brother: 19 A violent wind came on a sudden from the side of the desert, and shook the four corners of the house, and it fell upon thy children and they are dead, and I alone have escaped to fell thee. 20 Then Job rose up, and rent his garments, and having shaven his head fell down upon the ground and worshipped, 21 And said: Naked came I out of my mother's womb, and naked shall I return thither: the Lord gave, and the Lord hath taken away: as it hath pleased the Lord so is it done: blessed be the name of the Lord. 22 In all these things Job sinned not by his lips, nor spoke he any foolish thing against God.

Job 2:9 And his wife said to him: Dost thou still continue in thy simplicity? bless God and die. 10 And he said to her: Thou hast; spoken like one of the foolish women: if we have received good things at the hand of God, why should we not receive evil? In all these things Job did not sin with his lips.

In the lower border more events from the first chapter of this Old Testament Book are represented in three scenes (fig. 20). Inside a timber building are a woman and two men seated at a draped table laid with bowls and a covered cup. A bearded, hooded man, his shoulders hunched, exits through a doorway on the right. He looks back and shields his head with his hands. Above the door, a black devil holds in his paws half of the collapsing roof. The other half of the roof appears damaged and unstable. In the middle scene, in a landscape, a black devil accompanies three armed horsemen wearing armor, surcoats, and helmets, who attack three men dressed in hooded mantles. Next to them are two donkeys, oxen and sheep. A fourth man wearing a hooded mantle and a short tunic looks back over his right shoulder at the scene. Next to him, a man kneeling on one knee points backwards over his head while addressing Job. The white-haired and bearded Job stands in a tattered shirt, his right arm extended and raised. He holds a scroll inscribed: "Dominus dedit do(minus) ab(stulit)" (Job 1:21). Beside Job is his veiled wife.

The three scenes in the *bas-de-page* show the misfortunes that befall Job. In the first, his sons and daughters eat and drink in the home of their eldest brother (Job 1:18). The violent wind which causes the destruction of the house and the death of Job's children is represented as the devil breaking the roof of the house (Job 1:19). The man running out of the door is one of the messengers who will bring news of calamities to Job. The second scene shows the armed and mounted Sabeans stealing Job's oxen and donkeys and striking the servants with their swords (Job 1:15). The inclusion of the devil indicates that this is Satan's handiwork. The animals in the foreground are the sheep mentioned in Job 1:16. The man in the hooded mantle and short tunic looking over his shoulder and the one genuflecting are the servants who manage to escape the carnage and relate the tragic events to Job. In the final scene of the *bas-de-page*, Job is shown rending his clothes (Job 1:20) and lifting up a scroll inscribed with the words he uttered (Job 1:21): "Dominus dedit do(minus) ab(stulit)" (the Lord gave, and the Lord hath taken away). In the final scene of the *bas-de-page*, Job is accompanied by his wife who is not mentioned in the first chapter of the book but rather in the following one where she tells Job to compromise his integrity by cursing God (Job 2:9). Since moralist discourse often gendered malicious speech as feminine, the decision to depict Job's wife may have been made in response to the words written on the verso of folio 43 (Psalm 119:2): "Domine libera animam meam a labiis iniquis a lingua dolosa 3 quid detur tibi et quid adponatur tibi ad linguam dolosam" (O Lord, deliver my soul from wicked lips, and a deceitful tongue. 3 What shall be given to thee, or what shall be added to thee, to a deceitful tongue).[152]

The words written on the scroll serve to underline the ephemeral nature of man's creature comforts in this world. The verses from Psalm 114 written in the lines above the lower margin, "8 For he hath delivered my soul from death: my eyes from tears, my feet from falling. 9 I will please the Lord" (8 quia eripuit animam meam de morte oculos meos a lacrimis pedes meos a lapsu 9 placebo Domino), along with the images on this folio, show the necessity to serve God.

The reader is provided with images from Job with whom she can empathize: his despair at the loss of his family and property, his admission of transgressions and sin, and his faith in the Lord. The text on f. 43v reassures the supplicant that the Lord is merciful and just, f. 43v, Psalm 119:1: "ad Dominum cum tribularer clamavi et exaudivit me" (In my trouble I cried to the Lord: and he heard me). In the figure of Job's wife on the folio of the final liturgical division of her manuscript, she would have encountered a negative role model of femine behavior, one which might have called to mind the abbess's nuns at the opening of the Hours of the Virgin, who, like Job's wife, are associated with malicious speech and deceit.

The Office of the Dead in the Bodleian Psalter-Hours, f. 244, is also illuminated with subjects from Chapter One of the Book of Job. Before the seated Lord in the first scene are a group of robed, wingless figures and Satan. In the following scene, three figures sit at a table inside a house with a collapsing roof (Job 1:18–19). In the third, there are two men with swords; one attacks a ploughman, the second a smaller figure who is restrained by a fifth man (Job 1:14). In the final scene, fire falls on women and sheep (Job 1:16) while a man, to their left, turns to flee. Inside the initial, a messenger kneels before Job who rends his clothes. Next to Job's mouth is an effaced scroll with the text: "D(omi)n(u)s dedit ab(stulit dominus)" (Job 1:20).

Conclusion

The intended owner of Thott 547, 4° would have been presented with hieratically organized subjects. The most important were those of the historiated initials, drawn from Christ's Infancy, Passion, and Afterlife, whose principal subjects were the humanity and divinity of the Savior. The *bas-de-page* scenes, smaller in size and placed underneath the major illuminations, played a role in molding the viewer's understanding of these central beliefs of

Christianity. In the manuscript, the idea that the salvation and redemption of humanity was possible because of Christ's sacrifice is reinforced through the association of the historiated initial with the *bas-de-page*, of the Nativity with legend of the Jew of Bourges (plate 3), the Crucifixion with the Soul Saved (plate 7), the Resurrection with the Drowned Sacristan (plate 8), and the Last Judgment with the separation of the elect from the damned (plate 10). The chosen imagery in the manuscript also expresses repeatedly the necessity for mankind to ask actively for mercy and forgiveness in order to attain salvation.

In the drama of Christian redemption, which unfolds in the illuminations of the Office of the Virgin, Mary plays a vital role. She is depicted as compassionate, forgiving, and merciful towards her supplicants as well as an instrument of their salvation. The belief that the Virgin's motherhood, and her close and empathic relationship to her Child, gave her the authority and capacity to intercede with the Lord is illustrated time and again, for example in the *bas-de-page* on f. 22v (fig. 13), and f. 24v (fig. 14), as well as in the historiated initial on f. 32v (fig. 17).

Illuminations in the *bas-de-page* show that praying to sculptures of the Virgin, such as those on ff. 6v, 18, 20, 24v, 28v (figs. 6, 10, 11, 14, 16), are a means of accessing her. Only their smaller size and placement on altars distinguish sculptures of Mary from the figures, similar in appearance and dress, intended to represent the actual Virgin. The viewer is shown the Virgin's constant presence in her images and her power to answer prayers and perform miracles. Consequently, the audience of the manuscript is led to recognize that the images depicted in the devotional book have that type of potential power.

Praying figures in the manuscript's *bas-de-page* can be interpreted as models for the book owner to emulate, e.g. f. 6v and f. 24v (figs. 6, 14). In nearly all the *bas-de-page* legends, Mary offers protection to her devotees no matter how great their sin. One of the narratives can be read as encouraging supplicants to continue praying even when disheartened. In the legend of the Child Image taken hostage, f. 18 (fig. 10), the dejected mother initially believes that the Virgin has turned a deaf ear to her petitions, but in the final episode she understands that her prayers were heard.

The images in the manuscript might also have provided the female reader with the opportunity to contemplate not only the divine maternity of the Virgin but also that of the female protagonists in the miracle scenes as well as her own. The Annunciation, the pivotal event in the life of the Virgin, could be understood as every woman's submission to bringing children into this world. Another episode from Christ's Infancy, the Visitation, depicting the tender meeting of the two pregnant women, may on one level have provided women with an image of motherhood as a shared feminine experience. The Nativity may also have held meanings about the expectations of the relationship between a mother and her infant. Not only would the Virgin's tenderness for her Son have carried religious meanings but it would also have portrayed the ideal mother as someone who is affectionate and nurturing towards her child.

Conversely, three miracles dealing with women and their male children, namely the Legend of the Unchaste Abbess, of the Jew of Bourges, and of the Child Image taken Captive, could be read as cautionary tales about maternity. The three women are in no way superlative mothers. The first has broken her pledge of chastity and ends up separated from her child; the second and third are helpless in protecting their sons from calamity. In comparison with these deficient human mothers, Mary is represented as perfect and powerful.

The intended viewer is shown the necessity to distinguish good from evil for the sake of her own salvation as well as to be mindful of temptation and of behavior which disturbs social order.[153] In the *bas-de-page* she is shown the presence of those who oppose the Virgin, namely Jews and the devil. In three *bas-de-page* tales, Jews are allotted various negative roles. They are enemies not only of the Virgin but, more broadly, of the Christian faith. In the Theophilus legend, f. 6, the Jew is associated with sorcery and is depicted as the devil's assistant. In the miracle of the Jew of Bourges, the father is portrayed as a would-be child-murderer, while in the legend of the Merchant of Constantinople on f. 28v the Jewish lender is associated with avarice, deception, and theft. The otherness of the Jews is denoted by their Semitic features and their headgear as well as the proportions of their heads and bodies, which differ from those of Christians.

Admittedly, this type of subject matter appeared in English devotional manuscripts of an earlier date and anti-Jewish sentiment is present in the literary sources from which the *bas-de-pages* illuminations were drawn. However, by leaving out the concluding episodes dealing with conversion described in the texts, the tales depicted in the *bas-de-page* are given a different emphasis from their literary sources, in which consternation about non-Christians is hinged together with the desire to bring them into the fold. In the illustrations in the lower margins of Thott 547, 4°, the Jews are not redeemed. More generally, the images of the Jew and the devil represented in Thott 547, 4° can be regarded as warnings to Christians of the presence of the forces of evil while the inclusion of the tales of the unchaste abbess and the drowned sacristan reflect anxieties about inappropriate sexual conduct.

As we have seen, a number of images represented in Thott 547, 4° were made in response to textual components of the manuscript. Some of these are conventional. For example, the portrait of the book owner placed at the opening of the Hours of the Virgin, f. 1 (fig. 2), near the words "Domine labia mea aperies. Et os meum annunciabit laudem tuam" (O Lord, thou wilt open my lips: and my mouth shall declare thy praise), could be understood as representing the intended reader uttering these lines from Psalm 50. Another image of a woman, situated in a less customary place, f. 28v (fig. 15), and in the vicinity of the text "to turn off [his] anger from us," similarly illustrates the reader appealing to God. Images also draw the reader's attention to words and phrases as well as lines of text. For example, on f. 22v (fig. 13) directly below the word "misericordie" (mercy), is an image which embodies the meaning of this concept, namely of the Virgin baring her breast and in this attitude of supplication interceding for mercy with the Lord. Folio 6v, headed with the text of Psalms 69:2, "Deus in adiutorium meum intende. Domine ad adiuvandum me festina" (O God, incline unto my aid. O Lord make haste to help me), depicts at the bottom of the page Theophilus, the protagonist of the Marian legend, praying to Christ and his mother for assistance (pl. 2). These illuminations focused the reader's attention on ideas which were singled out as important. They also helped her commit passages to memory, and, since medieval manuscripts were not paginated, assisted her in finding her place in the book. The images were probably also intended as aids to meditation and a means of coming into contact with the sacred realm.

The armorial display in Thott 547, 4, as was common in private devotional books, served a commemorative purpose. They reminded the book owner to pray for deceased family members as well as being emblematic of prayers that had already been said for the dead. Devices were interwoven with religious imagery, placed in the backgrounds of or in close proximity to historiated initials depicting Christological scenes, and incorporated into initials of the opening words of sacred texts in the hope that the book owner's prayers would be more efficacious.[154] The closeness of the armorials to the sacred images in the historiated initials also had an eschatological connotation: it was an attempt to maintain the family's social position on earth and secure it in heaven for eternity.[155] This wish is probably reflected in the decision to insert the shield with the Bohun arms at the gates of Paradise (fig. 15). The hierarchical social order is also mirrored in the placement of shields on the page. Those displaying the arms of the Plantagenets appear above those of the Bohuns. Furthermore, the proximity of sacred image to coats of arms also can be viewed as expressing the idea that the position of the families in this world is divinely ordained. Because the armorial range in Thott 547, 4°, in comparison to other Bohun manuscripts, is narrower and focuses on the book owner's paternal family and members of the royal house, it would have allowed her to see herself and the Bohuns as part of the highest stratum of society. Thus, the coats of arms commemorate the family, celebrate the prestige of their line, and remind the living to pray for their dead ancestors.

If we compare the cycle of Christological themes in the historiated initials with cycles in other Bohun manuscripts, we find that there were certain subjects and motifs to which the artists returned time and again, for example the illustration of the Seven Penitential Psalms. However, none of the scenes are exactly alike. Sandler's analysis of the imagery in the *Lichtenthal Psalter* and other Bohun manuscripts suggests that the program designers of the Bohun manuscripts had a high degree of Biblical knowledge. It would also appear from the examination of the miracles in the Copenhagen manuscript presented here, which do not appear to illustrate texts in one collection, that they were were well-acquainted with Marian legends.[156] Pictorial narratives were created that had different focuses than their textual sources and which were not overtly reliant on established iconographies. Some of the represented motifs, such as Mary sheltering naked souls under her cloak, were unusual and could have held meanings significant for their intended viewers. If we compare the illuminations of the Bodleian Library Psalter-Hours and those of the Copenhagen Hours accompanying the Office of the Virgin, we find that there are different juxtapositions between the Christological images and Marian legends. Of the eight miracles of the Virgin illustrated in the Bodleian Library Psalter-Hours and the Copenhagen Hours, five, perhaps six, have the same subject matter but none mark the same subdivision.[157] The miniatures in this part of the Oxford manuscript were not painted by the main artist of the Copenhagen Hours and the page design, the style of the paintings, and the compositions of the scenes are quite different. The meanings that are constructed by the image/text juxtapositions are not the same and would have led their reader to understand them in other ways.

Turning back to the question of the identity of the intended reader of the Copenhagen Hours, I have argued that the book owner's heraldic garments, decorated with the pre-1340 arms of England over Bohun, depicted at the opening of the Hours of the Virgin, f. 1, suggest that the portrait represents one of the Bohun heiresses after her marriage. The loose, uncovered hair of the young woman probably connotes that she is an adolescent and perhaps still had not attained majority. She is also unlikely to represent a mother of numerous children. During the course of the 1380s, Eleanor gave birth to four children while Mary gave birth to three.[158] Because of the manner in which the book owner is represented, it is probable that the portrait was begun after her marriage but probably no later than the birth of her second surviving child. It is unlikely that an adolescent who had given birth to three children or more would have been depicted with long unbound hair.[159]

The book could have been intended for either Eleanor or Mary de Bohun, who were both closely related and associated with the royal family. The repeated representations of the Bohun arms on four of the illuminated folios and the arms of the crown on two are evidence of pride in the intended reader's lineage and royal connections. But the arms of Bohun were the arms of the seventh earl's heirs. In contemporary documents, the sisters are referred to as heirs of the earl of Hereford.[160] The epitaph on Eleanor de Bohun's funerary effigy draws explicit attention to the elder sister's status as one of her father's heirs: "Here lies Eleanor de Bohun, the eldest daughter and one of the heirs of the honorable lord Sir Humphrey de Bohun, Earl of Hereford, Essex and Northampton, and Constable of England, wife of the mighty and noble prince Thomas of Woodstock, son of the excellent and mighty prince Edward, King of England, the third since the Conquest, Duke of Gloucester, Earl of Essex and Buckingham, and Constable of England, who died October 3, 1399."[161] The imagery of her sepulchral brass, like the inscription, shows pride in Eleanor's lineage as well as her husband's. The central pinnacle is decorated with the Bohun's swan and on either side are heads of lions (badges of the kingdom).[162] Additionally, these two figures are represented at the side corbels, the lion on the right and the swan on the left. Swans are also depicted at the foot of the brass and next to the epitaph. On either side of the reposing Duchess are three shields: on the dexter side, the arms of Eleanor's husband; France and England quarterly with a border; and below these, those of Bohun (*azure a bend argent between two cotises and six lions rampart or*). At the foot of the canopy are the arms of the Constableship (the arms of Miles of Gloucester, first Earl of Hereford), an office held by Eleanor's father and inherited through Eleanor by Thomas of Woodstock.[163] On the sinister side are Eleanor's arms, England and France quarterly impaling Bohun quartering the Constableship of England. Below these are those of her mother, Joan, Bohun impaling Fitzalan and Warenne quarterly.[164] The shield below is missing. It has been suggested that it showed the arms of the Earldom of Essex, which passed to the Bohuns in 1239 through Maud de Mandeville and was invested in Thomas of Woodstock by virtue of his marriage to Eleanor. The manner in which Eleanor is dressed, and the inscription and the heraldry depict her as widow of a high-born nobleman, Prince Thomas of Woodstock, Duke of Gloucester, son of Edward III. However, unlike many medieval tombs made for married noblewomen, the inscription and imagery on Eleanor's brass are very powerful statements about her status as one of her father's heirs, to the titles and offices she brought her husband and her noble lineage on both her mother's and father's side of the family.[165]

The absence of the *fleurs-de-lis* of France, a very significant component of the arms of Thomas of Woodstock, on the first folio of the Copenhagen Hours, tips the balance somewhat in favor of identifying the intended reader of the manuscript as Mary de Bohun. Regardless of whether the manuscript's original owner was Mary or Eleanor de Bohun, the manuscript's intricate visual content and beauty of execution surely were meant to actively engage its female viewer; the imagery provided her with instruction and aided her religious meditation. Presented also in a visual language for the manuscript's viewers, the lady, her husband, children, and later owners, were the social and personal components of the Bohun heiress's identity; she is depicted as educated, virtuous, devoted to the Virgin and to prayer for her ancestors, and her elevated position in society is constructed as God-given. Ownership of the exquisite and complex manuscript, made by artists who had worked for her father and great-uncle, would have conveyed status and attested to her position as one of the main heirs of a family which placed great importance on books.[166]

Part Two

Chapter Three

Description of Thott 517, 4°

THOTT **517,** 4° CONTAINS three texts, The Passing of Mary, ff. 1–10v, The Life and Passion of Saint Margaret, ff. 10v–22v, and the Apostolic and Eremitic Life of Mary Magdalene, ff. 22v–38. Its primary decoration consists of three superb six-line historiated initials placed at the beginning of each of the works. The manuscript is further embellished with attractive four-sided and partial rectilinear borders, finely painted, three- and one-line decorative initials as well as abstract and vegetal line endings. Thott 517, 4°, unlike Thott 547, 4°, does not contain any *bas-de-pages*, *haut-de-pages*, marginalia, or heraldry. In this chapter, we begin with a codicological assessment of the manuscript. Then we continue with an examination of the manuscript from front to back, ending with a discussion of the binding. A comparison of Thott 517, 4° and Thott 547, 4°, their codicology, decoration, and scribal hands, is presented next. Conclusions are drawn about the manuscripts' chronology and it is argued that Thott 517, 4° was made before Thott 547, 4°.

The Collation, Page and Text Block Dimensions, Condition

Thott 517, 4° is composed of 38 folios measuring 176 × 130 mm. The folios have been trimmed. The dimensions of the text block, demarcated in lead, are 111 × 70 mm. The manuscript consists of five gatherings, four quaternions, and one ternion.[1] At the end of the fourth gathering, at the bottom of folio 32v, there is a catchword. The final folio of the manuscript, f. 38v, is ruled but has no text.

In the left margin at the top of the folio and below the text block are scarcely legible impressions of words from a folio, which used to preface f. 1. The inscription at the bottom of f. 1: "Vite trium sanctarum et illustrium Virginum S. Mariae. S. Margarethae.et S. Magdalenae," was added by a later scribe who imitated the writing of the thirteenth-century hand.

The manuscript's collation and textual contents, which will be discussed below, are not in opposition to Thott 547, 4°, being a complete collection of legends.

The vellum is much heavier and not of the same fine quality as that used in Thott 547, 4°. Many of the hair-side folios are not smooth but are velvety to the touch.

The Texts

The three texts narrate episodes from the lives, deaths, entombments, and afterlives of three female saints. Various terms have been used by scholars to designate the types of writings recounted in Thott 517, 4°, including the general term, saints' lives, as well as legends and *livret des saints*.[2] A legend, most literally, is a thing to be read and the application of this term to describe hagiography alludes to the practice of reading saintly biographies on feast days or other occasions.[3] *Livret des saints* is a designation which primarily refers to the small dimensions of the manuscript devoted to saintly biography and is used to express the book's difference in size from larger manuscript compendiums of hagiographic material.[4] In this study, I will refer to the texts in Thott 517, 4° as saints' lives and legends.

The Historiated Initials

The major decoration of Thott 517, 4° consists of three six-line historiated initials placed at the beginning of each of the legends and one three-line historiated initial introducing a prayer. The scenes within the historiated letters are painted black, white, grey, tan, brown, dusty pink, dark and light blue, and reddish orange. On f. 22v some green is introduced and on f. 1 some yellow. The letters themselves are painted pink, light blue, and white, while the one on f. 1 is additionally painted reddish orange and dark blue. Within the shape of the initial "Q," f. 1 (fig. 21), are ridged ornaments in pink and blue from which short red and white lines extend. Portions of this type of ornament are outlined in white. The interior of the shape of the letter "Q" is further embellished with red circles with small white circular centers. The initial "S," f. 10v (fig. 22), is decorated with foliate motifs and white dots. Within the left vertical stem of the initial "A," f. 22v (fig. 23), are two stylized leaves, one blue, the other pink. White circles are painted on and outside the foliate motifs. Pink, blue, white, and orange stylized vines sprout from the historiated initials.

The Background Panels of the Historiated Initials

Each of the three historiated initials, ff. 1, 10v, and 22v, is placed on a gold-tooled background panel, which on one or more of its sides follows the shape of the letter and its extensions. Some of the outlines of background panels have semi-circular indentations into which are placed gold balls with squiggles. The gold-tooled background of the initial "A" on f. 22v includes semicircles painted white, pink, or blue, and decorated with gold. The panels in Thott 517, 4°, unlike those in Thott 547, 4°, do not contain heraldic motifs, figures, or architecture.

The Secondary Decoration

All the pages of the manuscript are decorated with secondary ornamentation such as borders and ornamental initials. A few pages additionally have line fillers. A more limited combination and range of colors was used for the secondary decoration than for the miniatures. Gold is used on every folio.

The Borders

The four-sided borders, ff. 1, 10v, and 22v, on the folios with historiated initials, are outlined in black and embellished with tooled gold and decorated with pink, blue, and white paint. The borders have scalloped-edged medallions encompassing a single leaf or clusters of leaves. Attached to the borders, some by a thin black line, are ivy leaves in tooled gold or painted pink or blue with white veins. In between the leaves are small gold balls from which black irregular lines extend. There are fewer medallions, leaves, and balls with squiggles than in Thott 547, 4°. Unlike Thott 547, 4°, the text on some folios runs outside of the lead rulings, and on ff. 1, 10v, and 22v the right hand border wraps around projecting letters. The four-sided borders, although simpler than those in Thott 547, 4°, are very similar to them. Unlike the first folio of Thott 547, 4°, the four-sided border on f. 1 of this manuscript did not receive any special decoration for emphasis.

Except for the four-sided borders on the three folios with the historiated initials, all other ones are three-sided. They are outlined in black, embellished with gold and paint, encompass scalloped medallions and terminate in a spray of leaves.

The Ornamental Initials

There are thirty-five three-line initials decorated in a variety of manners. The letters, painted grey-blue and white or dull pink and white, are encompassed by gold framing devices, which follow the shape of the initial and are outlined in black. The letters have extensions. The palette of colors chosen for the interiors of the three-line initials is murkier than the one used in the historiated initials. The colors employed are mauve, red brown, orange brown, grey blue, brown, black, and, in small amounts, orange red. Some of the initials are composed of zoomorphic elements, for example part of the rounded shape of the letter "E" is marlin-like, f. 14, while attached to the letters on f. 9 and f. 2 are bird and bat wings, respectively. The motifs which decorate the interiors of the three-line initials are: birds (an owl, f. 15), dragons (ff. 11v, 15v, 22v), human heads (a man's, f. 13v, a monk's, f. 20v), grotesques, geometric decoration, as well as foliate motifs and other types of vegetal elements. Some of the initials contain ridged ornament, ff. 2v, 4v, 10, etc., similar in type to the kind found in the historiated initials, e.g. f. 1. Figurative elements also project from the letters, such as human heads (a woman's, f. 2, a man's, f. 9), bearded profile heads, demonic or satyr-like in appearance (f. 8, f. 1v) as well as zoomorphic heads in profile (bird-like creature, f. 11v, f. 16).

Thott 517, 4° has thirteen one-line initials and twenty-seven line fillers, which is significantly fewer than in Thott 547, 4°. Some of the motifs found in the decorative initials in Thott 517, 4° are similar to those in Thott 547, 4° but a more limited repertoire of decorative initials was employed than in the Hours. The reason for this difference is that the text of Thott 517, 4°, which is mostly prose, required fewer line fillers and one-line initials than a devotional book in which the different parts of the text – e.g. psalms, prayers, antiphons, verses, responses, etc. – are clearly separated from each other.

The Line Fillers

Gold line fillers, outlined in black, are either left unadorned or decorated with geometric patterns, foliate or floral motifs painted in blue, white, and/ or pink. Unlike in Thott 547, 4°, there are no fantastic animals employed as decoration of the line fillers.

The Scribe

The text of the *Lives* is written in Gothic semi-quadrata in black ink by one scribe. This hand is also discernible in Thott 547, 4°, ff. 1v–66v, as well as in four other Bohun manuscripts, namely the Bodleian Library Psalter-Hours, the Pommersfelden fragment, and the *Lichtenthal Psalter*.[5]

The Illuminators

As previously observed by Dennison, the same two artists who executed the decorations in Thott 547, 4° also illuminated Thott 517, 4°.[6] Hand One carried out the historiated initials and borders on the folios at the divisions of the text, while Hand Two painted the decorative initials and borders on the rest of the folios of the manuscript.

The Binding

The manuscript has a gold-tooled, red morocco binding. On the front cover are two four-sided framing devices, one larger than the other. Stylized plants extend from the four corners of the smaller rectangle. The central decorative unit is made up of drawer handles, suns with schematized eyes, brows, nose, and mouth, as well as floral motifs. The composition of the back binding is almost the same except for the central motif which is smaller. On its spine are five raised bands, decorated predominantly with geometric motifs. The area in-between the top two bands bears the title "VITAE TRIUM STAR VIRG," while the spaces between the other bands are embellished with stylized floral motifs.

The same shop was responsible for the bindings of Thott 517 4° and Thott 547 4°.[7] Leather of a similar color was used for the two Copenhagen volumes and the same marbled end papers in blue, red, green, and yellow, were added in both manuscripts. The edges of Thott 517, 4° are decorated with similar colors and patterns as those of Thott 547 4°, and the bands of both books are similarly stitched with red and white thread. None of the stamps used to decorate the binding of Thott 547, 4° were applied to Thott 517 4°, but some of the motifs, like the drawer handle, are similar. The manuscripts do not have the same size bindings. While Thott 547, 4° measures 137 × 187 mm, Thott 517, 4° measures 139 × 184 mm.

The Relationship between Thott 547, 4° and Thott 517, 4°

The Hours and the *Lives* have the same number of text lines and almost the same page dimensions.[8] The concordance between the measurements of the pages is due to the fact that the folios were trimmed before being rebound. There is more empty space at the top of the folios in Thott 547, 4° than Thott 517, 4°, which does not have any *haut-de-pages*. The external measurements of the rulings of the text block are not exactly alike, 108/9 × 67/68 mm and 111x 70 mm, respectively.

The same scribe worked on both manuscripts. Scribe One wrote 1v–66v in Thott 547, 4° and all of *Lives*. The script in Thott 517, 4° is larger than in Thott 547, 4°, making the text easier to read. While medieval people would have been quite familiar with the texts in Books of Hours, it might have been thought a help to make the unfamiliar text of the legends more legible.

A further difference between the Hours and the *Lives* is that the text of the *Lives* is written in black ink while that of the Hours is, for the most part, written in gold-colored ink. The *Lives* are more sparsely decorated than Thott 547, 4° and the palette of pigments used in Thott 517, 4° is more restricted in range than Thott 547, 4°. The pigment combinations result in a more somber effect. Vibrant colors, like yellow and green, are sparsely used, while some of the more lively pigments, such as purple, employed in Thott 547, 4°, are absent in Thott 517, 4°. The wings of angels, for example, are much more colorful in Thott 547, 4° than in Thott 517, 4°.

The same hands and division of labor is apparent in Thott 517, 4° and Thott 547, 4°. The folios on which the major illuminations appear were painted by Hand One while Hand Two painted the decorative initials and borders on the rest of the folios of the manuscript. In both manuscripts the figures have similar proportions and facial features. On f. 1, some of the apostles and the Lord have long, narrow mustaches and pointed beards. Some of the apostles on f. 32v of Thott 547, 4° sport this style of facial hair. On the whole, the clothing worn by the figures in Thott 517, 4° is simpler. The robes of the primary figures portrayed in the *Lives* have few embellishments and the draperies of the secondary figures have few folds. Some of the clothing of the secondary figures is clumsily painted, like, for example, the orange draperies worn by the angels standing before the Virgin's tomb on f.1. However, the artist skillfully painted the garments of the some of the more central figures, such as those worn by the Magdalene and by the priest on f. 22v, and created a sense of their three-dimensionality and texture. Also on f. 10v, the painter created the illusion of different kinds of materials; for example, the stone architecture of the prison and the demon's fur. Some of the figures, like the dragon on f. 10v, are less successfully executed than other figures in this manuscript.

Only one of the major miniatures in Thott 517, 4° employs architectural elements. This structure on f. 10v (fig. 22) is similar to one represented in the third scene in the *bas-de-page* in Thott 547, 4°, f. 18 (fig. 10). The upper portion of both structures is composed of an arch with battlements, behind which is a cupola atop of a roof. The other two scenes in the historiated initials of Thott 517, 4° take place in the world outdoors, and, like the Crucifixion and Resurrection in Thott 547, 4°, do not employ architectural elements. In both manuscripts, narrative scenes unfold before gold backgrounds. However, the scenes within the historiated initial in Thott 517, 4° do not spill into other areas of the page, as they do in Thott 547, 4°.

Some of the types of abstracted forms and decoration are present in both manuscripts. At the top of the scene inside the historiated initial f. 1 of Thott 517, 4° (fig. 21) is a blue cloud with a white edge, waved like a folded ribbon. A similar type of cloud is found in Thott 547, 4° in the historiated initial on f. 32v depicting the Last Judgement (fig. 18). However, the narrative paintings in Thott 547, 4° are much more developed in terms of the organization of objects and figures in space and the complexity of abstract ornamental forms. Compare also, for example, the ornament embellishing the interiors of the historiated initials. On f. 1 of Thott 517, 4°, the letter is filled with pink and blue wavy ornament against red and dark blue backgrounds and further decorated with blue or orange circles with white dots in their centers. The interior of the initial on f. 32v in Thott 547, 4° similarly includes sinuous decoration outlined in white. In Thott 547, 4° blue is not paired with pink, but more dramatically with gold, and red is not applied in circular areas but rather more freely on top of the gold. The result is a much more unified, sophisticated, and visionary composition.

The backgrounds of the initials are rendered in different ways. In Thott 517, 4°, on f. 10v and 22v, the backgrounds have semi-circular indentations into some of which are placed gold balls with squiggles. The borders in Thott 517, 4° are simpler and have a more limited repertoire of components than those in Thott 547, 4°.

Both Nordenfalk and Sandler have observed that the rendition of the light in the Copenhagen Bohun Hours is unique.[9] In Sandler's words, the principal painter of this manuscript "was a master of the illusion of light, of atmosphere, and the more visionary the theme, the more spectacular the representation."[10] In Thott 547, 4°, the main artist sought to express the Christian idea of equating God with light (John 8:12: "I am the light of the world"). In some representations in Thott 547, 4°, God is surrounded by red and gold lines, signifying divine radiance. For example, the Father and the Son are surrounded by luminous rays in the *bas-de-page* of f. 22v (fig. 13), in the historiated initial and the third *bas-de-page* scene respectively on f. 24v (fig. 14), while in the illumination depicting the Coronation of the Virgin, f. 28v (fig. 15), beams of light fan out behind the Lord seated on a bench. In the Annunciation, f. 1 (fig. 1), the Holy Spirit "coming upon" the Virgin is represented by rays of light emanating from the window of a turret and terminating near Mary's head.

Some heavenly beings or entities emanate or are made of red and gold lines, like the star that is a supernatural portent in the scene of the Adoration of the Magi, f. 18 (fig. 9). In the Annunciation, f. 1 (fig. 1), Gabriel's wings are made of bands of light and rays emanate from his halo as well as from an angel appearing to one of the shepherds on f. 14v (fig. 7). Golden rays may impart a supernatural quality to otherwise ordinary things, as for example on f. 14v (fig. 8) where the fire in the furnace creates a halo of gold and red light around the Jewish boy.

These kinds of effects of light are not present in the illuminations accompanying the *Lives*. That is not to say that there is lack of interest in light. Episodes chosen for illumination in the *Lives* draw on passages of texts describing celestial light. But the manner in which it is suggested is different. For example, if we compare the vignette in the historiated initial at the opening of the legend of the Magdalene (fig. 23) of the priest shielding his eyes while witnessing the Miracle at Baume to the scene in the Copenhagen Hours, f. 14v, in which a shepherd shades his eyes from the rays of light emanating from an angel (fig. 7), the differences become apparent. In the *Lives*, the artist utilized the gold leaf effectively to suggest supernatural light. Not only is there a contrast between the texture of the smooth and punched surfaces but also between paint and gold. In the Hours, he created the effect of brilliant supernatural light by placing gold and red striations on top and next to areas of contrasting colors of green and blue. The different textures and vertical lines of contrasting colors radiating from the angel create a sense of energy and drama which differs from the more subdued light reflected from the pool of gold surrounding the Magdelene.

In sum, my analysis of Thott 547, 4° and Thott 517, 4°, supports the conclusions of Dennison and Sandler that it is unlikely that the two Copenhagen volumes were originally part of one manuscript.[11] First of all, the text of the *Lives* is written in black ink while that of the Hours is executed predominantly in gold-colored ink. Secondly, the vellum on which the sparsely illuminated *Lives* are executed is thicker and coarser than that of Hours. Thirdly, there are differences in the degree to which, and the manner in which, the two manuscripts were decorated. Unlike Thott 547, 4°, Thott 517, 4° does not have any *haut-* or *bas-de- page*, heraldry, or marginalia, and has fewer line fillers and one-line initials. The style of the illuminations, as well as the depiction of supernatural light, is less developed in Thott 517, 4° and the color range more restricted. Fourthly, as Sandler has observed, no parallel of a combination of Hours of the Virgin and saints' lives occurs in English fourteenth-century Psalters or Hours. While Dennison has judged that Thott 547, 4° and Thott 517, 4° are close in date, I believe that the stylistic and compositional differences described here are due to the fact the *Lives* were executed before the *Lichtenthal Psalter* and some years before the Copenhagen Hours.[12]

Chapter Four

Principal Texts and Illuminations in Thott 517, 4°

In this chapter, each of the texts in Thott 517, 4° are first presented, summarized, and analyzed. The principal illuminations in the manuscript – the three six-line historiated initials and the three-line initials – are then described and examined. Next, similarities between the illuminations as well as common themes in the three texts are discussed; and finally, the identity of the intended reader of the manuscript is explored.

The Texts

The texts in Thott 517, 4°, written by one scribe, are primarily three Anglo-Norman French works composed by different authors, each recounting episodes from the life and afterlife of one of the three of the most popular female saints in England at that time, Mary, the mother of Christ, Margaret, the virgin martyr, and the Magdalene, the repentant harlot.[1] One of the lives, that of St. Margaret, is followed by an antiphon, a versicle, and a prayer. Each life opens with a historiated initial.

Lynda Dennison and, more recently, Lucy F. Sandler have both come to the conclusion that Thott 517, 4° was made as an independent volume.[2] Medieval books of small size, containing hagiographic biography and concerning a single saint or, occasionally, two or three saints, were most often written in Latin and produced between 950–1200 for abbeys.[3] Thott 517, 4° is a different kind of little book (*libellus*) of saints' lives, one designed for one or more members of a household.[4] English illuminated manuscripts of this format containing a few select lives and for this kind of readership are not all together common.

The works selected for the Copenhagen manuscript are of the type found in large hagiographic collections.[5] Two of the texts, the *Transitus mariae* and the life of Mary Magdalene, are represented in an unillustrated manuscript

(London, British Library, MS Additional 6524) containing fifty legends in Anglo-Norman French, copied in England around the end of the thirteenth century or in the early fourteenth century.[6] The third text, the Anglo-Norman translation of the life of St. Margaret, is preserved only in Thott 517, 4°. It is, therefore, possible that the first two lives could have been copied from a larger manuscript compendium of hagiographic material, while the life of St. Margaret was, perhaps, a new translation from the Latin.

Books concerned with the lives, miracles, and passions of saints were of interest to the Bohun family and are documented in their collection at Pleshey. The inventory of books taken when Thomas of Woodstock's property was seized by Richard II in 1397 lists a book in French of the Miracles of Our Lady, a large book containing different Saints' passions, a French Life of St. Thomas of Canterbury, a book in French called the Crown of Tribulation and the lives of the saints, and a book of Barlaam and Josaphat.[7] Thomas's wife, Eleanor de Bohun, is documented as owning a manuscript of *De Vitis Patrum*, which she bequeathed to her daughter, Isabelle, and a copy of the *Golden Legend* in French that she left to her daughter, Anne.[8]

I. *Transitus mariae* (The Passing of Mary), ff. 1–10v

The first text in Thott 517, 4°, an account of the death and assumption of the Virgin, is a vernacular translation of one of the two Latin recessions of the *Transitus mariae* (the Passing of Mary), erroneously ascribed in the Middle Ages to Melito of Sardis (d. c. 200).[9] The text has been judged to have been composed several centuries after Melito's death, at the end of the sixth century at the earliest.[10] Numerous medieval copies of the Pseudo-Melito text exist in Latin as well as the vernacular.[11] The translation of the *Transitus* in Thott 517, 4° is faithful to the style and content of its Latin source.

The following is a brief summary of the *Transitus mariae* as it appears in the Copenhagen manuscript:

Jesus while on the cross entrusted his mother to the care of St. John the Evangelist. After the departure of the apostles to preach and convert pagans to Christianity, Mary settled in the house of St. John's parents. A year after Christ had ascended to heaven, an angel appeared before the weeping Mary, who longed for her son. The angel told her that he had brought a palm branch from paradise, which would be carried before her bier. Mary requested that she be allowed to see the apostles. The angel told her that on that same day, all the disciples would come to her. Mary asked the angel to bless her at that hour in which her life shall go out of her body, and to spare her from seeing the prince of darkness. The angel replied that the Lord had blessed her eternally and by the power of him whom she had carried in her womb she would not see the prince of darkness. After the angel departed, Mary took the palm which she had received and returned to her dwelling.

St. John, who had been preaching in Ephesus, was raised up by a cloud and brought before Mary's dwelling. When Mary saw him, she was overjoyed. She related to him that the Jews were planning to burn her body after her death. She also showed St. John the robe of her burial and the palm which she had received from the angel and instructed him that he should have it carried before her couch when she was dead. St. John asked her how he would perform the funeral rites alone. Then all the apostles were brought before Mary's house and St. John told them why they had been brought together. Three days later the Lord came with a multitude of angels to take his mother to paradise. Mary then went to recline upon her couch, and giving thanks to God, gave up her soul. The apostles saw her soul, which was of such whiteness that it surpassed the whiteness of snow, and of every metal. The Savior instructed St. Peter where to take Mary's body while her soul was delivered to the archangel Michael. When three virgins took off Mary's clothes, the sacred body shone with so much brightness that it could not be seen. After they had washed and dressed her, the light gradually dimmed. An odor of great sweetness was emitted from the body. Then the apostles laid the Virgin on the bier, and St. Peter instructed St. John to carry the palm before her. While the apostles sang and carried Mary's body, there appeared above the bier a company of singing angels. People wondered about the source of the sweet sound and someone told them that Mary had departed from the body and that Jesus's disciples were singing. Then a large crown appeared above Mary's couch. Filled with fury and rage at the sight, the chief priest of the Jews tried to overturn the bier and throw the body down to the ground. Immediately his hands dried up and stuck to the couch. And when the apostles raised the bier, the chief priest felt great pain. And the angels smote the people with blindness. The chief priest cried out to St. Peter to end the torment and St. Peter replied that if he was to believe in Jesus Christ, his hands would be released from the bier. And when the chief priest said that he did, his hands were released but his arms were dried up, and the pain did not go away. Then St. Peter told him to kiss the couch, and say: I believe in God, and in the Son of God, Jesus Christ, whom she bore. When the chief priest did as St. Peter asked, he no longer felt any pain. St. Peter then told him to take the palm from St. John, and go and tell the blind of the great deeds of our Lord, promising that whoever should believe in Christ would have their sight restored. When he found the blind and told them how he had been cured, they believed in the Lord. When he touched the blind with the palm, they recovered sight. But five of them who remained hard of heart died.

The apostles brought Mary to the place chosen by the Lord, laid her in the tomb, and closed the sepulcher. Suddenly Christ appeared with a multitude of angels, addressed the apostles, and asked them what He should do? St. Peter and the other apostles responded that He should raise up the Virgin's body and take her to heaven. Then the Savior ordered the archangel Michael to bring the soul of Mary, and Gabriel removed the stone from the tomb; then he told Mary that she should rise. After Our Lady had risen from the tomb, she blessed her son. Prostrated at the Lord's feet, she could not render sufficient thanks. The Lord delivered her to the angels, so that they could carry her to paradise. Then the Lord and the angels returned back to heaven, carrying Mary to paradise. And each of the apostles was returned to the place where he preached.[12]

The focus of the *Transitus mariae* is on how Mary departed this life. It encompasses themes which are common to the earliest narratives: her meeting with the apostles, Christ's reception of his mother's soul, the hostility of the Jews towards Mary, and the transfer of the Virgin's body and soul to Paradise.[13] In the *Transitus mariae,* Mary is distinguished from all other women by her virgin maternity. This distinction justifies her corporeal assumption: the body which had given birth without corruption should not suffer destruction in death.[14] Mary is also set apart from the rest of humanity and, implicitly, connected to her son by the ascent of her body and soul to heaven a short time after death. But the text also portrays Mary's human maternity, her affection for her son and the emotional pain she suffered because he was taken from her. Christ's compassionate humanity is also noted. His concern for and devotion to his mother leads him to leave her in the care of St. John and give her the assistance for which she asks, fulfilling her wish not to see the prince of darkness.

II. A. The Life and Passion of St. Margaret, ff. 10v–22v

The Copenhagen Anglo-Norman life of St. Margaret is based on the tenth-century Latin version called *Mombritius* after its earliest editor, Boninus Mombritius (1424–1500).[15] This version of Margaret's legend was popular in medieval Europe and can be found in a great number of texts.[16] It was already known in pre-conquest England and was translated into Old English.[17] After the conquest it was translated into Anglo-Norman French as well as Middle English and was the source of inspiration for a number of writers.[18] The Anglo-Norman translation in Thott 517, 4° is not based on any of the known vernacular translations and might have been undertaken for the Bohuns from the Latin.[19]

The account in Thott 517, 4° can be broadly summarized as follows: St. Margaret, the daughter of the patriarch of Antioch, was filled with the Holy Spirit. She was taken to the countryside to a nurse who was a Christian. This woman taught Margaret the Christian faith and the girl embraced her nurse's beliefs and consecrated her virginity to God. After the death of her mother and father, she remained with her nurse. One day, while the girl was tending her foster-mother's flock, Olibrius, a powerful man in the region, caught sight of her and was attracted by her great beauty. He wanted to marry the maiden if she was freeborn or take her as his concubine if a slave. He sent his servants to apprehend the girl. Hearing of Olibrius's intentions, Margaret passionately prayed to the Lord to protect her. Despite her objections, the maiden was seized. When presented to Olibrius, he demanded to know her name, lineage, and religion. She answered that her name was Margaret, that she was freeborn and a baptized Christian. Olibrius was pleased that the girl was freeborn but ridiculed her for her belief in a crucified god. While he determined how to induce Margaret to renounce her faith and submit to him, he had the girl imprisoned. When brought once again before Olibrius, her resolve still had not been broken. She remained determined to follow Christ and not to marry. Therefore Olibrius commanded she be beaten. Margaret prayed to the Lord. As a result of the executioners' beating, blood flowed like streams from a fountain from her beautiful and tender body. Onlookers were moved by pity and told Margaret to give in to Olibrius. The saint scoffed at their advice and spoke derisively of Olibrius, insisting that God would deliver her. Enraged by the maiden's words, Olibrius ordered her hung and her flesh torn. Margaret remained steadfast and would not recant, asking God to send the Holy Spirit and make her strong. Bleeding profusely, she was re-imprisoned and visited by demons. First a dragon appeared and swallowed her, but after making the sign of the cross she was freed from its belly. Afterwards a devil came to torment her. Catching him by the head, she threw him to the ground and demanded to know why he had come. The demon counseled her to obey Olibrius and worship his gods. Margaret did not follow his advice.

When brought to Olibrius, she once again refused his demands. Before a great crowd, an attempt was made to burn her. Left unharmed by the flames she was then bound and thrown into a cauldron of boiling water. Miraculously, her bonds were broken and she stood up uninjured. Finally Olibrius ordered her to be beheaded. Before the sentence was carried out, she was permitted to pray and asked the Lord to keep from peril any woman in labor who called on her. She also asked that any children of her supplicants be delivered without injury to body or limb, and that anyone who dedicated a church or chapel to her or owned a copy of her passion be forgiven for his sins and shielded from demons.

Then, there was a great earthquake and the Holy Spirit descended from heaven in the form of a dove, carrying a golden crown and told the maiden to come and join Christ. Margaret commanded Malachus the executioner to take his sword but he refused. Margaret warned him if he did not do as she asked, he would not join her in paradise. Malachus then beheaded her. After the maiden's martyrdom, Theotimus took her relics and placed them in a new stone tomb in the city of Antioch in the house of St. Tecla.

The legend of St. Margaret in Thott 517, 4° is somewhat freely translated from its Latin source. Some changes were made to the order of presentation (e.g., f. 17, f. 17v) and details are placed in a more contemporary context by the translator. For example, in the Mombritius recension, the passage in which Olibrius promises Margaret that she would be above all his household, "tibi erit super omni familia mea," is translated in Thott 517, 4°, f. 13 as she would be second only to him in his palace and lady of his household ("apres moi la souereine de mou[n] paleis et dame serroiez sour toute ma menee.") The translator shortened many of the oral communications in the Latin text, namely the prayers, monologues, and dialogues. Thus some of the layers of meaning and symbolism in the Mombritius text are eliminated. Examples of these types of abbreviations are: the curtailing of Margaret's prayers (while in prison, f. 16 and f. 16v, during her ordeal in the vessel, f. 19v, and after the appearance of the dove of the Holy Spirit, f. 21), as well as of her speeches (especially her vehement exchange with the demon is significantly abbreviated, ff. 17–17v). It is puzzling that a part of the Mombritius text which seems especially relevant for a lay audience, namely the confirmation of Margaret's powers of intercession by the Holy Spirit, is truncated in Thott 517, 4°, f. 21.

Other portions of the Latin source are expanded on. For example, in Margaret's first prayer, f. 12, she compares herself to a lamb, bird, fish, and deer, while in the Mombritius text she compares herself to a sparrow and a fish. The incorporation of the extended animal imagery suggests that the translator was aware of versions of Margaret's legend other than the Mombritius one.[20] Generally speaking, the Anglo-Norman French translation heightens the emotional content of events related in the Latin original and provides more details about the events unfolding in the narrative. For example, in relationship to the Latin original the translator of the Copenhagen text expands on the details of Margaret's torture after her ordeal with the demon, ff. 19–19v.[21]

One of the most significant changes to the dramatic structure of the story in the Copenhagen manuscript is the diminished role of Margaret's father, Theodosius. The Latin Mombritius text, as well as other medieval compositions dealing with the saint's life, pit pagan father against Christian daughter, emphasizing Theodosius's great displeasure at his daughter's embrace of her nurse's religion, to the point that he comes to despise Margaret: "Odiosa erat patri: dilecta domino Iesu Christo" (Mombritius, 190, 35; She was hated by her father: she was loved by the Lord Jesus Christ). In contrast to the Mombritius text (Mombritius, 192, 21–23, and 193, 53–54), in Thott 517, 4°, f. 16, Margaret, while imprisoned, does not mention that she is her father's only child and that he has abandoned her, nor are her father and mother named by the demon as his followers. While Margaret's mother, in the Mombritius text, acts as a foil to the heroine's Christian and affectionate nurse (Mombritius, 190, 33), the Thott text tells the reader very little about Margaret's relationship to her parents, f. 11: "En un temps son pier[e]& sa mere demurent & ele remist orpheine" (after some time her mother and father died and she was an orphan).

Affective imagery already present in the Mombritius recension of Margaret's legend is expanded on in the Copenhagen text. The translator increased the number of references to Margaret's heart, ff. 11, 13, 14, as well as to her love of Christ. The Thott text uses language that shows the saint's personal emotional attachment to the Lord, for example, the manner in which Margaret's love for Christ is described, f. 11, "en seon noun de fist seint marger[ete] baptizer & einz seon queor. vers ih[es]u crist grant amour conseen en taunt ke lautre amour aver ne savoit" (in His name Margaret was baptized and in her heart she conceived so much love for Jesus Christ that she could know no other love), and the characterization of Jesus as her "ami" (lover, friend, or suitor), ff. 13v, 16 and 19v. Unlike the Mombritius recension, in the Thott text the language of romantic love is used to describe Olibrius's feelings for Margaret. While in the Mombritius version (Mombritius, 191, 15–16), Olibrius thinks about what devices he can use to deflower Margaret: "quali machinatione eius uirginitatem perderet," in the Thott translation, f. 13, he thinks of a way to enchain Margaret's heart (penser une maneire p[ar] quel il purreit enchiner le queor margarete de alui assentir). Olibrius's romantic feelings for Margaret are also noted elsewhere in Thott 517, 4°. While Margaret is being tortured, the people witnessing her torments cry out with pity and tell her, f. 14v, "assentir a Olibrius q[u] i tant desir[]tamour" (give in to Olibrius who greatly desires your love). In contrast, in the Mombritius recension, this type of language is not used; the crowd warns the girl that the prefect is angry and counsels her to save herself by believing in his gods, "præfectus iste iracundus est et perdere te festinat et delere de terra memoriam tuam: Crede illi et uiues" (Mombritius, 191, 44–45). The characterization of Olibrius's relationship to Margaret is more explicitly emotional than in the Mombritius text and juxtaposed to Margaret's romantic but chaste dependence on Christ. Thus, there is a greater sense in Thott 517, 4° that Margaret's piety is more affective than in the Latin source.

If we compare St. Margaret's prayer on behalf of those who worship her in Thott 517, 4°, f. 20, to its Latin source we find that the Copenhagen text is somewhat longer and more specific than the Mombritius version (Mombritius, 195, 2–13). In the Copenhagen manuscript, Margaret entreats the Lord to specifically protect women in labor and their children: "e a femmes q[ui] sont en travaillant denfa[n]t et que lirront ou orrount cestestoire, ne suffrez q[ue] les ne lour engendrure soient failes de corps ne de membre" (and to women who are in labor in childbirth and who read or hear this story, that they will not suffer nor will their progeny be ill in body or in limb). The Mombritius Latin version of Margaret's prayer makes no mention of women in childbirth. However, petitions on behalf of expectant mothers and women in labor are present in a number of English and Anglo-Norman accounts which predate the Copenhagen life.[22] Another detail present in the Copenhagen manuscript but absent from the Mombritius recension is the reference to the contemporary practice of purchasing (from scribes) an amuletic text, which could be folded or rolled and carried on the body, f.20v: "& ki estoire escriuera ou escrit a chatera & entour seon corps portera" (and whoever writes the story or purchases it and wears it around the body).[23] The modifications to the Mombritius text in the Copenhagen translation thus result from knowledge of other versions of St. Margaret's life and the practices of women associated with the saint's cult, specifically with the veneration of the saint by expectant mothers. The reasons for the differences between the Mombritius text and the vernacular translation might be due to the influence of the patron for whom Thott 517, 4° was translated and adapted.

There are documented examples of women in their childbearing years who owned books and images which could be used to venerate St. Margaret. Amongst the English women who owned these types of objects were Eleanor de Bohun, who in 1382 received from her brother-in-law, John of Gaunt, a picture of the saint and Eleanor's granddaughter, Anne Stafford, Countess of March (c. 1403–1432), who requested a life of St. Margaret from John Lydgate, probably in the 1420s.[24] French works include a prose life of St. Margaret, together with a miniature depicting the saint, found in a manuscript (*Hours of Jeanne II of Navarre*, Paris, Bibliothèque Nationale de France, nal 3145, ff. 133–134v, c. 1336–40) made for Jeanne II de Navarre (1311–1349), who by 1336 had given birth to four of her eight children, and a small book of the life of St. Margaret commissioned for the French queen, Isabeau de Bavière (1371–1435), shortly before the birth of her ninth child.[25]

In sum, while in the Mombritius Latin text the prayers of the saint provide the bulk of the legend, in the Copenhagen vernacular translation less space is devoted to Margaret's words. There is more of a focus on events and the actions of the protagonists in the Thott translation, which includes more concrete and colorful imagery than is found in the Latin version of the text. The prayer St. Margaret utters in the Mombritius Latin text is expanded in the Copenhagen translation and the saint specifically promises to intercede at confinements on the behalf of women and their children. Thus it can be concluded that not only was the text of the life of St. Margaret in all likelihood translated for the intended owner of Thott 517 4° but also that it was adapted for its audience. The importance St. Margaret must have held for the intended owner can also be attested to by the ensuing texts and illumination.

II.B. Antiphon, Versicle and Prayer, f. 22v

The three Latin texts that follow the vernacular life of Margaret are of the type found in commemorations of the saints and have common elements with *memoriae* in three Bohun devotional manuscripts.[26] The first, introduced by the decorated letter "E," is an antiphon, a text of simple character intended to be sung and which contains the fundamental thought of the lines that follow it. It states: "Erat a[utem] margareta annor[u]m quindecim cum ab impio olibrio tradebatur i[n] carcerem" (Moreover Margaret was fifteen years of age when she was sent to prison by the impious Olibrius). Next comes the versicle in which the reader calls upon blessed Margaret to pray for us so that we may prove worthy of the promises of Christ (Ora p[ro] nobis, beata margareta. Ut digni efficiamur p[ro] missionib[u]s xpi.]). The last Latin text on this folio is a prayer in which Margaret is invoked as an example for the supplicant: "God who on this day causeth the blessed virgin Margaret to reach heaven through the martyr's palm, grant to us, we beseech you, that by following her examples we may deserve to come to thee" (Deus qui beatam virginem margareta[m] hodierna die ad celos p[er] martirii palmam uenire fecisti, concede nob[is] q[ue]s[umus] eius exempla sequentes ad te p[er]uenire mer[e]amur).

Following the text of the versicle in which Margaret is asked to pray for us in Thott 517, 4° is the portrait of the orant saint in the interior of the initial "D," f. 22v, marking the opening of the prayer. The golden-haired Margaret, clad in an orange gown, is shown emerging from the dragon that had swallowed her. The image illustrates not only the text of the versicle preceding it but also the scene related in the legend in Thott 517, 4°, ff. 16 v–17, which describes her emerging without blemish to her body from the dragon's burst-open belly and thanking God for saving her.

III. The Apostolic and Eremitic Life of Mary Magdalene, ff. 22v–38

The events recounted in the section devoted to the Mary Magdalene chronicle her post-ascension life. The legend is made up of two distinct parts, originally completely separate Latin compositions.[27] The first, "the Pilgrim episode," describes the voyage of Mary and her companions to Marseille, their arrival in the city, the saint's missionary activities in southern France where she converted many pagans to Christianity, and her involvement with the pagan rulers of Marseille.[28] The second part is concerned with the many years of her life spent in the wilderness, which were devoted to heavenly contemplation as well as to her death and burial.[29]

The Copenhagen Life relates the legend of the childless pagan ruler of Marseille and his wife. Hoping for an heir, the couple sacrifice to idols. The Magdalene forbids them to continue their idolatrous practices and the couple agree to cease worshiping their gods if the lady conceives. A boy is born to them at sea during a pilgrimage to Rome. Tragically, the mother, believed to have died during childbirth, and her infant are left on a beach next to a mountainous coast. The child's father continues his pilgrimage and meets St. Peter who shows him the sights associated with Christ. On the return trip to his homeland, he spots the place where he left his family and on the beach he sees a child playing. After disembarking from the boat the father finds his son nursing from the uncorrupted body of his mother. The lady miraculously awakens and then recounts how the saint, who had helped her during her labor, protected the child and made it possible for her to accompany her husband on his pilgrimage. When the reunited family returns to Marseille, they find the Magdalene with her disciples and are baptized by Maximin. The Magdalene then retires to lead a hermitic life. She lives ascetically, alone in a cave for thirty years, and devotes herself to contemplation. Seven times each day she is lifted up in the air by angels, and fed, and then is brought back by the angels to earth. This miraculous event is witnessed by a priest, who reports all he has seen to Maximin and gives him a message from the Magdelene to meet her alone in the monastery. On the day and hour specified by the saint, she appears among angels to Maximin. Mary bids him to come before her and to summon all the priests and clerics, and after taking communion she dies before the altar on Sunday, the eleventh of August, at the hour of Prime, leaving behind her a sweet fragrance that persists for seven days. Her body is placed in a white marble tomb, which Maximin had ordered for the monastery. When Maximin learns that he is about to die, he orders a tomb for himself that will be placed beside the Magdelene's. St. Maximin dies on the 8th of June and is crowned by our Lord.

Mary Magdalene's life may have been chosen for inclusion in Thott 517, 4° because the saint's penitence, self-sacrifice, and life of prayer made her an ideal role model for the faithful who themselves confronted temptation. Her life had a broad appeal.[30] It was of value to men and to women who were or had been sexually active as well as to virgins.[31] Isabel Plantagenet, wife of Henry Bouchier, Count of Eu and Eleanor de Bohun's grandson, commissioned Osbern Bokenham to write a life of Mary Magdalene for her personal devotional reading. Bokenham writes that Isabel said, "I have for a long time had a special devotion of pure affection to that holy woman who is called "apostle of the apostles;" I mean blessed Mary Magdalene whom Christ made pure and clean from sin, as the writers say. I desire to have her life made in English, and if you would undertake this work for my sake and for reverence of her, I would ask you to do it."[32]

Mary Magdalene had particular importance for the Bohun family. A relic of the Magdalene, much in demand by women in labor, was said to have been given by Empress Matilda (1102–1167) to the priory of St. Mary Magdalene at Farleigh, a dependent house of the priory of Lewes, founded by Maud de Bohun (b. c. 1084) and her son, Humphrey III.[33] The Bohuns were important benefactors of the priory throughout the medieval period.[34] When Eleanor de Bohun came of age in 1380, the advowson of Farleigh priory passed to her and her husband.[35] In 1386, however, Thomas of Woodstock granted Henry of Bolingbroke the advowson of the priory.[36]

The saint also figures in a number of other Bohun manuscripts. A young female member of the Bohun family appears to have held the saint in particular reverence. In the Bodleian Library's Psalter-Hours, f. 181v, Mary Magdalene is given a place of significance in a full-page miniature, in which she presents a young female member of the Bohun family to the Virgin and Child (fig. 4). Four Bohun manuscripts commemorate the saint in the *memoriae*. Three commemorations are prefaced by an initial with her portrait, while a fourth shows Christ appearing to the Magdalene after he had risen.[37]

Mary Magdalene is depicted first among female saints of the third tier in the pictorial tables of saints in the Bodleian Library's Psalter-Hours and in the Pommersfelden manuscript, and is shown with an ointment jar and a crown.[38] Lucy Sandler has judged the crown an exceptional motif, evidently unique to the Bohun manuscripts.[39] It should be noted that Mary Magdalene is not always represented crowned in the Bohun manuscripts – for example, in the initials in the Bodleian Library's Psalter-Hours, f. 218v, and in the Exeter College's Psalter, f. 123, as well as in the historiated initial prefacing her legend in Thott 517, 4°. In the Copenhagen *Lives* it is Margaret, f. 10, who receives the crown, and not the Virgin or Magdalene. In the narrative scenes depicting the Magdalene in MS Egerton 3277, f. 142 and 145v, she is not crowned. It should also be pointed out that all of the female saints in the third level of the pictorial tables are crowned, not just the martyrs. St. Ethelreda was not a martyr but is depicted crowned because she was Queen of Northumbria. It might have been seen as odd perhaps, that Mary Magdelene was represented as the only uncrowned saint.

For the most part, then, the texts in Thott 517, 4° are, or are based on, orthodox and widely disseminated accounts of these holy women's legends that had been in circulation for centuries and were originally read by clerics. But it is likely that there are reasons other than these that the particular versions of the saints' legends in Thott 517 4° were chosen to be copied and bound together. The narratives of the three legends have common threads. The first and most important is the holy women's relationships to Christ. Two of them, the Virgin and Mary Magdalene, were present at many of the central events of Jesus's life. In the legend of the Magdalene, some of these key episodes are noted: the washing of the Creator's feet with her tears and drying them with her hair (f. 34v), the Lord's appearance to her before all others, and her mission to inform the apostles that Christ has risen (f. 37v). As stated in the text of the Life of the Magdalene, f. 32, Jesus himself provided both his mother and Mary Magdalene with companions, St. Maximin and St. John, respectively.[40]

Both the *Transitus* and the legend of Mary Magdelene are involved with events following the Ascension, especially those occurring just before and shortly after the holy women's deaths as well as their burials. The text of the *Transitus* concentrates almost entirely on the end of the Virgin's life, her meeting with the apostles, her death and Assumption, while the legend of Mary Magdalene deals with a longer period of time, her apostolic and hermitical life in France, and only towards the end of the text with her death and burial.

Margaret's *vita* traces her entire life, focusing on the events leading to her martyrdom. She is exceptional in the trilogy in that she did not live while Christ was on this earth. However, her close relationship to the Lord is represented in a different manner. Although not explicitly stated in the text, Margaret imitates Christ. She acts on behalf of humanity and willingly suffers so that others will be saved. Margaret's defeat of the dragon and the demon evoke Christ's victory over Satan. Her triumph over death, her emergence from the belly of the dragon, is not dissimilar from the resurrected Christ's emergence from his tomb. Margaret, as well as the other two holy women whose legends are described in Thott 517, 4°, play an active role in the conversion of non-Christians. In the Copenhagen *Lives* pagans embrace the Christian faith after witnessing miracles at the Virgin's funeral, seeing Margaret's ordeals, and after hearing the Magdalene preach.

The Major Illuminations in the Copenhagen Bohun *Lives*

Thott 517, 4° contains three six-line historiated initials depicting episodes described in the texts they introduce.

Plate 12. Folio 1.
Historiated Initial "Q": Assumption of the Virgin

> f. 9 the Lord Jesus Christ came with a great multitude of angels, and light flashing with great brightness, and spoke to the apostles saying: [...] What, do you wish that I should do with her? St. Peter and the other apostles f. 9v said: Lord, Thou did choose before all others this thine handmaiden to become thine immaculate chamber [...] thou shouldest raise up the body of thy mother and take her into heaven. Then the Savior said: Be it done according to your will. And He ordered the archangel Michael to bring the soul of St. Mary. And, the archangel Gabriel rolled back the stone from the tomb; and the Lord said: Arise, my beloved and my nearest relation; thou who hast not been corrupted by union with a man, suffer not destruction of the body in the sepulcher. And immediately f. 10 Our Lady rose from the tomb, and blessed her dear son, our Lord Jesus Christ, and falling forward at the feet of the Lord, adored Him, saying: I cannot render sufficient thanks to Thee for Thy boundless benefits which Thou hast deigned to bestow upon me Thine handmaiden. May Thy name, O Redeemer of the world, God of Israel, be blessed for ever. And kissing her, the Lord went back, and delivered her to the angels, to carry her into paradise.[41]

In a mandorla held by the Lord and supported by four angels, and under the gaze of the twelve apostles, the young, slim, and beautiful Virgin Mary ascends from her tomb. Two angels, situated on either side of the Lord and descending from a cloud, swing censers. Mary, whose hands are joined in prayer, has loose, long blond hair, white skin, and wears a tight fitting rose-colored gown.

The Assumption of the Virgin into heaven is described on ff. 9–10 of the manuscript. Some of the elements depicted in the historiated intial are recounted in the text, for example, Mary rising from her tomb in the presence of apostles, angels and the Lord. The absence of St. Michael, who plays an important role in the Pseudo-Melito text, was not uncommon in visual renditions of the Assumption. The visualization of the scene of the Assumption is, for the most part, based on the by then established pictorial tradition of showing Mary carried up by angels to join her son.[42] For example, in two earlier English manuscripts, the *Tiptoft Missal* (New York, Pierpont Morgan Library, M.107, c. 1320), f. 253v and a religious miscellany (Oxford, Bodleian Library, MS Douce 79), f. 3, we find some of the same compositional components as in Ms Thott 517 4°, such as the depiction of the Virgin with joined hands in a mandorla held by angels and the Lord. Other details present in Ms Thott 517 4° can also be found in earlier representations of the Virgin's Assumption. For example, the censing angels, which are not mentioned in the text of the *Transitus*, were depicted in scenes of the Assumption on portals of cathedrals. Some elements are of a symbolic nature. The Virgin who at the time of her death would have been middle-aged is represented in the historiated initial as an adolescent; her youthful beauty symbolizes her faultlessness and her long loose hair is a sign of her maidenhood. Her attire too adds to her attractive physical appearance. In the miniature she is clothed in a tight-fitting rose color gown and not in "the robe of her burial" which she is described as wearing in the text, f. 6.

Plate 13. Folio 10v.
Historiated Initial "S": St. Margaret Delivered from the Dragon

From a window in an architectural structure with battlements, turrets, and a dome, St. Margaret's veiled and wimpled nurse holds in her hands a plate and a pitcher. She witnesses her foster daughter emerging from the gash in the dragon's abdomen and battling a black, hairy demon. The saint, seen from the belly up, has loose long golden hair, white skin, and is dressed in a pink gown and a blue cloak. A nimbed angel hovers above the triumphant saint with a crown ready to be placed on her head.

The scene illustrates a number of events described in the legend which took place in the prison where Margaret was held captive (for example, the saint's nurse bringing bread and water to her foster daughter, narrated on f. 16v) and other events which occur later in the *vita*, namely Margaret emerging unharmed from the dragon's belly, f.17, the saint attacking the demon, ff. 17–17v, and the descent of the crown from heaven, f. 19v. Margaret is represented not only as an adolescent, which according to the antiphon on f. 22v was the age when she was imprisoned, but also, as is stated throughout her legend and in the prayer, as a maiden. She is slim, narrow-waisted, and small bosomed and has uncovered loose hair. While the text on f. 17 states that the saint made the sign of the holy cross so the dragon's belly burst open and Margaret emerged without blemish to her body, in the miniature she spears the beast. Such a depiction of Margaret's liberation was not unusual in the pictorial arts.[43] In fact, in a number of other Bohun manuscripts she is shown with loose long blond hair, emerging from the belly of the dragon and transfixing the beast with a cross-spear, namely in the *memoriae* following Lauds in the British Library's manuscript, f. 120, and in the pictorial tables of saints in the Bodleian Psalter-Hours, f. 238, and the fragmentary manuscript in Pommersfelden, f. 10.[44] Another component of the narrative which draws on pictorial tradition is that Margaret is shown about to be crowned, not by the dove of the Holy Spirit holding a crown in its beak, as described on f. 19v, but, rather, by an angel descending from heaven.[45]

A few details in the miniature illustrate aspects of the description of the dragon narrated in the legend. For example, the text, f. 16v, states that the dragon's hair and beard gleamed just like gold and in the miniature the creature is golden brown. However, the creature is depicted as having white teeth and not teeth "the color of iron," as stated on f. 16v, nor is fire exuding from its nostrils, nor does it have a long tongue. On the whole the representation of the beast is based on visual precedents.

The representation of the erect and black demon takes into account the description on f. 17, which states that the devil appeared in the form of a man blacker than an Ethiopian: "en forme de homme plus noir cum vn ethiopien." However, he is also portrayed as bestial: he is horned, has two paws and two cloven feet. According to the text, Margaret grabbed the demon by the hair, threw him to the ground, and trampled him underfoot. In the Copenhagen manuscript, Margaret attacks the demon in another fashion: she thrusts an object into his mouth.[46]

Plate 14. Folio 22v.
Historiated Initial "A": Mary Magdalene Borne Up by Angels

> f. 33v A priest, who desired to lead the life of a hermit, took a cell for himself not far from the Magdalene. Monday before Easter our Lord opened the eyes of the priest, and he showed him the place where the Magdalene lived. He saw how the angels carried her up and after an hour, singing, they brought her back.

Mary Magdalene, with comely features and uncovered, long, loose, wavy, brown and golden hair is supported by four angels above the entrance to a cave. She is barefoot, dressed as a hermit, and clutches a gold ointment jar to her chest. Mary's slender body, except for her feet and lower arms, is completely covered by hair, her own, and that of the beast's whose hide she wears. To the left of the cave stands a bearded man in a grey hooded cloak. With his left hand he shields his eyes and with his right he holds a stick.

The miniature depicts the scene described in the second half of the legend in which a priest living as a hermit witnesses Mary Magdalene in the arms of angels hovering above the place in which she dwelt. Some of the aspects of the representation of the Miracle at Baume in Thott 541, 4° are based on a pictorial tradition. The text does not mention an ointment jar, nor does it describe the Magdalene's disheveled tresses or primitive attire. The ointment jar was the attribute by which she was commonly identified in the visual arts. Mary's clothing and hair are symbolic of her penitence, humility, and removal from society.

In summary, the compositions of all three major illuminations while based largely on pictorial tradition were also influenced by contents of the texts they accompany. Certain aspects of the texts were highlighted by the illuminations and an attempt was made to show common aspects in the three legends. The scenes in all three historiated initials portray the heavenly favors bestowed on each of the holy women and the revelation of their celestial rewards to chosen witnesses, the apostles, Margaret's nurse, and a priest, respectively. Because the scenes are placed at the opening of narratives recounting their lives, the juxtaposition of text and images could be understood as implying that the heavenly rewards bestowed on each of them are the consequence of the lives they led. One of the lives, that of St. Margaret, is followed by a prayer in which the virgin saint is presented as an exemplum for the faithful. The manner in which the three holy women are depicted in the historiated initials, on earth but in contact with heaven, may also be read as an allusion to these saints' roles as intercessors for prayers. Furthermore, the Virgin, St. Margaret, and Mary Magdalene were named in the Litanies of devotional manuscripts associated with the Bohun family, while St. Margaret and the Magdalene were invoked in some of the *memoriae*.[47] Because the holy women were important for their powers of intercession and because of the manner in which they were depicted in Thott 517, 4°, it would seem reasonable to suppose that the images in the manuscript might have been used for prayer and meditation.

The Intended Reader

The manuscript has no arms or portraits. It was certainly made by the Bohun atelier, but at whose command and for whom? The most likely candidates for the book's patron and owner are the seventh earl's daughters, his wife, or one of his son-in-laws. Lynda Dennison has leaned toward the view that Thomas of Woodstock and Eleanor de Bohun were the chief patrons of the Bohun atelier after the death of the seventh earl. She points to their documented interest in books, primarily noted in Eleanor's will and the inventory of Thomas's property taken in 1397.[48] Dennison also judges that it was Thomas who built up the library at Pleshey Castle.

However, as noted below, it is possible that the Bohun atelier produced manuscripts at Joan de Bohun's behest. Like Thomas of Woodstock and Eleanor de Bohun, the dowager countess has been connected to a number of literary works and manuscripts.[49] Thomas Hoccleve claimed that he undertook for her his devotional poem, *The Complaint of the Virgin*, a translation into English of a section of Guillaume de Deguileville's *Le Pèlerinage de l'âme*.[50] She is documented as having given a Missal and Breviary to her grandson, Henry V.[51] Sandler has argued that Joan de Bohun was the patron of a number of manuscripts made for Mary de Bohun and Henry of Bolingbroke. While there is no inventory or will that records books owned by Mary de Bohun, heraldic and other types of evidence in two manuscripts indicate that she was the indended reader. The inclusion of the arms associated with the countess's husband, Henry of Bolingbroke (*gules three leopards or, a label of three points azure floretty or*) above those of her paternal family in the *Lichtenthal Psalter*, at Psalm 119, f. 124v, suggests that it could have been made for Mary.[52] Another manuscript that the countess is likely to have owned is the Bodleian Library's Psalter-Hours. It contains depictions of the arms born by Henry, Duke of Lancaster, and by Henry of Bolingbroke as well as an inserted portrait of the manuscript's female reader wearing a gown embellished with the arms of Bohun and a surcoat with the arms of the kingdom.[53] Sandler has argued that Henry of Bolingbroke was the intended reader of the Fitzwilliam Psalter, executed by the Bohun atelier and which she dates to c. 1380–1394.[54] His interest in books and writers is well documented in the 1390s and during the period of his reign.[55] He made presents of manuscripts to others and owned works of history, bibles, and at least two Psalters, as well as other texts.[56]

We now turn to Thott 517, 4° itself for any indications about its patronage and intended audience. The Bohuns, like other layfolk, would have heard hagiographic biographies read on saints' feast days and in sermons.[57] The choice of material included in Thott 517, 4° suggests that the patron might have wanted a manuscript which could have been read out loud from or studied in the household. Both the legend of the Magdalene and of St. Margaret have engaging narratives, which must have appealed to audiences of both genders and have similarities with romances that were read by the family.[58] The life of Mary Magdalene describes the perilous journey undertaken by a pregnant noblewoman who gives birth at sea, is taken for dead, and is abandoned on an island with her still living infant. The translator of the life of St. Margaret could be said to have created a more dramatic narrative than the author of its Latin source. An aspect of the legend is its portrayal of a love-struck tyrant set on possessing the object of his affections and when he finds he cannot have her, he slowly and cruelly takes her life. Both the legend of the Magdalene and of St. Margaret also include lessons about faith and conduct, appropriate for a reader of either gender. Features of these legends might have instructed their secular audience about desirable social and religious mores as well as providing them with relevant and validating examples. Included in Margaret's life are promises of protection, which could have appealed not only to a female audience but to a wider one as well. For example, the saint asks the Lord for the grace to amend their life and pardon their sins of all those who read or hear the story of her passion, f. 20, and to deliver from peril and torment those who remember her passion and invoke her with their heart, f. 20v. However, there are a number of reasons to believe that this collection of the lives of three saints was primarily intended for a female audience or a particular woman.

Individual female saint's lives tended to be perceived as particularly relevant for women, and, by extension, a collection of holy women's lives would be seen as fitting the needs of a female audience.[59] A number of female hagiographies in the vernacular were specifically written or translated for noblewomen.[60] While laywomen were interested in the lives of male saints, few laymen appear to have been the primary audience of female saint's lives, let alone a series of three.[61]

The analysis presented here suggests that the Copenhagen *Lives* have a special focus on saints associated with motherhood and childbirth. As we have seen, both St. Margaret and Mary Magdalene were specifically associated with the protection of mothers and children. The image of St. Margaret being delivered whole from the belly of the beast came to represent the mother's hope for a similar fate for her child.[62] Because of the attachment of the Marseille miracle to Mary Magdalene's *vita* since the twelfth century, and widely known from its inclusion in the *Golden Legend*, the childless Magdalene came to be largely regarded as a saint who specialized in issues related to motherhood.[63] In versions of the legend which include the Marseille miracle, like the one in Thott 517, 4°, the Magdalene helps the barren lady conceive, and during her labor the saint acts as a midwife.[64] She was also responsible for a lactation miracle, allowing the newborn to nurse at his dead mother's breast and offered continuous protection to the mother and child after they had been abandoned.[65] The Marseille miracle inspired childless women and mothers to turn to the saint for help.[66] This particular version of the Magdalene's life, with its long and detailed account of the miracle of Marseille, may have been thought particularly appropriate for a female reader. It should be remembered that the church canonized few mothers and that women might have looked to holy virgins and women who were no longer sexually active for help with issues relating to motherhood.[67]

While St. Margaret and Mary Magdalene did not have children themselves, the Virgin Mary had experienced motherhood and, as is made clear in the *Transitus*, knew both maternal joy and pain. There was a long-standing belief that the Virgin came to the assistance of women in childbirth.[68] A secondary relic of the Virgin's, her girdle, was claimed to help women in labor. It was brought to Henry III's queen, Eleanor, to be used in preparation for the birth of her child in 1242 and to Edward III's queen, Philippa, during her confinements in 1338 and in 1354, when she gave birth to Lionel of Antwerp and Thomas of Woodstock, respectively.[69] Also, as we have seen in the Copenhagen Bohun Hours, the Virgin is shown assisting a mother with the birth of her child, f. 1 (fig. 3).

It would seem from the analysis of the texts and images presented here that the likely intended audience for the illuminated *Lives* was a woman who was about to enter or already was in her child-bearing years.[70] However, it cannot be ruled out that the *Lives* were executed for Joan de Bohun after she became a widow in 1373. The *Transitus* and the legend of Mary Magdalene deal with issues like faith, conduct, and death, which might have relevance for a widow. The focus of the *Transitus* text on the Virgin Mary might have had an additional attraction for the dowager countess. After her husband's death, Joan de Bohun became an important benefactress of Walden, a Benedictine abbey founded by Geoffrey de Mandeville, Earl of Essex (d.1144), and dedicated to the honor of St. Mary and St. James the Apostle.[71] The dowager countess had been delivered the advowson of the abbey as part of her dower in 1374 and at her death was buried there.[72] Joan's interest in the life of the Virgin in her later years can also be seen in her commission of Thomas Hoccleve's devotional poem, *The Complaint of the Virgin.*[73] This poem is similar to the *Transitus mariae* in that the subject of both works is the lamenting mother of Christ. It is, therefore, not impossible that the texts in Thott 517, 4° would have held some interest for Joan de Bohun and that the Copenhagen manuscript was intended for her. However, it is also conceivable that the *Lives* were not meant for the exclusive contemplation of one person. Both Joan and one of her daughters could have been the intended audience of the *Lives*. In wealthy families, mothers often played a role in the education of their children, usually overseeing their instruction.[74] As already discussed here, it is known that in the first few years of Mary de Bohun's marriage the young lady lived with her mother. Thus, Mary could have heard and read the legends with her mother while in her care.

One final point may be added. Because Thott 517, 4° and Thott 547, 4°, the two Bohun manuscripts in Copenhagen, survived together we need to entertain the possibility that they stem from the collection of one particular member of the Bohun family. We know on the basis of manuscript evidence that Thott 547, 4°, which I believe was executed later than the *Lives*, was made for a young female member of the Bohun family, in all likelihood for either Mary or Eleanor. The absence of the *fleurs-de-lis* of France, a very significant component of the arms of Eleanor's husband, Thomas of Woodstock, on the first folio of Thott 547, 4° tips the balance somewhat in favor of identifying the intended reader of the manuscript as Mary de Bohun. It seems, therefore, possible that Thott 547, 4° was in Mary's collection and that the *Lives* may be of the same provenance. The dowager countess, who was likely to have been the patron of the *Lives*, may have given her daughter the manuscript – for example, when Mary left her mother's household to live with Henry of Bolingbroke, or on another fitting occasion, perhaps during one of her pregnancies.

Conclusion

WITH THE EXCEPTION OF the scholarship of Lucy Freeman Sandler, most of the existing studies of the Bohun manuscripts that discuss patronage tend to present Humphrey, the sixth earl, Humphrey, the seventh earl, and the men related by marriage to the Bohun women as the primary commissioners. My study has dealt more fully with the issue of female patronage and has taken a close look at the implications of the texts and images in the two Copenhagen manuscripts for women viewers.

I have presented and analyzed the visual and textual components of the two Copenhagen manuscripts and have argued that both Thott 547, 4° and Thott 517, 4° not only portray powerful miracle-working female saints for the audience to contemplate and venerate, but also holy women whose patience, faith in the Lord, and strength of character in the face of adversity, could be emulated. Some of the representations, such as those of the Virgin in the *bas-de-page* of the Hours, and of St. Margaret in the Lives, show holy women who are active rather than passive, and in these, and in many of the other images, it is women's strength and effectiveness that are emphasized.

Other women in the Hours act as foils to the representations of the virtuous women in the historiated initials and are meant as anti-models of appropriate female behavior. Job's wife and the nuns depicted in the *bas-de-page* of f. 1 appear to embody vices often associated with their gender in the period. However, as I have argued, the Bohun lady represented on the same folio as the scheming and disloyal nuns is clearly depicted as far above the negative comportment in which they engage. While there is a preoccupation in both manuscripts with virginity and sex, with holy women in the *Lives* conquering temptations of the flesh and with the abbess succumbing to them in the Copenhagen Hours, unchastity is not gendered as purely female. In the pictorial program of the *bas-de-page* of Thott 547, 4°, a legend concerning a lecherous sacristan also features. Moreover, most of the figures who are portrayed negatively in the Hours, and who embody one or more vices, are men, particularly Jewish ones. What is interesting is how much of a focus there is in the pictorial program of the Copenhagen Hours on women's relationships, not with men but with the divine, with children, and with other women, and how much both manuscripts demonstrate the abundance of female virtue.

Considering all the positive attributes associated with holy women, and, in particular, with the Mother of God in the Copenhagen Hours, we can view the portrait of the Bohun heiress, who resembles the Virgin, as constructing a powerful and flattering image of the young lady. The placement of saintly women in a fourteenth-century interior and their resemblance to women of the period also suggests a high degree of identification between the viewer and virtuous women.

It is representations of the arms of the heiress's natal family that are displayed most often in the Hours, appearing on four of the illuminated folios. I have suggested that they can be understood as evidence of pride in the intended reader's lineage, and her status as countess in her own right. The arms of the crown embellishing her surcoat in her portrait, and on one of the fully-illuminated folios, proclaim her royal connections. The majority of the representations of women in these two very beautiful manuscripts, made for a great and noble family, offered a female audience a variety of relevant role models and experiences with which they could identify, and which they could admire and imitate.

Plate 1. Thott 547, 4°, f. 1. Historiated Initial "D" at Matins: Annunciation. Borders: Portrait of the Book-Owner, Angel Musicians. *Bas-de-Page*: Legend of the Unchaste Abbess.

Plate 2. Thott 547, 4°, f. 6v. Historiated Initial "D" at Lauds: Visitation. Two-line initial "D": Shield with the Bohun Arms, Earls of Hereford and Essex (*azure a bend argent two cotises and between six lions rampart or*). *Bas-de-Page*: Legend of Theophilus.

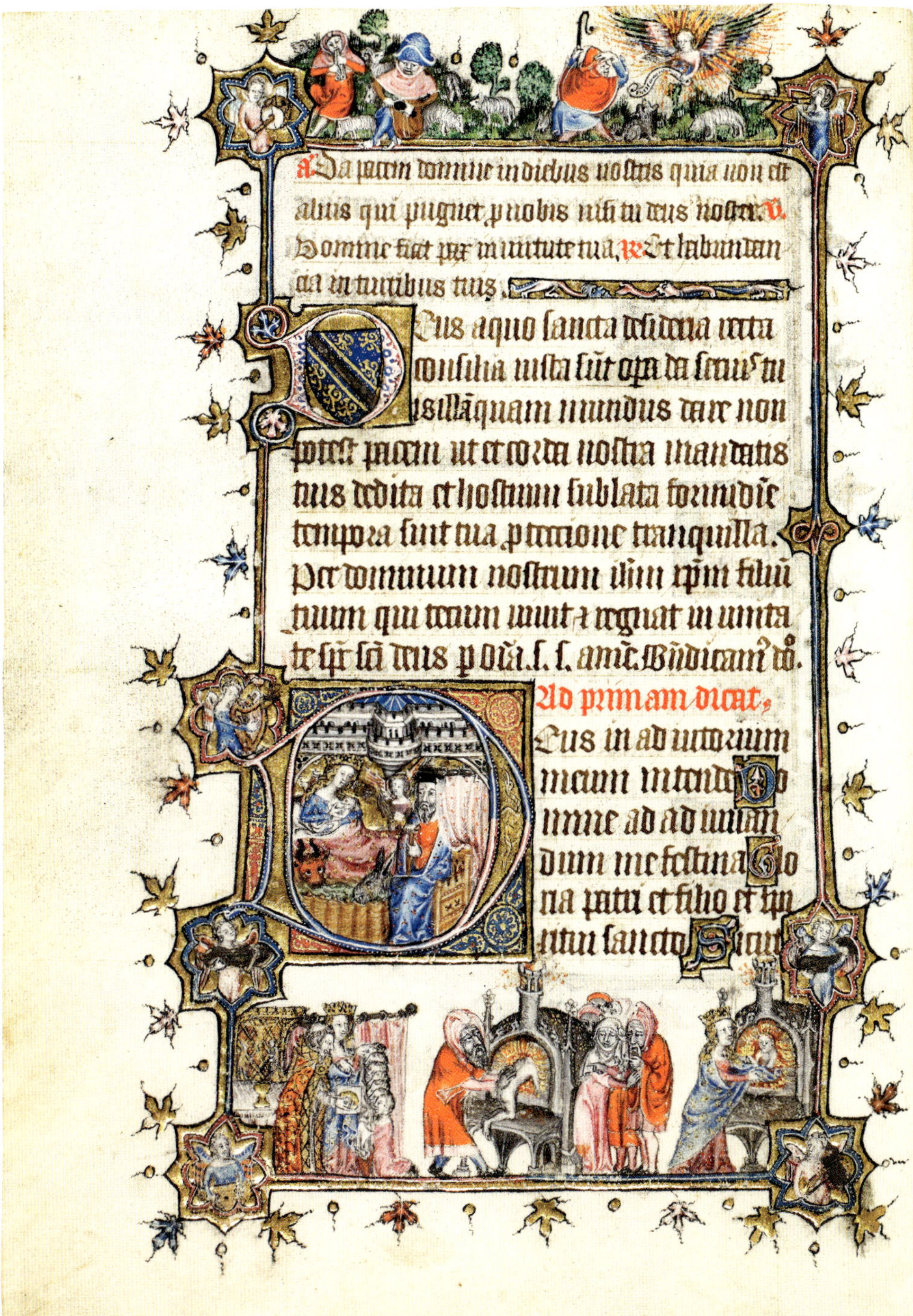

Plate 3. Thott 547, 4°, f. 14v. *Haut-de-Page*: Annunciation to the Shepherds. Historiated Initial "D" at Prime: Nativity. Three-line initial "D": Shield with the Bohun Arms. Borders: Seven Medallions with Angel Musicians. *Bas-de-Page*: Legend of the Jew of Bourges.

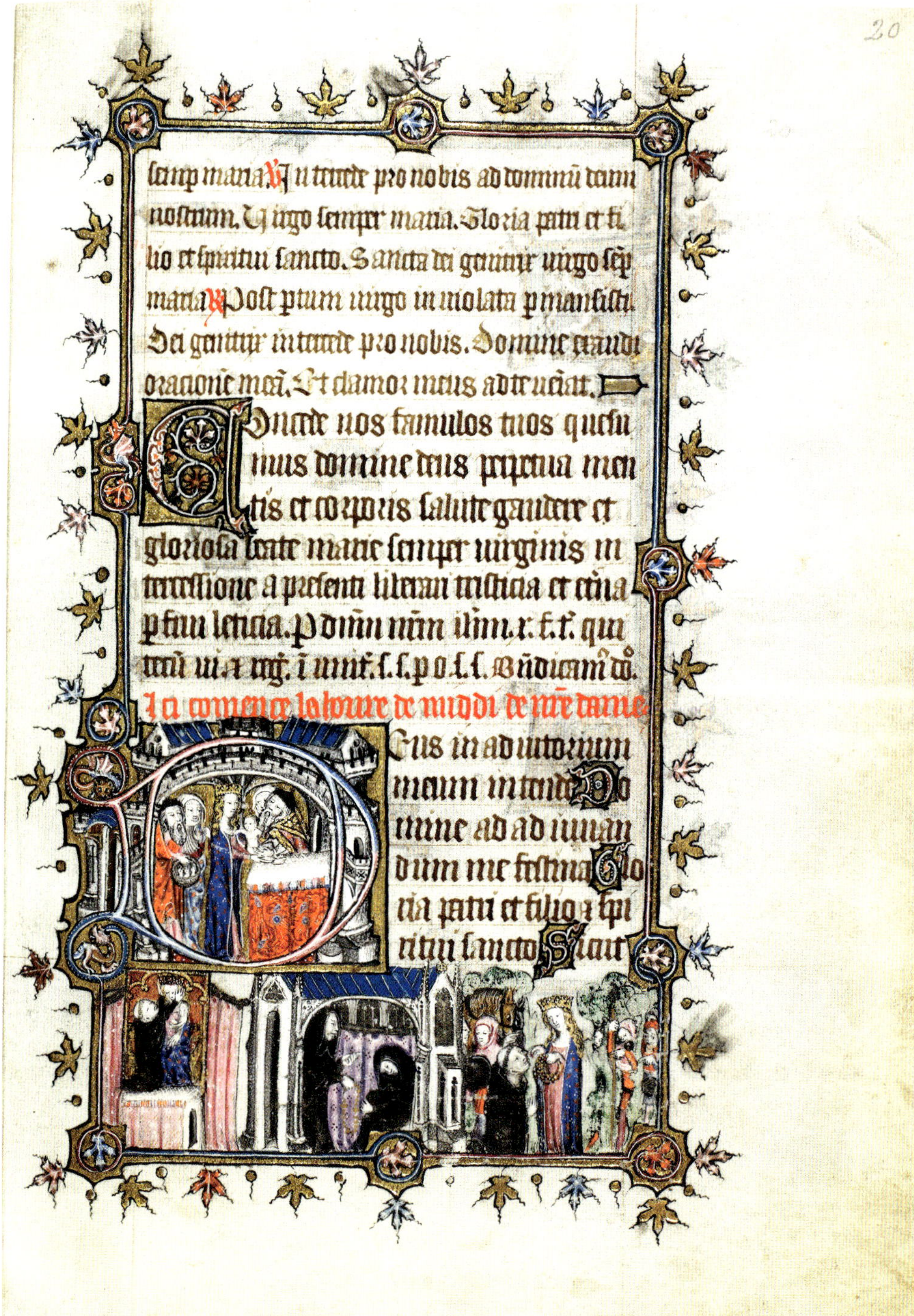

Plate 6. Thott 547, 4°, f. 20. Historiated Initial "D" at Sext: Presentation of the Child in the Temple and Purification of the Virgin. *Bas-de-Page*: Legend of the Monk and the Roses.

Plate 7. Thott 547, 4°, f. 22v. Historiated Initial "D" at None: Crucifixion. *Bas-de-Page*: Miracle of the Soul Saved. Borders: Longinus, Two Angels, Head of God.

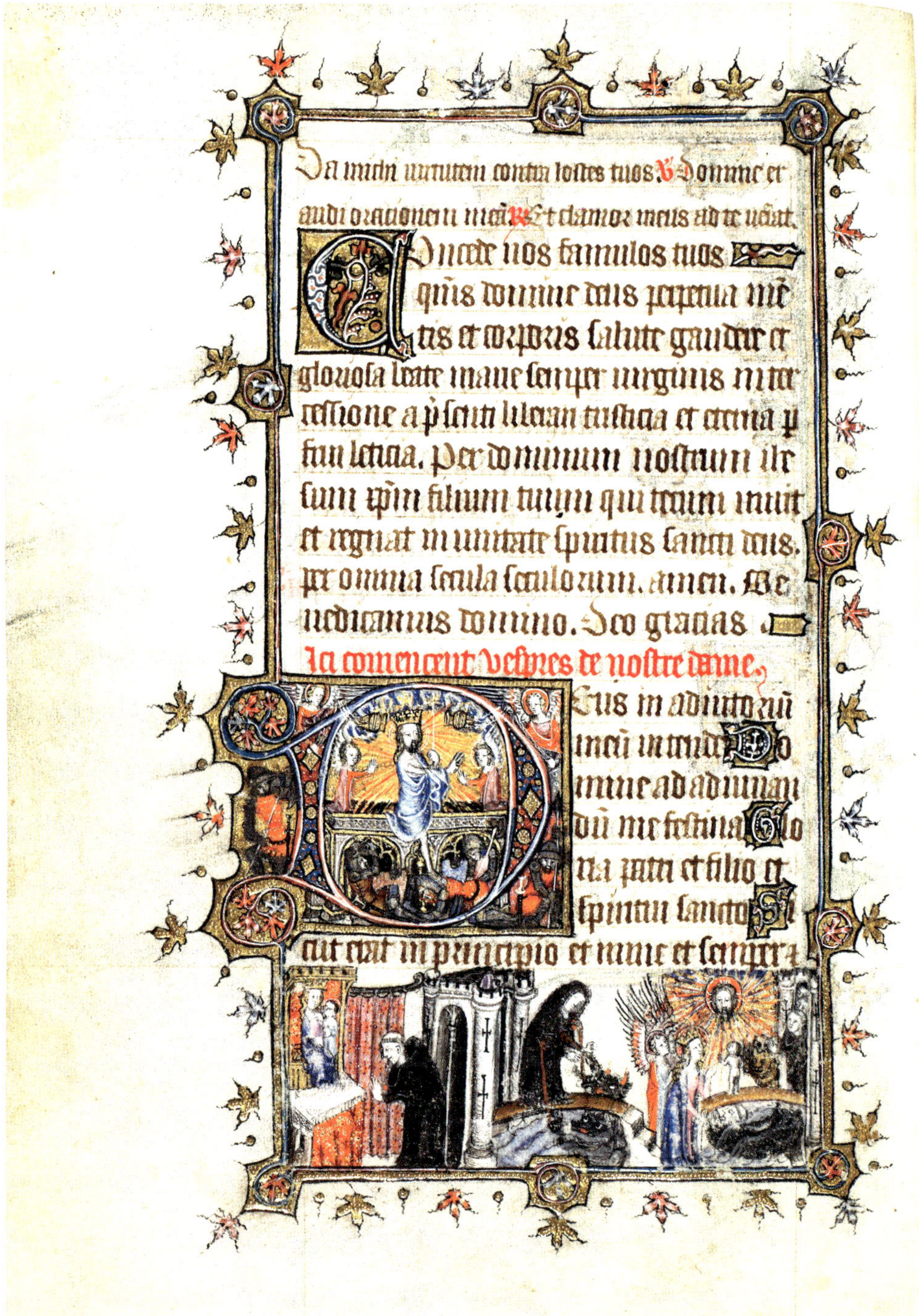

Plate 8. Thott 547, 4°, f. 24v. Historiated Initial "D" at Vespers: Resurrection. *Bas-de-Page*: Legend of the Drowned Sacristan. Border: Soldier Guarding Christ's Sepulcher.

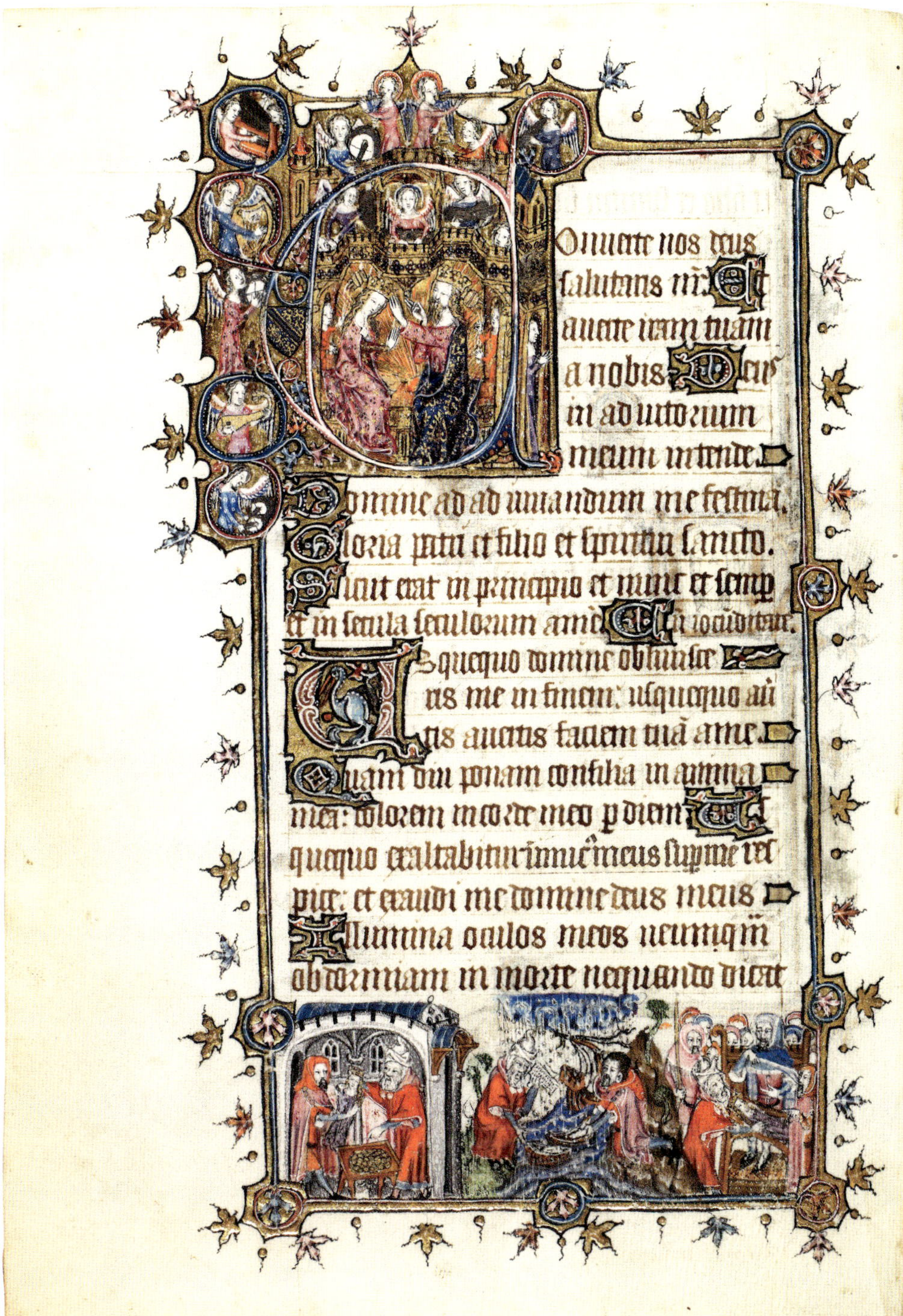

Plate 9. Thott 547, 4°, f. 28v. Historated Initial "C" at Compline: Coronation of the Virgin. *Bas-de-Page*: Legend of the Jew and the Merchant. Border: Angel Musicians.

Plate 10. Thott 547, 4°, f. 32v. *Haut-de-Page*: The Just in the New Jerusalem. Historiated Initial "D" at the Seven Penitential Psalms: Last Judgement. *Bas-de-Page*: The Dead are Raised. Separation of the Saved from the Damned. Borders: Angels, Souls, Devils.

Plate 11. Thott 547, 4°, f. 43. Historiated Initial "D" at the Office of the Dead: Job and Satan before God. *Bas-de-Page*: Three Scenes from the Book of Job (1:18, 19, 15, 20, 21, 2:9).

Plate 12. Thott 517, 4°, f. 1. Historiated Initial "Q:" Assumption of the Virgin.

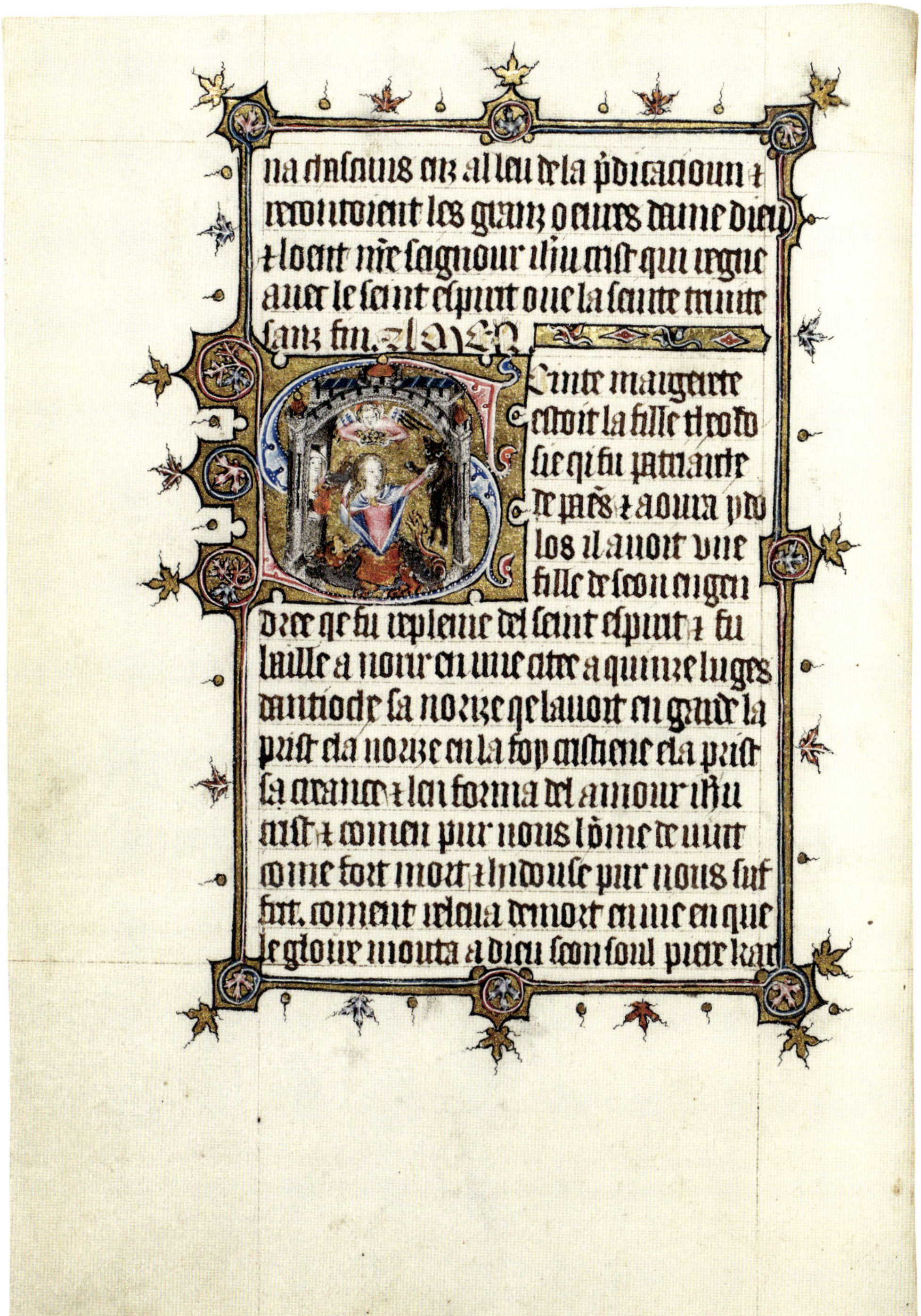

Plate 13. Thott 517, 4°, f. 10v. Historiated Initial "S:" St. Margaret Delivered from the Dragon.

Plate 14. Thott 517, 4°, f. 22v. Historated Initial "A:" Mary Magdalene Borne Up by Angels.

Plate 15. Thott 547, 4°. Front Binding.

Plate 16. Thott 547, 4°. Back Binding.

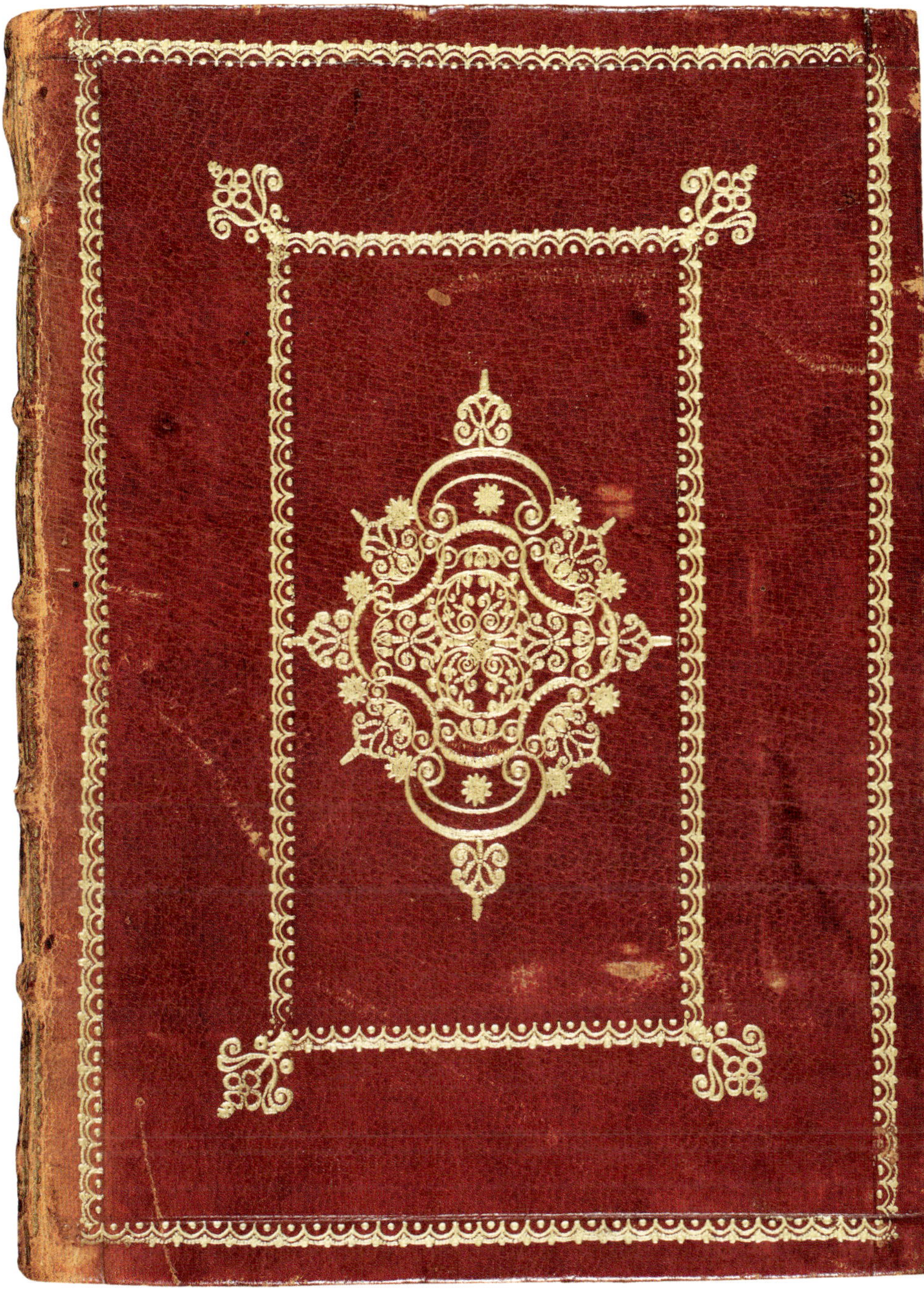

Plate 17. Thott 517, 4°. Front Binding.

Plate 18. Thott 517, 4°. Back Binding.

Figure 1. Thott 547, 4°, f. 1. Detail. Historiated Initial "D" at Matins: Annunciation.

Figure 2. Thott 547, 4°, f. 1. Detail. Border: The Book Owner, Portrait of the Book Owner.

Figure 3. Thott 547, 4°, f. 1. Detail. *Bas-de-Page*: Legend of the Unchaste Abbess.

Figure 4. Oxford, Bodleian Library, MS Auct.D.4.4, f. 181v. Virgin and Child with Mary Magdelene and a kneeling woman clad in arms of England and Bohun.

Figure 5. Thott 547, 4°, f. 6v. Detail. Historiated Initial "D" at Lauds: Visitation,

Figure 6. Thott 547, 4°, f. 6v. Detail. *Bas-de-Page*: Legend of Theophilus.

Figure 7. Thott 547, 4°, f. 14v. Detail. *Haut-de-Page*: Annunciation to the Shepherds.

Figure 8. Thott 547, 4°, f. 14v. Detail. Historiated Initial "D" at Prime: Nativity. Detail. *Bas-de-Page*: Legend of the Jew of Bourges.

Figure 9. Thott 547, 4°, f. 18. Detail. Historiated Initial "D" at Terce: Adoration of the Magi.

Figure 10. Thott 547, 4°, f. 18. Detail. *Bas-de-Page*: Legend of the Child Image taken Hostage.

Figure 11. Thott 547, 4°, f. 20. Detail. Historiated Initial "D" at Sext: Presentation of the Child in the Temple and Purification of the Virgin. Detail. *Bas-de-Page*: Legend of the Monk and the Roses.

Figure 12. Thott 547, 4°, f. 22v. Detail. Historiated Initial "D" at None: Crucifixion.

Figure 13. Thott 547, 4°, f. 22v. Detail. *Bas-de-Page*: Miracle of the Soul Saved.

Figure 14. Thott 547, 4°, f. 24v. Detail. Historiated Initial "D" at Vespers: Resurrection. Detail. *Bas-de-Page*: Legend of the Drowned Sacristan.

Figure 15. Thott 547, 4°, f. 28v. Detail. Historiated Initial "C" at Compline: Coronation of the Virgin.

Figure 16. Thott 547, 4°, f. 28v. Detail. *Bas-de-Page*: Legend of the Jew and the Merchant.

Figure 17. Thott 547, 4°, f. 32v. Detail. *Haut-de-Page*: The Just in the New Jerusalem. Historiated Initial "D" at the Seven Penitential Psalms: Last Judgement, Christ Displays His Wounds.

Figure 18. Thott 547, 4°, f. 32v. Detail. *Bas-de-Page*: the Dead are Raised.

Figure 19. Thott 547, 4°, f. 43. Detail. Historiated Initial "D" at the Office of the Dead: Job and Satan before God.

Figure 20. Thott 547, 4°, f. 43. Detail. *Bas-de-Page*: Three Scenes from the Book of Job (1:18, 19, 15, 20, 21, 2:9).

Figure 21. Thott 517, 4°, f. 1. Detail. Historiated Initial "Q": Assumption of the Virgin.

Figure 22. Thott 517, 4°, f. 10v. Detail. Historiated Initial "S:" St. Margaret Delivered from the Dragon.

Figure 23. Thott 517, 4°, f. 22v. Detail. Historiated Initial "A:" Mary Magdalene Borne Up by Angels.

Notes

Introduction

1. The manuscripts attributed to have been made for individuals of the Bohun family are: three fragmentary manuscripts containing components of a Book of Hours (Private Collection; Pommersfelden, Kunstsammlungen Graf von Schönborn, MS 348 and Copenhagen, Royal Library MS Thott 547, 4°), four extensively illuminated Psalters (Vienna, Österreichische Nationalbibliothek, MS 1826; Oxford, Exeter College, MS 47; Cambridge, Fitzwilliam Museum, MS 38–1950 and Baden-Baden, Lichtenthal Abbey, Archiv, MS 2), two Psalter-Hours (London, British Library, MS Egerton 3277 and Oxford, Bodleian Library, MS Auct.D.4.4.), and the manuscript under discussion here containing saints' legends (Copenhagen, Royal Library MS Thott 517, 4°). All of the manuscripts, with the exception of Thott 517, 4°, contain textual or heraldic references to the Bohun family. Five contain prayers to various saints in the name of "servus tuus Humfridus" (thy servant Humphrey). An early fourteenth-century French manuscript of the *Romance of Lancelot* (London, British Library, MS Royal 20.D.iv) contains two repainted miniatures by an artist working for the Bohuns. For a short description of the manuscripts and the scholarship dealing with these works, see Lucy Freeman Sandler, *The Lichtenthal Psalter and the Manuscript Patronage of the Bohun Family*, London: H. Miller, 2004, 163–165.
2. Scholarship dealing with wider issues concerning English fourteenth-century medieval painting or illumination and addressing the style of Bohun manuscripts are: Margaret Rickert, *Painting in Britain: The Middle Ages*, Harmondsworth: Penguin, 1954; and Amanda Simpson, *The Connections between English and Bohemian Painting during the Second Half of the Fourteenth Century*, Outstanding Theses from the Courtauld Institute of Art, New York: Garland Publishing, 1984.
3. C. Bruun, "De illuminerede Haandskrifter fra Middelalderen i Det store kongelige Bibliotek," *Aarsberetninger og Meddelelser fra Det store kongelige Bibliotek*, Copenhagen: Gyldendal, 1870–1902, 192–196. The identification of the *bas-de-pages* on f. 22 and f. 28 as scenes from Joseph's death and of the father who sold his daughter to a knight, respectively, are doubtful. For a discussion of the heraldry which Bruun and others believed to be that of Lancaster, see Lucy Freeman Sandler, "Lancastrian Heraldry in the Bohun Manuscripts," in *The Lancastrian Court: Proceedings of the 2001 Harlaxton Symposium*, ed. Jenny Stratford, Donington: Shaun Tyas, 2003, 221–232. Thott 547, 4° is summarily described in Ellen Jørgensen, *Catalogus codicum latinorum mediiaevi Bibliothecae Regiæ Hafniensis*, Copenhagen: Prostat in aedibus Gyldendalianis, 1926, 232–233.
4. Bruun, "De illuminerede Haandskrifter,"193.
5. Bruun, "De illuminerede Haandskrifter," 197. Thott 517, 4° is included in N. C. L. Abrahams, *Description des manuscrits français du moyen âge de la Bibliothèque Royale de Copenhague*, Copenhagen: Imprimerie de Thiele, 1844, 9–11. Both Copenhagen manuscripts are briefly described in Kåre Olsen and Carl Nordenfalk, *Gyldne Bøger: Illuminerede middelalderlige håndskrifter i Danmark og Sverige*, Copenhagen: Nationalmuseet, 1952, 61–62.
6. Paul Meyer, "Légendes hagiographiques en Français," *Histoire littéraire de la France*, vol. 33, Paris: Imprimerie nationale, 1906, 443. Meyer judged that the account of the Assumption of the Virgin in Thott 517, 4° is the same as in Brussels, Bibliothèque Royale de Belgique, MS 10326, London, British Library MS Add. 6524, London,

British Library, MS Royal 20. D. VI, Paris, Bibliothèque Nationale de France, français 17229, and Paris, Bibliothèque Nationale de France, français 6447.

7. Meyer, "Légendes hagiographiques," 443.
8. Meyer, "Légendes hagiographiques," 443. It was not included by R. Dean and M. B. M. Boulton in their *Anglo-Norman Literature: A Guide to Texts and Manuscripts*, London: Anglo-Norman Text Society, 1999.
9. *The Bohun Manuscripts, A Group of Five Manuscripts Executed in England about 1370 for Members of the Bohun Family*, described by Montague Rhodes James, with an introductory note on the group by Eric George Millar, Oxford: Printed for the Roxburghe Club by J. Johnson at the University Press, 1936.
10. James and Millar, *The Bohun Manuscripts*, 1–2. Thott 547, 4° does not contain prayers to saints in the name of Humphrey.
11. Lucy Freeman Sandler, "A Note on the Illuminators of the Bohun Manuscripts," *Speculum* 60 (1985): 364–372.
12. Lucy Freeman Sandler, *Gothic Manuscripts 1285–1385*, ed. J. J. G. Alexander, *Survey of Manuscripts Illuminated in the British Isles*, vol. 5, part 2, London: Harvey Miller, 1986, 161. See also her catalogue entry in Jonathan Alexander and Paul Binski, eds., *Age of Chivalry Art in Plantagenet England 1200–1400*, London: Royal Academy of Arts, 1987, 503.
13. Lynda Dennison, "The Stylistic Sources, Dating and Development of the Bohun Workshop," Ph.D. thesis, University of London, 1988.
14. Dennison, "The Stylistic Sources," 172, 174–175, and 342.
15. Lynda Dennison, "The Fitzwarin Psalter and its Allies: A Reappraisal," in *England in the Fourteenth Century: Proceedings of the 1985 Harlaxton Symposium*, ed. W. M. Ormrod, Woodbridge: Boydell Press, 1986, 42–66. Dennison returned to the Flemish Hand's origins and career in later articles, most extensively in Lynda Dennison, "Transformation, Interaction and Integration: The Career and Collaboration of a Fourteenth Century Flemish Illuminator," in *Manuscripts in Transition: Recycling Manuscripts, Texts and Images: Proceedings of the International Congress held in Brussels (5–9 November 2002)*, ed. Brigitte Dekeyzer and Jan Van der Stock, Paris: Uit geverij Peeters, 2005, 173–191.
16. Lynda Dennison, "Oxford, Exeter College MS 47: The Importance of Stylistic and Codicological Analysis in its Dating and Localization," in *Medieval Book Production: Assessing the Evidence: Proceedings of the Second Conference of the Seminar in the History of the Book to 1500, Oxford, July 1988*, ed. L. L. Brownrigg, Los Altos Hills: Anderson-Lovelace, 1990, 41–59.
17. Lynda Dennison, "British Library, Egerton MS 3277: A Fourteenth-Century Psalter-Hours and the Question of Bohun Family Ownership," in *Proceedings of the 1997 Symposium: Family and Dynasty in Late Medieval England*, ed. Richard Eales and Shaun Tyas (Harlaxton Medieval Studies, N.S., 9), Donington: Shaun Tyas, 2003, 122–155.
18. Felix Heinzer, "Un témoin inconnu des Bohun Manuscripts: le MS. 2 des Archives de l'abbaye de Lichtenthal," *Scriptorium* 43 (1989): 259–266. A manuscript in a private collection containing a fragmentary Hours was recognized by Christopher de Hamel to have been made for an individual of the Bohun family. De Hamel described its contents and dated it to c. 1345–50. See Christopher de Hamel, "A New Bohun," in *The English Medieval Book: Studies in Memory of Jeremy Griffiths*, ed. A. S. G. Edwards, Ralph Hanna and Vincent Gillespie, London: British Library, 2000, 19–26.
19. Heinzer, "Un témoin," 261–264.
20. See *The Lives of St Mary Magdalene and St. Martha (MS Esc. H-I-13)*, ed. John Rees Smith, Exeter: University of Exeter Press, 1989, xxi–xxii, and 12–22 for the transcription of ff. 29–38.

21. For a study of the three illustrated Psalters, see Lucy Freeman Sandler, "The Illustration of the Psalms in Fourteenth-Century English Manuscripts: Three Psalters of the Bohun Family," in *Reading Texts and Images: Essays on Medieval and Renaissance Art and Patronage in Honour of Margaret M. Manion*, ed. Bernard J. Muir, Exeter: University of Exeter Press, 2002, 123–151. For a study of the imagery in the Bohun Psalter in Vienna, see Lucy Freeman Sandler, "Word Imagery in English Gothic Psalters: The Case of the Vienna Bohun manuscript: ÖNB, cod. 1826," in *The Illuminated Psalter: Studies in the Content, Purpose and Placement of its Images*, ed. F. O. Buttner, Turnhout, Belgium: Brepols, 2005, 387–395. Lucy Freeman Sandler, "Bared: The Writing Bear in the British Library Bohun Psalter," in *Tributes to Jonathan J. G. Alexander: The Making and Meaning of Illuminated Medieval and Renaissance Manuscripts, Art and Architecture*, ed. Gerald B. Guest and Susan L'Engle, London: Harvey Miller/Brepols, 2006, 269–282.
22. Lucy Freeman Sandler, "Political Imagery in the Bohun Manuscripts," in *Decoration and Illustration in Medieval English Manuscripts, English Manuscript Studies 1100–1700*, ed. A. S. G. Edwards, London: British Library, 2002, 114–153.
23. Sandler, "Lancastrian Heraldry," 221–232.
24. Sandler, "Lancastrian Heraldry," 222.
25. Sandler, "Lancastrian Heraldry," 231–232.
26. Sarah Glover, "Illustrations of the Miracles of the Virgin in English Books of Hours c. 1200–1400," Ph.D. thesis, University of Virginia, 2003. Earlier but much briefer explorations into some aspects of the iconography of the *bas-de-page* scenes of the Jew of Bourges in Thott 547, 4° are to be found in an essay on Marian miracles and anti-Jewish sentiment by Denise L. Despres, "Mary of the Eucharist: Cultic Anti-Judaism in Some Fourteenth-Century English Devotional Manuscripts," in *From Witness to Witchcraft: Jews and Judaism in Medieval Christian Thought*, ed. Jeremy Cohen (Wolfenbütteler Mittelalter-Studien, 11), Wiesbaden: Harrassowitz, 1996, 395–396; and by Miri Rubin in her analysis of the narrative discourse in tales of Jews desecrating the host, dating shortly before 1300. See Miri Rubin, *Gentile Tales: The Narrative Assault on Late Medieval Jews*, New Haven, CT: Yale University Press, 1999.
27. Glover, "Illustrations of the Miracles," 143 and 152.
28. Lucy Freeman Sandler, *The Lichtenthal Psalter and the Manuscript Patronage of the Bohun Family*, London: H. Miller, 2004.
29. Sandler, *The Lichtenthal Psalter,* 126.
30. Sandler, *The Lichtenthal Psalter,* 119–121.
31. Sandler, *The Lichtenthal Psalter,* 126 and 164.
32. http://www.chd.dk/gui/thott547_HV_gui.html
33. They can be viewed at: http://base.kb.dk/manus_pub/cv/manus/ ManusIntro.xsql?nnoc=manus pub&pManusId=76&p_Lang=alt and http://base.kb.dk/manus_pub/cv/manus/ManusIntro.xsql?nnoc=manus pub&p ManusId=75&p_Lang=alt
34. Lucy Freeman Sandler, "Mary de Bohun's 'Livret de saintes' in Copenhagen," in *Tributes to Nigel Morgan: Contexts of Medieval Art; Images, Objects & Ideas*, ed. Julian M. Luxford and M. A. Michael, Turnhout: Brepols, 2010, 65–76. Since completing this Introduction I have learned from Prof. Sandler that she has published an additional article dealing with the two Copenhagen manuscripts. See Lucy Freeman Sandler, "One Hundred and Fifty Years of the Study of the Illuminated Book in England, The Bohun Manuscripts from the Nineteenth Century to the Present," in *Gothic Art and Thought in the Later Medieval Period: Essays in Honor of Willibald Sauerländer*, ed. Colum Hourihane, University Park, PA: Pennsylvania State University Press, 2011, 243–263, as well as that my comment to her that there might be more to be learned about the provenance of Thott 547, 4° and Thott 517, 4° from their bindings has resulted in her

showing pictures to Mirjam M. Foot. See Sandler, "One Hundred and Fifty Years of the Study," 252. For Dr. Foot's findings, see "An Eighteenth-Century Dutch Patron of Bookbinding," *Quaerendo* 41 (2011): 193–207.

The Historical Background

1. They were related in the fourth degree and received papal dispensation in September of 1359 to marry. See *Calendar of Entries in the Papal Registers Relating to Great Britain and Ireland: Papal Letters, 1342–1362*, ed. W. H. Bliss, vol. 3, London: for Her Majesty's Stationery Office, 1897, 606.
2. K. B. MacFarlane, *The Nobility of Later Medieval England*, Oxford: Clarendon Press, 1973, 86.
3. For the marriage of Thomas Holland and Alice Fitzalan, see *Register of Edward the Black Prince Preserved in the Public Record Office*, Part 3 (Palatinate of Chester), A.D. 1351–1365, London: Stationery Office, 1932, 480–481.
4. See CPR, Edward III, vol. 10, 1354–1358, August 4, 1357, 595. For the Mautravers's estate, see CIPM, vol. 11, 452–455.
5. Margaret Aston, *Thomas Arundel: A Study of Church Life in the Reign of Richard II*, Oxford: Oxford University Press, 1967, 7–8.
6. Until 1363 Humphrey is described as Edward III's ward; see CPR, Edward III, vol. 12, 1362, 173, 177, etc. For his early years in the king's service, see CPR Edward III, vol. 12, February 1, 1363, 299, and March 8, 1364, 528.
7. Mary proved her age (14) in December, 1384. See CCR, Richard II, vol. 2, 512–516.
8. CPR Edward III, vol. 15, 1370–1374, February 16, 1374, 476, and CIPM, Edward III, vol. 13, 130–146.
9. CCR, Edward III, vol. 13, May 20, 1373, 505–506. For the king's letters patent concerning the administration of the property of the late Humphrey de Bohun, see CPR, Edward III, vol. 15, March 9, 1373, 261, March 18, 1373, 261, June 15, 1373, 325, February 22, 1374, 476, etc. CPR, Edward III, vol. 16, November 15, 1374, 57, March 29, 1375, 85, May 28, 1375, 112, etc.
10. CCR, Edward III, vol. 13, March 9, 1373, 494–495, and March 29, 1373, 495. CPR, Edward III, vol. 15, April 2, 1373, 267, and September 2, 1373, 334.
11. CCR, Edward III, vol. 13, March 9, 1373, 495.
12. CPR, Edward III, vol. 15, April 2, 1373, 267 and September 2, 1373, 334. CFR, Edward III, vol. 8, July 26, 1373, 217, December 16, 1373, 231. CCR, Edward III, vol. 16, June 2, 1374, 28.
13. See CCR, Edward III, vol. 16, May 10, 1374, 22–25, and May 10, 1374, 25–26, respectively.
14. M. M. Bigelow, "The Bohun Wills, II," *American Historical Review* 1 (1896): 639.
15. A second husband would have shared use of her dower. See Sue Sheridan Walker, "Feudal Constraint and Free Consent in the Making of Marriages in Medieval England: Widows in the King's Gift," *Historical Papers* 14 (1979): 99.
16. Joel T. Rosenthal, *Patriarchy and Families of Privilege in Fifteenth-Century England*, Philadelphia, PA: University of Pennsylvania Press, 1991, 194.
17. Rosenthal, *Patriarchy*, 17; and Rowena E. Archer, "Rich Old Ladies: The Problem of Late Medieval Dowagers," in *Property and Politics: Essays in Later Medieval English History*, ed. Anthony James Pollard, Gloucester: Sutton, 1984, 19.
18. Bigelow, "The Bohun Wills, II," 634. For women as supervisors of wills, see Rowena E. Archer and B. E. Ferme, "Testamentary Procedure with Special Reference to the

Executrix," *Reading Medieval Studies* 15 (1989): 5; and Rosenthal, *Patriarchy*, 186. For her father's will, see Aston, *Thomas Arundel, 17.*
19. CCR, Edward III, vol. 13, May 20, 1373, 505.
20. CFR, Edward III, vol. 8, February 20, 1374, 245. CPR, Edward III, vol. 15, February 22, 1374, 476. For Thomas de Maundevill acting as Joan's attorney, see CFR Edward III, vol. 8, July 26, 1373, 217. For a reference to Thomas de Maundevill as John of Gaunt's well-loved servant, see JGR, 1372–1376, vol. 1, February 20, 1372, 123.
21. CCR, Edward III, vol. 13, May 20, 1373, 505.
22. Sue Sheridan Walker, "Widow and Ward: The Feudal Law of Child Custody in Medieval England," *Feminist Studies* 3 (1976): 109. That heirs, in general, were not raised by their widowed mothers has been questioned in B. Gregory Bailey, Meaghan E. Bernard, Gregory Carrier, Cherise L. Elliott, John Langdon, Natalie Leishman, Michal Mlynarz, Oksana Mykhed and Lindsay C. Sidders, "Coming of Age and the Family in Medieval England," *Journal of Family History* 33 (2008): 43.
23. Walker, "Widow and Ward," 106.
24. For example, in 1285 John of Holland was sent to England at the age of one to be raised together with his future spouse, Elizabeth of Rhuddlan.
25. CPR, Edward III, vol. 15, April 3, 1374, 472.
26. CPR, Edward III, vol. 15, April 3, 1374, 472.
27. See JGR, 1372–1376, June 1, 1374, 225, no. 1431: "item que vous delivrez a nostre tres ame seur la dame de Wodstok le jour de son marriage un graunt hanape et un eawer d'argent surorrez a nous donez par nostre tres honore friere le Prince."
28. See James A. Brundage, *Law, Sex, and Christian Society in Medieval Europe*, Chicago, IL: University of Chicago Press, 1987, 238, and 433–434; Christopher N. L. Brooke, *The Medieval Idea of Marriage*, Oxford: Oxford University Press, 1989, 140; and Charles Donahue, Jr., "The Canon Law on the Formation of Marriage and Social Practice in the Later Middle Ages," *Journal of Family History*, 8 (1983): 144.
29. Brundage, *Law, Sex, and Christian Society*, 236.
30. A married girl of her class came of age at fourteen, an unmarried girl at sixteen. See Sue Sheridan Walker, "Proof of Age of Feudal Heirs in Medieval England," *Mediaeval Studies* 35 (1973): 307.
31. James S. Bothwell, "'Escheat with Heir': Guardianship, Upward Mobility, and Political Reconciliation in the Reign of Edward III," *Canadian Journal of History* 35 (2000): 241–273.
32. Elizabeth's inheritance was at least one-third of Ireland and the estates of the Clares, earls of Gloucester. Lionel and Elizabeth were betrothed as children and only married in 1347 when Lionel was about twelve. During some of the period of Elizabeth's nonage, her great inheritance was controlled by Queen Philippa, Edward's wife and Lionel's mother. See CPR, Edward III, vol. 5, May 5, 1341, 187. For the grant to Queen Philippa of the custody of Elizabeth's lands, see CPR, Edward III, vol. 7, May 10, 1346, 87.
33. Blanche had been betrothed in 1347 to John de Segrave who died 1353. See *Complete Peerage*, vol. 7, 410. For her father's property, see CIPM, Edward III, vol. 11, no. 118. For Blanche's share, see *CCR,* Edward III, vol. 11, 202–211.
34. CIPM, Edward III, vol. 11, no. 229.
35. Anthony Tuck, *Richard II and the English Nobility,* London: Edward Arnold, 1973, 7.
36. CPR, Edward III, vol. 16, December 27, 1375, 210, and July 11, 1376, 297, July 16, 1376, 298, and November 2, 373.
37. CPR, Edward III, vol. 16, June 10, 1376, 279.
38. CPR, Edward III, vol. 16, August 24, 1376, 337; October 6, 1377, 407.

39. CPR, Edward III, vol. 16, August 24, 1376, 337; October 6, 1376, 355; October 6, 1377, 407–408.
40. For the grant, see CPR, Richard II, vol. 1, July 13, 1377, 60.
41. CPR, Richard II, vol. 1, December 14, 1377, 99.
42. Chris Given-Wilson, *The English Nobility in the Late Middle Ages: The Fourteenth-Century Political Community*, London: Routledge & Kegan Paul, 1987, 44; W. M. Ormrod, *The Reign of Edward III: Crown and Political Society in England 1327–1377*, New Haven, CT and London: Yale University Press, 1990, 59; Anthony Goodman, *The Loyal Conspiracy; The Lords Appellant under Richard II*, London: Kegan Paul, 1971, 88–90; and Simon Walker, *The Lancastrian Affinity 1361–1399*, Oxford: Clarendon, 1990, 189.
43. In 1362 the king gave his close associate and advisor, Robert de Ufford, license to grant 300 marks yearly rent to the convent of Barking during the life of Maud de Mountagu, daughter of Edward, Lord Montagu (d. July 14, 1361). CPR, Edward III, vol. 12, July 19, 1362, 234. For Robert de Ufford's relationship to Edward III, see J. S. Bothwell, *Edward III and the English Peerage: Royal Patronage, Social Mobility, and Political Control in Fourteenth-Century England*, Woodbridge: The Boydell Press, 2004, 22–24. Maud (born 1350) and her sister Joan (born 1349), who married Robert de Ufford's son William, were to inherit the vast estates of their mother, Alice (d. 1352), the co-heiress of Thomas Brotherton, Earl of Norfolk. CPR, Edward III, vol. 9, November 16, 1351, 181; and February 15, 1352, 230. Upon the death of her half-brother, Joan later inherited the estates of her father. Since the girls had been wards of Edward III from the time of their mother's death, Joan de Mountagu's marriage and the placement of the twelve-year-old Maud into a nunnery could not have taken place without the king's permission.
44. See p. 29 above.
45. CPR, Richard II, vol. 1, March 20 1380, 471.
46. Thomas was owed £7,182 by the crown for the 1380–1381 expedition. See James Sherborne, *War, Politics and Culture in Fourteenth-Century England*, London: Hambledon Press, 1994, 65.
47. CPR, Richard II, vol. 1, May 8, 1380, 502.
48. CCR, Richard II, vol. 1, June 22, 1380, 390, and 394.
49. CPR, Richard II, vol. 1, July 27, 1380, 537.
50. Jean Froissart, *Chronicles of England France and Spain: and the Adjoining Countries, From the Latter Part of the Reign of Edward II, to the Coronation of Henry IV*, trans. Thomas Johnes, vol. 1, London: William Smith, 1839, 623–624.
51. JGR, 1379–1383, vol. 1, 179–180. For the celebration, the countess supplied various officials, including officers and valets of her chamber, suggesting that it took place at her manor.
52. Two entries in the Lancastrian account book have been interpreted as providing evidence that in April 1382 at the dowager countess's manor of Rochford, Mary bore a son who died almost immediately after birth. For the entries, see James Hamilton Wylie, *History of England under Henry the Fourth*, vol. 3, London: Longmans, Green and Co., 1896, 325, and vol. 4, 166; and *Women of the English Nobility and Gentry, 1066–1500*, trans. and ed. by Jennifer Ward, Manchester: Manchester University Press, 1995, 69, who provides a translation of the two entries from the account of Hugh de Waterton of the receipts and household expenses of Henry, Earl of Derby, 1381–1383 (London, National Archives DL 28/1/1, f. 5). Ian Mortimer (*The Fears of Henry IV. The Life of England's Self-Made King*, London: Vintage, 2007, 370) is right to point out that Wylie's transcriptions from the document are not accurate. Mortimer's own transcription of the first entry is more precise: Et dat[a] uni armigero voc[ato] Westcombe d[omi]ni

de Bokyngham portanti d[omi]no meo nova quod d[omi]na sua erat deliberat[a] de pu[er]o per mandat[um] d[omi]ni mei Lanc[astrie] xvj die Aprilis lxvjs viijd (Given by order of my lord on 16 April to an esquire of my lord Buckingham called Westcombe who brought my lord the news that his lady was delivered of a child, 66 s 8 d.) The second entry, transcribed by Michael H. Gelting, reads: Et apud Recheford(iam) d(omi) n(u)s dedit Magistre pu(er)i p(re)dict(i) xviij' die april(is) p(er) mandat(um) d(omi)ni mei Lanc(astrie) xl. s(olidos). Et eodem die dat(um) nutrici pueri p(re)dict(i) xxvj s(olidos) viij d(enarios) (And at Rochford On the 18th of April the lord gave to the mistress of the said child by mandate of my lord Lancaster, 40s. And given to the nurse of the said child, 26s 8d). Mortimer reads "domina sua" in the first entry as the messenger's lady, Eleanor de Bohun, and therefore it records a gift made in conjunction with the birth of Eleanor's child. Michael H. Gelting, in a note to me in support of Mortimer's translation of the entry, adds that the Countess of Derby was not only the earl's "domina," but also Hugh de Waterton's. Hence he would have expressed himself differently if the child had been Mary de Bohun's.

53. Henry III likened this practice to entrusting sheep to wolves. See Scott L. Waugh, *The Lordship of England: Royal Wardships and Marriages in English Society and Politics, 1217–1327*, Princeton, NJ: Princeton University Press, 1988, 198–199.
54. For the expenses for wedding gifts and those associated with the festivities, see JGR, 1379–1383, vol. 1, no. 556, March 6, 1381, 178–180.
55. Thomas was back in England by May 15, 1381 when he was appointed to investigate matters in the town of Gloucester. See Richard Holt, "Thomas of Woodstock and Events at Gloucester in 1381," *Historical Research* 58 (1985): 240.
56. JGR, 1379–1383, vol. 2, 309. The crown also contributed to cover her expenses. See CPR, Richard II, vol. 2, 95, February 6, 1382, in which it is stated that Joan received a pardon from the king of: "40 l. yearly farm payable to the king for the manor of Henton during the minority of Mary [...] married to the king's cousin the earl of Derby and staying with her mother; in aid of her maintenance."
57. John Carmi Parsons, "Mothers, Daughters, Marriage, Power: Some Plantagenet Evidence, 1150–1500," in *Medieval Queenship*, ed. John Carmi Parsons, New York, St. Martin's Press, 1998, 66–67, and 207, note 5.
58. Bliss, ed., *Calendar of Entries in the Papal Registers*, vol. 5, 385.
59. Joan's mother, Eleanor, and Blanche's father, Henry of Grosmont, 1st Duke of Lancaster, were sister and brother.
60. For Gaunt's appointment of Humphrey as a feoffee and their campaign in France, see Goodman, *The Loyal Conspiracy*, 275. For the expensive and elaborately executed gift Hereford gave Gaunt in 1372, see JGR, 1372–1376, vol. 2, 108. For the payment for 1,000 masses for the seventh earl's soul, see JGR, 1372–1376, vol. 2, 155.
61. Although some scholars are of the opinion that Richard named Roger Mortimer, grandson of Lionel of Antwerp, as his heir (1385/6–1398), others have argued against Richard ever officially taking this position. For a summary of this debate, see Ian Mortimer, "Richard II and the Succession to the Crown," *History* 91 (2006): 324–325, 328.
62. Michael Bennett, "Edward III's Entail and the Succession to the Crown, 1376–1471," *English Historical Review* 103 (1998): 591.
63. For the political instability caused by the prospect of Arthur of Brittany (1187–1203), heir of his uncle, Richard I (d. 1199), ascending the throne, see, for example, J. A. Everard, *Brittany and the Angevins, Province and Empire, 1158–1203*, Cambridge: Cambridge University Press, 2000; and M. Dominica Legge, "William the Marshal and Arthur of Brittany," *Historical Research* 55 (1982): 18–24. For the perilous state of affairs dur-

ing the minority of Henry III, see D. A. Carpenter, *The Minority of Henry III*, London: Methuen, London, 1990.

64. See Bennett, "Edward III's Entail," 591.
65. Mortimer provides evidence that by 1384 Richard himself believed that in the event of his death without male issue, he would be succeeded by Gaunt, and after the latter's death, by Henry of Bolingbroke. See Mortimer, "Richard II and the Succession to the Crown," 323.
66. Mortimer has argued that Richard made an announcement not in 1385 but in 1386, see Mortimer, "Richard II and the Succession to the Crown," 327.
67. Mortimer, "Richard II and the Succession to the Crown," 331.
68. Mortimer, *The Fears*, 368.
69. For the gifts, see JGR 1379–83, vol. 1, 230, 231; and for the gift to the squire, see p. 150, note 52 above.
70. Aston, *Thomas Arundel*, 202.
71. CCR, Richard II, vol. 2, 511–516.

The Illuminators

1. In Dennison's view, the Vienna Psalter was executed by five hands. The three earliest, which she calls Hands A, B, and C, started the enterprise. A second campaign was carried out by two further artists, Hands D and E, illuminators to whom she gives the names "the English Artist" and "the Flemish Hand." See Dennison, "The Stylistic Sources," 40–97.
2. For the British Library's Psalter-Hours, see Dennison, "The Stylistic Sources," 341–343; Sandler, "Political Imagery," 117 and 148, note 28, etc. For the folia inserted in the Bodleian Library's Psalter-Hours, see Sandler, *Gothic Manuscripts*, part 2, 159. For the overpainted miniatures in the *Romance of Lancelot*, see Sandler, *Gothic Manuscripts*, part 2, 155; and Dennison, "The Stylistic Sources," 343. And for the *Lichtenthal Psalter*, see Sandler, *The Lichtenthal Psalter*, 126.
3. The last campaign in the Exeter Psalter can be linked with books produced for other patrons. See Dennison, "Oxford, Exeter College MS 47," 56–57.
4. Sandler, "A Note on the Illuminators," 365.
5. "Nous devisoms auxint a frere Johan de Teye n're luminour x.li. a prier pur nous." See John Nichols, *A Collection of All the Wills, Now Known to Be Extant, of the Kings and Queens of England, Princes and Princesses of Wales, and Every Branch of the Blood Royal, From the Reign of William the Conqueror to that of Henry the Seventh Exclusive: with Explanatory Notes, and a Glossary*, London: printed by J. Nichols, 1780, 50. For the translation of the text, see Bigelow, "Bohun Wills, II" 634.
6. Nichols, *A Collection of all the Wills*, 52; and Bigelow, "Bohun Wills, II," 636.
7. Sandler, "A Note on the Illuminators," 365.
8. For the original document, see Rome, Archivio degli Agostiniani, Dd2, f. 17. It has been transcribed and published by Francis Roth, *The English Austin Friars, 1249–1538. II. Sources*, New York: Augustinian Historical Institute, 1961, vol. 2, 223, no. 559: "Concessimus Fratri Johanni Tye de provincia Anglie, quod possit vocare et retinere fratrem Henricum Hood per annum tantum ipsum instruendo in arte illuminandi libros, qui non sit ab eo amovendus nisi hoc sua demerita [seu] utilitas persuaderet" (We give permission to Brother John de Teye from the English province to summon and retain brother Henry Hood for a period of a year to instruct him in the art of book illumination. [Brother Henry Hood] may not be taken away from [Brother John de

Teye] unless either his faults [or] his usefulness requires it). The text is also transcribed and published by Arnulfus Hartmann, ed., *Bartholomæi Veneti O.S.A., Registra generalatus, 1383–1393,* Rome: Institutum Historicum Augustinianum, 1996, vol. 1, 64, no. 193.

9. Roth, *The English Austin Friars,* vol. 1, 370.
10. For Dennison's arguments that John de Teye is one and the same as the "English Artist," see Dennison, "British Library, Egerton MS 3277," 125; and for Sandler's, see Sandler, *The Lichtenthal Psalter,* 126–129.
11. Dennison, "The Stylistic Sources," 342.
12. Sandler, "A Note on the Illuminators," 371, judges that the production of illuminated manuscripts of the later fourteenth century was the domain of secular craftsmen. The only example Sandler found of the involvement of an Augustinian in the execution of a book in the fourteenth century is the *Tickhill Psalter* (New York Public Library, MS Spencer 26), which according to a fifteenth-century inscription was written and gilded by John Tickhill, prior of the Augustinian house of Worksop in Nottinghamshire. See Sandler, "A Note on the Illuminators," 372, note 24. For a few other examples, see Jonathan J. G. Alexander, *Medieval Illuminators and their Methods of Work,* New Haven, CT: Yale University Press, 1992, 29–30.
13. The family's close connection to the order of St. Augustine went back to the thirteenth century. See Aubrey Gwynn, *The English Austin Friars in the Time of Wyclif,* London: Humphrey Milford, 1940, 15–16.
14. The sixth earl rebuilt the friar's church in London on a lavish scale in 1354. See Gwynn, *The English Austin Friars,* 78. In his will he first bequeathed his soul to God in reverence of the Trinity and to St. Augustine for whom he had great affection. He also stipulated that he should be buried among the poor friars of the order of St. Augustine in London and entrusted three Austin friars, Brother William de Monklane, his confessor, Brother William Wilhale, and Brother Geoffrey Berderfeld, to appoint and pay for fifty friars to chant masses for his soul. Additionally, he made financial and other provisions for the retirement of his confessor. He also left bequests to the priory of Llanthony. See Nichols, *A Collection of all the Wills,* 44–56.
15. *The Prophecy of John of Bridlington*, dedicated to Humphrey de Bohun, may have been written by a member of this order. See Michael J. Curley, "John of Bridlington (c. 1320–1379)," in the *Oxford Dictionary of National Biography*, Oxford University Press, 2004. Joan was a patron of Bricett Priory, a house of Augustinian canons. In a letter of c. 1405 to Master William Milton, in which she states that she is a patron of the priory, the Dowager Countess of Hereford requested to examine the state of the Priory as it is being ill-governed. For the letter, see M. Dominica Legge, ed., *Anglo-Norman Letters and Petitions from All Souls Ms. 182*, Oxford: Blackwell, 1941, 388. For her visit to the Augustine friars at Lynn, see Aston, *Thomas Arundel*, 184.
16. In 1384 Mary de Bohun and Henry of Bolingbroke were given the livery of the advowson of LLlanthony Priory, but only two years later Bolingbroke granted it to Thomas, Duke of Gloucester, for the term of Henry's life. See CCR, Richard II, volume 2, December 22, 1384, 515; and London, National Archives, Piece reference DL 27/312. In her will of 1399, Eleanor de Bohun, like her great uncle Humphrey, remembered the priory of LLlanthony. See Bigelow, "Bohun Wills, II," 645. For Brother Thomas de Bradefeld, who was in the service of Thomas of Woodstock, see Roth, *The English Austin Friars,* vol. 2, 235 and 247.
17. L. E. Dennison, "Bohun," *Grove Art Online*, Oxford Art Online, 2010, http://www.oxfordartonline.com.ep.fjernadgang.kb.dk/subscriber/article/grove/art/T009619.

18. After Humphrey's death, Pleshey Castle was assigned to Thomas Maundevill, knight, until Eleanor and Mary came of age. CFR, Edward III, vol. 8, February 20, 1374, 245.
19. CPR, Edward III, vol. 16, October 6, 1376, 355.
20. For the books listed in the inventory, see J. Dillon and W. H. St. John Hope, "Inventory of the Goods and Chattels Belonging to Thomas, Duke of Gloucester, and Seized in His Castle at Pleshy, Co. Essex, 21 Richard II (1397); with Their Values, as Shown in the Escheator's Accounts," *Archaeological Journal* 54 (1897): 298 303.
21. See Léopold Delisle, *Recherches sur la librairie de Charles V*, 2 volumes, Paris, H. Champion, 1907; and Elisabeth Pellegrin, *La bibliothèque des Visconti et des Sforza, ducs de Milan*, Paris: CNRS, 1955. Charles V's brothers also had extensive libraries. In 1401 Jean de Berry's library contained 300 volumes and Philip of Burgundy's library inventory of 1404 comprised eighty volumes. For Philip's books, see Muriel J. Hughes "The Library of Philip the Bold and Margaret of Flanders, First Valois Duke and Duchess of Burgundy," *Journal of Medieval History* 4 (1978): 145–188. Isabelle of France, Edward II's queen, had at least thirty-four books in her possessions in 1358. For the books associated with Edward II's queen, see Susan H. Cavanaugh, "A Study of Books Privately Owned in England: 1300–1450," Ph.D. thesis, University of Pennsylvania, 1980, 456–460; and for the argument that these books comprised only a portion of her library, see Anne Rudloff Stanton, *The Queen Mary Psalter: A Study of Affect and Audience*, Philadelphia, PA: American Philosophical Society, 2001, 235.
22. Some of the books are described in the inventory as "veile"or "veit" (old). See Dillon and St. John Hope, "Inventory of the Goods and Chattels," 298–303. The sixth earl's will provides evidence of his owning a silver bound copy of the Gospels. See Bigelow, "Bohun Wills, II," 633. On the basis of stylistic and heraldic evidence, a number of manuscript commissions have been attributed to him. See Sandler, "Political Imagery," 117; and Dennison, "The Stylistic Sources," 341. An English translation of the French romance poem "Guillaume de Palerme" was commissioned by him in c. 1350 from a poet named William. A single surviving manuscript of the English version (Cambridge, King's College MS. 13) was written not long after the poem was composed for an unknown recipient. See *William of Palerne: An Alliterative Romance*, ed. Gerrit Hendrik Volken Bunt, Groningen: Bouma's Boekhuis, 1985. See also Sandler, *The Lichtenthal Psalter*, 15–18.
23. The Vienna Psalter, in Sandler's view, was probably completed for the seventh earl. Work on the Exeter and Egerton manuscripts, begun in the 1360s, was taken up again during his lifetime but the two books remained unfinished at his death. See Sandler, "Political Imagery," 117.

Part One

Chapter One: Description of Thott 547, 4°

1. 1(8)+2(8)+3(8)+4(8)+5(8)+6(8)+7(8)+8(8)+9(2).
2. F. Madan, "The Localization of Manuscripts," in *Essays in History Presented to Reginald Lane Poole*, ed. H. W. C. Davis, Oxford: Clarendon Press, Oxford, 1927, 5–29. See also Roger S. Wieck, *Time Sanctified: The Book of Hours in Medieval Art and Life*, New York:

George Braziller, in association with the Walters Art Gallery, 1988, 149–150; Nigel Morgan, "Texts and Images of Marian Devotion in Fourteenth-Century England," *England in the Fourteenth Century, Proceedings of the 1991 Harlaxton Symposium*, Stamford: Paul Watkins Medieval Studies, 1993, 35, note 4, and http://www.chd.dk/use/madantest.html.

3. Madan, "The Localization of Manuscripts," 26.
4. Susan Cavanaugh's study of about a thousand book owners in the period of 1300–1450 lists fifty-three women, but of these thirty possessed a Book of Hours as opposed to twenty-eight men. See Cavanaugh, "A Study of Books Privately Owned." See also Eamon Duffy, *Marking the Hours: English People and their Prayers, 1240–1570: The Riddell Lectures 2002*, New Haven, CT: Yale University Press, 2006, 8.
5. Christopher de Hamel, *A History of Illuminated Manuscripts*, Oxford: Phaidon, 1986, 160; and Duffy, *Marking the Hours*, 5–6.
6. Duffy, *Marking the Hours*, 8; and Sandler, *Gothic Manuscripts*, part 1, 38.
7. See Claire Donovan, *The De Brailes Hours: Shaping the Book of Hours in Thirteenth-Century Oxford*, London: The British Library, 1991, 60. As we shall see below, local practices and personal preferences influenced the contents of the *memoriae* as well as saints named in the Litany.
8. See, for example, the description of the widely-varied contents of the Bohun manuscript in a private collection in de Hamel, "A New Bohun," 21–24.
9. There are no rubrics in Thott 547, 4° before Lauds, f. 6v, and Compline, f. 28v. For the various Anglo-Norman prayers in the Bohun manuscript in a private collection, see de Hamel, "A New Bohun," 21 and 24.
10. James judged that the Calendar in the Bodleian Library's Psalter-Hours was added in the fifteenth century. Dennison ("Oxford Exeter," 50) has argued that the Calendar of the Exeter Psalter was added in the third campaign of the manuscript's execution. See James and Millar, *The Bohun Manuscripts*, 23.
11. Dennison, "Oxford, Exeter College," 50. The folia on which Calendars are written out can be part of one gathering and thus easily joined to the rest of the manuscript.
12. Sandler, *Gothic Manuscripts*, part 2, 162.
13. Charity Scott-Stokes, *Women's Books of Hours in Medieval England: Selected Texts Translated from Latin, Anglo-Norman French, and Middle English*, Woodbridge, UK and Rochester, NY: D. S. Brewer, 2006, 17; and Sandler, *Gothic Manuscripts*, part 1, 38.
14. The subjects of the miniatures that accompany each of the eight hours in the Office of the Virgin in French books are usually central events from the Infancy, which are ordered chronologically. In fully-illustrated Hours, the Office of the Virgin opens with a miniature of the Annunciation (Matins), followed by the Visitation (Lauds), the Nativity (Prime), the Annunciation to the Shepherds (Terce), the Adoration of the Magi (Sext), the Presentation in the Temple or Circumcision (None), the Flight into Egypt or Massacre of the Innocents (Vespers), and, frequently, the Coronation of the Virgin (Compline). See Wieck, *Time Sanctified*, 60; and Sandler, *Gothic Manuscripts*, part 1, 38–39.
15. Highly burnished gold leaf is not applied to the square background of the initial "D" on f. 6v. Instead the background is decorated with the arms of England quartered with the fleur-de-lis of France.
16. Thott 547, 4° is a fragmentary manuscript and it cannot be excluded that heraldry was or was planned to be displayed in sections of the book which are either now missing or were not carried out.
17. Compare, for example, f. 28v with f. 29v. For the observation about the appearance of the gold in the manuscript, see Dennison, "The Stylistic Sources," 167.

18. Adelaide Bennett, "A Thirteenth-Century French Book of Hours for Marie," *The Journal of the Walters Art Gallery* 54 (1996): 22.
19. *Breviarium ad usum insignis ecclesiae Sarum*, ed. Francis Procter and Christopher Wordsworth, Cambridge: Cambridge University Press, 1879–1886, vol. 2, 250.
20. James and Millar, *The Bohun Manuscripts*, 47. Sandler, *Gothic Manuscripts*, 162, describes the Litany as one "of a perfect standard sort."
21. The saints named in Thott 547, 4° are similar to those found in the Litany of the Vienna Bohun Psalter. A significant difference between the Litanies in the Copenhagen Royal Library's and Austrian National Library's manuscripts is that St. Augustine is included in the Vienna Psalter but not St. Dominic or St. Francis. For a transcription of the saints invoked in the Vienna Bohun manuscript, see Dennison, "The Stylistic Sources," 311.
22. See Erik Drigsdahl, "The Bohun Hours," http://www.chd.dk/gui/thott547_HV_gui.html. St. Francis and St. Dominic are only included in the Litanies of the Copenhagen Hours and the Egerton Psalter-Hours. In the second litany in the Egerton manuscript, ff. 137v–139, St. Francis precedes St. Benedict on f. 138 followed by St. Dominic on f. 138v. See http://www.bl.uk/catalogues/illuminatedmanuscripts/ILLUMINBig.ASP?size=big&IllID=16080
23. For the cult of St. George in England, see Samantha Riches, "Hagiography in Context: Images, Miracles, Shrines and Festivals," in *A Companion to Middle English Hagiography*, ed. Sarah Salih, Cambridge: D. S. Brewer, 2006, 25–46.
24. Knud Ottosen, *The Responsories and Versicles of the Latin Office of the Dead*, Aarhus: Aarhus University Press, 1993, 112, and http://www.chd.dk/use/OD_th547.html
25. http://www.chd.dk/gui/thott547_HV_gui.html
26. Sandler, *The Lichtenthal Psalter*, 119. For the role the scribes might have played in the Bohun household, see Sandler, *The Lichtenthal Psalter*, 20.
27. Dennison, "The Stylistic Sources," 174, attributes the text written on folios 1 and 1v to one scribe (Scribe C). Sandler attributes the recto of folio 1 to a different and firmer hand. See Sandler, *The Lichtenthal Psalter*, 121.
28. Foot, "An Eighteenth-Century Dutch Patron," 204.
29. Foot, "An Eighteenth-Century Dutch Patron," 204.
30. Although a number of authors have been under the impression that both Thott 547, 4° and Thott 517, 4° were brought to Scandinavia by Mary de Bohun's daughter, Queen Philippa, the wife of Eric of Pomerania, King of Denmark, Norway, and Sweden, there is no evidence to support this supposition. They may have jumped to this conclusion because of a misconception that the two Copenhagen Royal Library manuscripts have a royal provenance.
31. Foot, "An Eighteenth-Century Dutch Patron," 204. For Thott and his connections to the rare book market, see Harald Ilsøe, "Hvordan så Otto Thotts bøger ud?" *Fund og Forskning* 35 (1996): 66.

Chapter Two: Principal Illuminations in Thott 547, 4°

1. At Pleshey Castle there were copies of the *Golden Legend* and Miracles of our Lady, both in French. The dates of these manuscripts are unknown. For the *Golden Legend*, see Nichols, *A Collection of all the Wills*, 182; and for the Miracles of our Lady, see Dillon and St. John Hope, "Inventory of the Goods," 300. The resources of a monastic library

could also have provided the designer/designers with the knowledge of the contents of Marian legends. For the French miracles of the Virgin belonging to Augustinian canons at Llanthony, a priory patronized by the Bohuns, see M. Blaess, "Les Manuscrits français dans les monastères anglais au moyen âge," *Romania* 94 (1973): 331.

2. In the early Middle Ages isolated Marian legends were found in the works of Gregory of Tours, Bede, Ælfric, as well as saints' lives, etc. Adolfo Mussafia, in his pioneering and monumental study, identified a group of seventeen legends that he believed belonged to the oldest Mariales, from which others drew. Mussafia designated this collection as HM ("Hildefonsus-Murieldis"). Next in Mussafia's chronology is the Four Element series, a work by an unknown author who re-edited some earlier legends (Theophilus, the Jew of Bourges, Basil, and the Childbirth at Sea), to illustrate the Virgin's powers over the four elements (air, fire, earth, and water). Mussafia called the third oldest collection TS ("Toledo-Samstag"). See Adolf Mussafia, "Studien zu den mittelalterlichen Marienlegenden," *Sitzungsberichte der kaiserlichen Akademie der Wissenschaften in Wien, Philosophisch-historische Klasse* 113 (1886): 917–994; 115 (1887): 5–93; 119 (1889): 1–66; 123 (1890): 1–85; 139 and (1898): 1–74. The "TS" group is represented in three manuscripts: Toulouse, Bibliothèque de la ville de Toulouse, MS 482; Oxford, Balliol Library, MS 240; and London, British Library, MS Cotton Cleopatra C. X. For the Oxford manuscript, see Hilding Kjellman, *La deuxième collection anglo-normande des miracles de la Sainte Vierge et son original latin*, Paris and Uppsala: Edouard Champion and A.-B Akademiska Bokhandeln, 1922; and for an analysis of the Cotton manuscript, see H. L. D. Ward, *Catalogue of Romances in the Department of Manuscripts in the British Museum*, volume 2, London: British Museum, 1893, 600–618.
3. Richard W. Southern, in "The English Origins of the 'Miracles of the Virgin,'" *Mediaeval and Renaissance Studies* 4 (1958): 176–216, was critical of Mussafia's conclusions. He proposed that "HM" and "TS" were in some form a single series of stories and ascribed them to Anselm the Younger. See Southern, "The English Origins," 186 and 199.
4. Southern associated Dominic, Prior of Evesham, with the Four Element series and argued that it was originally a set of fourteen stories. See Southern, "The English Origins," 182–183.
5. William of Malmesbury's collection of Latin Marian miracles was probably a combination and adaptation of two existing miracle collections, "HM-TS" and "Elements." See Southern, "The English Origins," 200–201. For a critical edition of the text itself, see *El libro 'De laudibus et miraculis sanctae mariae' de Guillermo de Malmesbury, estudio y texto*, ed. J. M. Canal, Rome: Alma Roma Libreria Editrice and Edizioni Ephem, Mariol, 1968. William of Malmesbury's collection was the source for the miracles of the Virgin in Latin verse, containing eighteen stories by Nigel of Canterbury (1130–1200). See *Nigel of Canterbury: Miracles of the Virgin Mary in Verse*, ed. Jan Ziolkowski, Toronto, published for the Centre of Medieval Studies by the Pontifical Institute of Mediaeval Studies, 1986.
6. Southern, "The English Origins," 202.
7. D. R. Howlett, *The English Origins of Old French Literature*, Dublin: Four Courts Press, 1996, 96.
8. Jennifer Shea, "Adgar's Gracial and Christian Images of Jews in Twelfth-Century Vernacular Literature," *Journal of Medieval History* 33 (2007): 184.
9. Kjellman, *La deuxième collection*, publishes the texts of this Anglo-Norman collection of miracles and its Latin source, Oxford, Balliol Library, MS 240.

10. For the collection – named after Bernard Pez who printed it – see Thomas Frederick Crane, ed., *Liber de miraculis sanctae Dei genitricis Mariae*, Ithaca, NY: Cornell University, 1925.
11. See J.-Th. Welter, *L'Exemplum dans la litterature religieuse et didactique du moyen age*, Paris and Toulouse: Occitania, 1927, 113–118; and Caesarius of Heisterbach, *The Dialogue on Miracles*, trans. H. von E. Scott and C. C. Swinton Bland, with an introduction by G. G. Coulton, 2 vols., London: Routledge, 1929.
12. *Gautier de Coinci: Miracles, Music and Manuscripts*, ed. Kathy M. Krause and Alison Stones, Turnhout: Brepols, 2006, 268, 271, 407–442.
13. Adrian P. Tudor, "Telling the Same Tale? Gautier de Coinci's *Miracles de Nostre Dame* and the first *Vie de Pères*," in *Gautier de Coinci: Miracles, Music and Manuscripts*, ed. Kathy M. Krause and Alison Stones, Turnhout: Brepols, 2006, 303.
14. Claudine A. Chavannes-Mazel, "The Miroir Historial of Jean le Bon: The Leiden Manuscript and Its Related Copies," Ph.D. thesis, University of Leiden, 1988, 8.
15. Representations in fourteenth-century sculpture of the Miracles of the Virgin include those in the Lady Chapel of Ely Cathedral and on the back of the altar screen of Beverley Minster. See M. R. James, *The Sculptures in the Lady Chapel at Ely*, London: D. Nutt, 1895. Monumental paintings depicting Marian legends include an early fourteenth-century wall painting of Theophilus, the Jew of Bourges, and probably the Youth Betrothed to a Virgin (or the Miracle of the Bridegroom) in Chalfont St. Giles, Buckinghamshire. See E. W. Tristram, *English Wall Painting: The Fourteenth Century*, London: Routledge & Kegan Paul, 1955, 86. Scenes of miracles of the Virgin are rare in stained glass. For the early representations at Canterbury Cathedral, see Madeline Caviness, *The Early Stained Glass of Canterbury Cathedral, ca. 1175–1220*, Princeton, NJ: Princeton University Press, 1977, 118; for the thirteenth-century scenes at Lincoln Cathedral of Theophilus and the Jew of Bourges, see Nigel Morgan, *The Medieval Painted Glass of Lincoln Cathedral*, London: Oxford University Press, 1983, 30. For the Theophilus legend represented in thirteenth-century glass at St. Denys, Walmgate, and the early glazing of Canterbury, see Richard Marks, *Stained Glass in England during the Middle Ages*, London: Routledge, 1993, 71.
16. The majority of those found in English and French manuscripts illuminated before the middle of the thirteenth century most often represent the legend of Theophilus. An early example of an English work with illustrations from the legend is found in a Psalter (Cambridge, Fitzwilliam Museum, MS 330, leaf no. 4, c. 1230–40). A few other early thirteenth-century works in addition to the Theophilus legend include another miracle of the Virgin. For example, in the *De Brailes Hours* (London, British Library MS Additional 49999, and Dyson Perrins 4, c. 1240), ten historiated initials, ff. 32v, 33, 34, 36, 38, 39v, 40v, 41v, 42v, and 44, show the legend of Theophilus, and one on folio 44v represents the miracle of the Priest of One Mass Only. Depicted in the *Lambeth Apocalypse* (London, Lambeth Palace Library, MS 209, c. 1260–67) are scenes with Theophilus, ff. 46–46v, and the representation of the miracle of Julian the Apostate, f. 45v. It has been suggested that the frontispiece showing a monk polychroming a statue of the Virgin and Child, f. iiv, depicts the legend of the "Painter and the Devil." See Russakoff, "Imaging the Miraculous: Les Miracles de Notre Dame, Paris, BnF, n.acq.fr. 24541," Ph.D. thesis, New York University, 2006, 62–65.
17. See Russakoff, "Imaging the Miraculous," 65. In France, the most extensive cycle of Marian miracle illustrations of the fourteenth century are found in the Gautier de Coinci manuscripts. A long series is also included in illuminated manuscripts of the French translation of Vincent of Beauvais' *Speculum historiale*. See Russakoff, "Imaging the Miraculous," 67.

18. A single Marian miracle, the drunken monk that was rescued by the devil, is represented in the *Ramsey Psalter* (New York, Pierpont Morgan Library, M. 302, c. 1300–10), f. 5v. See Russakoff, "Imaging the Miraculous," 67–68. For a Marian miracle involving a mother and her child, f.104v, in the *Luttrell Psalter* (London, British Library MS Additional 42130, c. 1320–1340), see Michael Camille, *Mirror in Parchment: The Luttrell Psalter and the Making of Medieval England*, London: Reaktion Books, 1998, 138–140. The *Smithfield Decretals* (London, British Library, MS Royal 10. E. IV, c. 1330–40) is not a devotional book but rather a manuscript containing Decretals of Gregory IX with a prologue addressed to the University of Paris. It has many *bas-de-page* illustrations of miracles of the Virgin (ff. 161–228v.) See Russakoff, "Imaging the Miraculous," 70–71.
19. For the *Carew-Poyntz Hours*, see Sandler, *Gothic Manuscripts*, part 2, 143–145. For the miniatures in the *Queen Mary Psalter*, see *Queen Mary's Psalter: Miniatures and Drawings by an English Artist of the 14th century, Reproduced from Royal Ms. 2 B VII in the British Museum*, intro. by George Warner, London: The British Museum, 1912; Sandler, *Gothic Manuscripts*, part 2, 64–66; and Stanton, *The Queen Mary Psalter*.
20. The five extant miracles in the *Madresfield Hours* are: the Miracle of the Unchaste Abbess, f. 17, the Miracle of the Monk and the Roses, ff. 31v–32, Theophilus, ff. 59v–60, the Dead Knight Raised, ff. 72v–73, and the Clerk of Chartres, ff. 93v–94. See Sandler, *Gothic Manuscripts*, part 2, 42–43 and Glover, "Illustrations of the Miracles of the Virgin," 71–76. For the six Marian miracles represented in the *Taymouth Hours* see M. R. James, *A Descriptive Catalogue of the Second Series of Fifty Manuscripts (Nos. 51 to 100) in the Collection of Henry Yates Thompson*, Cambridge: Cambridge University Press, 1902, no. 57, 50–74, Sandler, *Gothic Manuscripts*, part 2, 107–109, see M. R. James, *A Descriptive Catalogue of the Second Series of Fifty Manuscripts (Nos. 51 to 100) in the Collection of Henry Yates Thompson*, Cambridge: University Press, 1902, no. 57, 50–74 and Sandler, *Gothic Manuscripts*, part 2, 107–109.
21. The miracles represented are Theophilus, the Unchaste Abbess, the Miracle of the Virgin's Milk, and the Monk who Knew only the *Ave Maria*. See Sandler, *Gothic Manuscripts*, part 2, 127–129; and Kathryn A. Smith, *Art, Identity, and Devotion in Fourteenth Century England: Three Women and their Books of Hours*, Toronto: University of Toronto Press, 2003, 222–231.
22. See Sandler, *Gothic Manuscripts*, part 2, 157–159; and Glover, "Illustrations of the Miracles of the Virgin," 153–188.
23. See Sandler, *Gothic Manuscripts*, part 2, 151–154.
24. Depicted on pre-1340 arms of the crown are three golden lions, facing outwards, with their right foreleg raised on a red field. After 1340 the arms of the Kingdom of England were quartered with those of France (azure three *fleurs-de-lis or*).
25. Lesley Smith, "Scriba, Femina: Medieval Depictions of Women Writing," in *Women and the Book: Assessing the Visual Evidence*, ed. Lesley Smith and Jane H. M. Taylor, London and Toronto: British Library and University of Toronto Press, 1997, 22.
26. For a discussion of this belief, see Leo Steinberg, "'How Shall This Be?' Reflections on Filippo Lippi's Annunciation in London," *Artibus et Historiae* 16 (1987): 25–44.
27. A source for the belief that Mary descended from King David is Isaiah 11:1–2: "et egredietur virga de radice Iesse et flos de radice eius ascendet 2 et requiescet super eum spiritus Domini spiritus sapientiae et intellectus spiritus consilii et fortitudinis spiritus scientiae et pietatis" (Then a shoot shall grow from the root of Jesse, and a flower shall ascend from his root. 2 And the spirit of the Lord shall rest upon him; the spirit of wisdom and understanding, the spirit of counsel and fortitude, the spirit of knowledge and of godliness). In the Middle Ages it was interpreted that the Virgin sprang from the root of Jesse because the word *virga* (shoot) was associated with *virgo*

(virgin). However, according to the Gospels (Matthew 1:1–16), it was Joseph whose ancestry could be traced back to David. See A. Watson, *The Early Iconography of the Tree of Jesse*, Oxford: Oxford University Press, 1934, 3.

28. Ilene H. Forsyth, *The Throne of Wisdom: Wood Sculptures of the Madonna in Romanesque France*, Princeton, NJ: Princeton University Press, 1972, 24–26.
29. For the locations of depictions of book owners in thirteenth-century Psalters, see Nigel Morgan, "Patrons and their Devotions in the Historiated Initials and Full-Page Miniatures of 13th-Century English Psalters," in *The Illuminated Psalter: Studies in the Content, Purpose and Placement of Its Images*, ed. F. O. Büttner, Turnhout: Brepols, 2004, 309–319.
30. For the feminine ideal of beauty in medieval England, see Kim M. Phillips, *Medieval Maidens: Young Women and Gender in England, 1270–1540*, Manchester: Manchester University Press, 2003, 45.
31. For this and other meanings of long, uncovered, and loose hair in late-medieval English culture, see Kim M. Phillips, "Maidenhood as the Perfect Age of Woman's Life," in *Young Medieval Women*, ed. Katherine J. Lewis, Noël James Menuge and Kim M. Philips, Stroud: Sutton, 1999, 6–8.
32. For a description of the manuscript, see Sandler, *Gothic Manuscripts*, part 2, 36–37; and *The Cambridge Illuminations: Ten Centuries of Book Production in the Medieval West*, ed. Paul Binski and Stella Panayotova, London: Harvey Miller, 2005, 191–193.
33. Another example are the portraits in the *Luttrell Psalter*, f. 202v, of Agnes de Sutton, wife of Geoffrey Luttrell, and her daughter-in-law, Beatrice le Scrope, in which both women wear heraldic surcoats with the Luttrell family arms on one half of the surcoat and those of their fathers on the other. These married women wear their hair plaited and covered by a veil.
34. For the observation that if the young woman is intended to represent Mary Bohun, the arms of her husband are not painted accurately, see Sandler, *Gothic Manuscripts*, part 2, 153.
35. In Westminster Cathedral's St. Stephen's chapel, painted in 1361, each of Edward III's five sons was represented wearing a jupon decorated with the arms of France and England quarterly. See Emily Howe, "Divine Kingship and Dynastic Display: The Altar Wall Murals of St. Stephen's Chapel, Westminster," *Antiquaries Journal* 81 (2001): fig. 7. In the depiction of their shields, the arms were displayed as quarterly France and England, differentiated by a label, with the exception of the six-year-old Thomas of Woodstock's shield, which did not have any marks of differencing. For the armorial shields, see John Thomas Smith, *Antiquities of Westminster, The Old Palace, St. Stephen's Chapel*, London: printed for J. T. Smith and sold by R. Rejan and J. Manson, 1807, fig. 13. Seals and tombs dating from the late 1380s and 1390s show Thomas of Woodstock's arms as those of the kingdom within a *bordure argent*. See, for example, Roger H. Ellis, *Catalogue of Seals in the Public Record Office: Personal Seals*, London: Her Majesty's Stationery Office, 1978, vol. 2, 13, P1059.
36. The arms were inherited from Henry of Bolingbroke's maternal grandfather, Henry, Duke of Lancaster, after whom he was named. John of Gaunt was entitled to these arms after the death of his father-in-law in 1361 but he did not make use of them. See Robert Somerville, *History of the Duchy of Lancaster: 1265–1603*, vol. 1, London: The Chancellor and Council of the Duchy of Lancaster, 1953, 154, note 1; J. H. and R. V. Pinches, *The Royal Heraldry of England*, London: Heraldry Today, 1974, 86; Weston Styleman Walford, "On Some Marks of Cadency Borne by the Sons of King Edward III, and by Others of the of the Family of Plantagenet," *Archaeological Journal* 7 (1850): 159; and Charles Boutell, *A Manual of Heraldry, Historical and Popular*, London: Winsor and Newton, 1863, 191, and no. 493.

37. In the full-page bordered miniature on f. 181v, a beautiful girl, attended by Mary Magdalene, kneels on a cushion before the crowned and nimbed Virgin Mary and the cross-nimbed Christ Child. The girl's surcoat is made of a bright red fabric decorated with gold leopards and trimmed with white fur. Underneath the surcoat, she wears a blue gown with a slit, edged with white fur, and embellished with the arms of the Bohun family, earls of Hereford and Essex. The supplicant has the same color tresses and wears her hair long down her back like the Virgin and the Magdalene.
38. A miniature shield in the Copenhagen Hours, f. 6v, four times larger than the area used for the surcoat, is marked with a label (fig. 5).
39. Armorials referring to the marriage of Elizabeth of Rhuddlan to Humphrey de Bohun, the 4th earl, are found in the Vienna Psalter, f. 100, at Psalm 109. In the stem of the initial "D" are the pre-1340 arms of England over Bohun. The arms are reversed in the bowl of the initial "D." For quartered arms referring to marriages, see the will of Margaret de Courtenay, née Bohun, in Bigelow, "The Bohun Wills, II," 641, which mentions a pair of basins with the arms of Hereford and Courtenay quartered. For the seal of Joan de Bohun, née Fitzalan, which shows the arms of Bohun quartering Warren, see London, National Archives, D/DAy T1/14.
40. Trans. Renate Blumenfeld-Kosinski, "Gautier de Coincy, Miracles of the Virgin Mary," in *Medieval Hagiography: An Anthology*, ed. Thomas Head, New York: Garland, 1999, 631.
41. For the tale of the Unchaste Abbess in the work of Dominic of Evesham, see J. C. Jennings, "The Writings of Prior Dominic of Evesham," *The English Historical Review* (1962): 301; in William of Malmesbury's *De miraculis beatae virginis Mariae*, see Canal, ed., *El libro*, 154–156; and in the Pez collection, see Crane, ed., *Liber*, 51–55. See also Ward, *Catalogue*, vol. 2, 626. For the story attributed to Adgar, see J. A. Herbert, "A New Manuscript of Adgar's Mary-legends," *Romania* 32 (1903): 415–421; and in the second Anglo-Norman collection of miracles of the Virgin in verse, see Kjellman, *La deuxième collection*, 62–67. For this legend in Vincent de Beauvais, *Speculum historiale*, see Michel Tarayre, *La Vierge et le miracle: Le Speculum historiale de Vincent de Beauvais*, Paris: Honoré Champion, 1999, 48–55; in Gautier de Coincy's *Miracles*, see *Gautier de Coincy: Les miracles de Nostre Dame*, ed. V. Frederic Koenig, Geneva: Droz, 1955–70, vol. 2, 181–196. For the "Abesse grosse" in *La Vie des Pères*, see Félix Lecoy, ed., *La vie des pères*, Paris: Société des anciens textes français, 1987, vol.1, 300–316; and Tudor, "Telling the Same Tale?" 319–329. For these and other versions of the legend, see Frederic C. Tubach, *Index exemplorum: A Handbook of Medieval Religious Tales,* Helsinki: Suomalainen Tiedeakatemia, 1969, 9; Ruth Wilson Tryon, "Miracles of Our Lady in Middle English Verse," *PMLA* 38 (1923): 369; and *The Stella Maris of John of Garland*, ed. Evelyn Faye Wilson, Cambridge, MA: Medieval Academy of America, 1946, 156.
42. The Copenhagen *bas-de-page* does not appear to show the redaction of the "Abbess" legend found in some collections of English origin, including Adgar's. In these the abbess confesses her plight to one of her nuns who reports her superior's transgression to the archdeacon, who then tells the bishop. See Herbert, "A New Manuscript," 416.
43. Tarayre, *La Vierge,* 51; and Head, ed., *Medieval Hagiography*, 631.
44. Tarayre, *La Vierge,* 53; and Head, ed., *Medieval Hagiography*, 633.
45. Tarayre, *La Vierge,* 53; and Head, ed., *Medieval Hagiography*, 633.
46. In the visualization of this episode from the tale of the Unchaste Abbess in the *bas-de-page* of the *Taymouth Hours*, f. 157v, similarly the bishop squeezes one of the abbess's breasts. I am grateful to Kathryn A. Smith for this information. See http://www.bl.uk/catalogues/illuminatedmanuscripts/ILLUMIN.ASP?Size=mid&IllID=29245 and James, *A Descriptive Catalogue*, 71. In the conclusion of the literary renditions of the

legend of the unchaste abbess, the bishop, finding no proof of the crime of which the abbess is accused, declares her innocent. Furious with the sisters who accused their superior, the bishop demands they leave the convent. The abbess prevents the expulsion of the nuns by relating the miracle. Clerks are then sent to the hermitage where the hermit tells all that had transpired, including that the Virgin had asked him to keep the boy until he reached the age of seven. When the child is no longer obliged to stay with the hermit, the bishop has him educated and later elected to the see.

47. For the Virgin as Ecclesia in the writings of St. Augustine, see, for example, *De sancta virginitate*.

48. In the miniature in the Oxford manuscript, f. 188, the abbess, wearing a grey habit and black hood, has fallen asleep over a fadstool while kneeling in prayer before an altar with an image of the Virgin and Child and a chalice. Behind the abbess, the Virgin points with her index finger at the naked infant held by an angel. In the doorway of a building, behind the angel, stands a man in a grey, hooded cape holding a staff. The legend was also depicted in the *Queen Mary Psalter*, ff. 208v–209. On f. 208v, the abbess prostrates herself before a statue of the Virgin and Child within a niche on a draped altar. On f. 209, an angel gives the swaddled newborn to the hermit.

49. Sandler, *Gothic Manuscripts*, part 2, 162, notes that the Visitation taking place in a bedroom was a usual iconographic motif.

50. For Abelard exhorting women to see their commonality with Mary, see Penny Schine Gold, *The Lady and the Virgin: Image, Attitude, and Experience in Twelfth-Century France*, Chicago, IL: University of Chicago Press, 1985, 68. For furnishings for the bedchamber listed in contemporary inventories and wills, see, for example, Dillon and St. John Hope, "Inventory of the Goods," 289–291; and for Eleanor de Bohun's bequests of curtains and bed furnishings to her children, see Nichols, *A Collection of all the Wills*, 180–183.

51. Amongst the numerous examples of this type of depiction in manuscripts are the ones in: the *Saint Albans Psalter* (Hildesheim, Cathedral Library, St. Godehard 1), f. 10v; the *Leiden Psalter* (Leiden, Bibliotheek der Universiteit, MS 76 A), f. 15; the *Winchester Psalter* (London, British Library, Cotton Nero.C.IV), f. 10; the *De Brailes Hours*, f. 13v; and the *Queen Mary Psalter*, f. 84v.

52. Sandler, "Lancastrian Heraldry," 224–225.

53. Sandler, "Lancastrian Heraldry," 230.

54. Sandler, "Lancastrian Heraldry," 230.

55. For the iconography of the imagery on Philippa's tomb, see Anne McGee Morganstern and John A. Goodall, *Gothic Tombs of Kinship in France, the Low Countries and England*, University Park, PA: Pennsylvania State University Press, 2000, 95–101.

56. The original account was written in Greek in the sixth century. It was translated into Latin in the ninth century by Paul, the Deacon of Naples. Ælfric (c. 950–c. 1010) narrated the legend of Theophilus in Anglo-Saxon in his First Homily for the Assumption of the Virgin. See *Ælfric's Life of Saint Basil the Great: Background and Context*, ed. Gabriella Corona, Woodbridge, UK and Rochester, NY: D. S. Brewer, 2006, 53–54, note 10. It was included in the Latin collections of Dominic of Evesham, William of Malmesbury, etc., and related in Anglo-Norman French by the poet William Adgar. See *Adgar's Marienlegenden nach der Londoner Handschrift Egerton 612*, ed. Carl Neuhaus, Heilbronn: Henninger, 1886, 81–115. In the thirteenth century, Vincent de Beauvais included the miracle in the *Speculum historiale* (XXI, 69). See Michel Tarayre, *La Vierge*, 157–159. The legend was also widely known through its dissemination in the *Golden Legend*. See Jacobus de Voragine, *The Golden Legend: Readings on the Saints*, trans. William Granger Ryan, Princeton, NJ: Princeton University Press, 1993, vol. 1, 157. An expanded ver-

sion is found in the *South English Legendary*. For the legend in general, see Anders Hugo Hjalmar Lundgren, *Studier öfver Theophiluslegendens romanska varianter*, Uppsala: K. W. Appelbergs Boktryckeri, 1913. See also Tubach, *Index exemplorum*, 277.

57. Michel Tarayre, *La Vierge*, 157–163.
58. For the representation of the legend of Theophilus in English fourteenth-century manuscripts, see for example Smith, *Art, Identity, and Devotion*, 223–224 and Glover, "Illustrations of the Miracles of the Virgin," 85–87, 91, 154–156.
59. For example, in the *De Brailes Hours*, f. 40, the Virgin accosts the devil, while in the *Neville of Hornby Hours*, f. 21v, she birches Satan, and in the *Taymouth Hours*, f. 160, she scourges him. See Donovan, *The De Brailes Hours*, fig. 44; Smith, *Art, Identity, and Devotion*, fig. 116, and http://www.bl.uk/catalogues/illuminatedmanuscripts/ILLUMIN.ASP?Size=mid&IllID=29250, respectively.
60. See Corona, ed., *Ælfric's Life*, 51.
61. Placing these two events from the Infancy of Christ, the Annunciation to the Shepherds and the Nativity, on the same folio was more common in fifteenth-century Books of Hours than in earlier ones.
62. For the observation that images of the Virgin nursing her infant at the Nativity appear with some regularity in French and English art from the late thirteenth century on, see Smith, *Art, Identity and Devotion*, 234. English examples of the Virgin nursing at the Nativity noted by Smith are found in the: *Brussels Peterborough Psalter*, f. 10v; *Queen Mary Psalter*, f. 85 and f. 148 v; and *Luttrell Psalter* f. 86v. For a discussion of the significance and evolution of the image of the Virgin *Lactans*, see Beth Williamson, *The Madonna of Humility: Development, Dissemination and Reception, c. 1340–1400*, Woodbridge: Boydell Press, 2009.
63. For a discussion of naturalism in fifteenth-century Italian representations of the Virgin's breast, see Megan Holmes, "Disrobing the Virgin: The Madonna Lactans in Fifteenth-Century Florentine Art," in *Picturing Women in Renaissance and Baroque Italy*, ed. Geraldine A. Johnson and Sara F. Matthews Grieco, Cambridge: Cambridge University Press, 1997, 167–195.
64. The story, of Greek origin, spread to the west and is recorded in the works of Gregory of Tours (d. 595), Paschasius Radbertus (d. c. 860), Honorius of Autun (d. c. 1150), and others. See Ward, *Catalogue*, vol. 2, 586, 587, and 588, respectively. It appears in early Mariales produced in England (e.g. Oxford, Balliol College Library MS 240, ff. 137–148; London, British Library, MS Cotton Cleopatra C. X., f. 101v). See Carl Neuhaus, *Die Lateinischen Vorlagen zu den alt-franzosischen Adgar'schen Marienlegende*, Aschersleben: H. C. Bestehorn, 1886–1887, vol. 1, 10–12. It was widely disseminated in Vincent de Beauvais's *Speculum historiale* (XXI, 78), and the *Golden Legend*. For the former, see Tarayre, *La Vierge*, 163–165; and for the latter, see *The Golden Legend*, trans. Ryan, vol. 2, 87–88. It also appeared in *La Vie des Pères*, see Lecoy, ed., *La Vie des Pères*, vol. 1, 14–26. For the different versions of the tale and works in which it appeared, see Tubach, *Index exemplorum*, 164–165; Wilson, ed., *The Stella Maris*, 157–159; Tryon, "Miracles," 324; and Rubin, *Gentile Tales*, 8–17.
65. In Vincent's and Gautier's versions, the crowd rushes to the furnace and extinguishes the fire. To their amazement, the child is unharmed. The boy tells them how the lady from the church came and covered him with a garment – in Vincent's version with her cloak, in Gautier's with her veil.
66. See Head, ed., *Medieval Hagiography*, 634–636. In the Pez collection and *Golden Legend*, the cries of the boy's mother collect many Christians and Jews together. In Gautier's poem the whole city assembles, while in the *Speculum* it is only Christians who gather together.

67. In the *Golden Legend*, Jacobus does not mention that the Virgin used her clothing to protect the boy.
68. For example, in Vincent's and Gautier's accounts it is a sculpture of the Mother and Child that the boy sees above the altar. See Tarayre, *La Vierge*, 165, and Head, ed., *Medieval Hagiography*, 635, respectively.
69. For the Jewish mother's role in the narrative of the Jew of Bourges, see Rubin, *Gentile Tales*, 7–27, esp. 10.
70. For discussions of the tradition of viewing Joseph as a just man and caring foster father, see Cynthia Hahn, "'Joseph Will Perfect, Mary Enlighten and Jesus Save Thee': The Holy Family as Marriage Model in the Mérode Triptych," *Art Bulletin* 68 (1986): 54–66; and Adelaide Bennett, "Leaves of a Fourteenth-Century Franco-Flemish Antiphonary Owned by John Ruskin (1819–1900)," in *Tributes to Lucy Freeman Sandler: Studies in Illuminated Manuscripts*, ed. Kathryn A. Smith and Carol H. Krinsky, London and Turnhout: 2007: 235–251, esp. 242. I would like to thank Kathryn A. Smith for alerting me to these references.
71. For the association of the lactating Virgin with the Eucharist, see Caroline Walker Bynum, *Holy Feast and Holy Fast: The Religious Significance of Food to Medieval Women*, Berkeley, CA: University of California Press, 1987, 271.
72. Leah Sinanoglou, "The Christ Child as Sacrifice: A Medieval Tradition and the Corpus Christi Plays," *Speculum* 48 (1973): 494.
73. Sinanoglou, "The Christ Child as Sacrifice," 496.
74. Sinanoglou, "The Christ Child as Sacrifice," 491–509.
75. The tale was used by Paschasius in the Eucharistic Controversy. See Peter Carter, "The Historical Content of William of Malmesbury's Miracles," in *The Writing of History in the Middle Ages: Essays Presented to Richard William Southern*, ed. R. H. C. Davis and J. M. Wallace-Hadrill, with the assistance of R. J. A. I. Catto and M. H. Keen, Oxford: Clarendon Press, 1981, 139. See also Despres, "Mary of the Eucharist," 375–401; and Rubin, *Gentile Tales*, 22–23. As noted by Rubin, the tale appears in the thirteenth-century *Alphabetum narrationum* and its fifteenth-century English translation, *The Alphabet of Tales*, under the rubric dealing with the Eucharist, with the caption "The Eucharist received by an unbeliever, saves him from fire." See Rubin, *Gentile Tales*, 17. For the text, see Mary Macleod Banks, ed., *An Alphabet of Tales: An English Fifteenth-Century Translation of the Alphabetum narrationum of Etienne de Besançon, from Additional MS. 25,719 of the British Museum*, London: Kegan Paul, Trench, Trübner and Co., 1904, vol. 1, 210–211.
76. For a discussion of the association of Jews with the ritual killing of children, see Carole Stone, "Anti-Semitism in the Miracle Tales of the Virgin," *Medieval Encounters* 5 (1999): 368–370.
77. An example of a legend of this type is the Legend of the Child slain by the Jews. See Stone, "Anti-Semitism," 369–370.
78. It was also represented in other English manuscripts of the period, including the *Carew-Poyntz Hours*, the *Queen Mary Psalter*, and the *Sherborne Missal*.
79. Glover, "Illustrations of the Miracles of the Virgin," 170–171.
80. In this manuscript, which follows the use of Sarum, this collect is found on f. 11v, 17v, 20, 22, 24v, and 28. Only the initial on f. 17v is decorated with armorials.
81. For this miracle of the Virgin, see DAL Morgan, "The Banner-Bearer of Christ and Our Lady's Knight: How God Became an Englishman Revisited," in *St. George's Chapel, Windsor, in the Fourteenth Century*, ed. Nigel Saul, Woodbridge: Boydell Press, 2005, 55. Examples of Books of Hours with representations of Mary reviving St. George are:

the *Taymouth Hours*, f. 154; the *Carew Poyntz Hours*, f. 152v; and probably the *Madresfield Hours*, f. 73.

82. For St. George as the English monarchy's protector and the patron of the Order of the Garter, see *St. George's Chapel, Windsor, in the Fourteenth Century*, ed. Nigel Saul, Woodbridge: Boydell Press, 2005, 3. For the quarrel between the Teutonic Knights and the English Crusaders over the use of the St. George banner in 1364, see *Scriptores rerum Prussicarum: die Geschichtquellen der preussischen Vorzeit bis zum Untergange der Ordensherrschaft*, Theodor Hirsch, Max Toeppen, and Ernst Strehlke, vol. 2, Leipzig: Hirzel, 1863, 544.
83. For the arms of St. George below the figural representations of the king and his immediate family on Edward III's tomb in Westminster, see Howe, "Divine Kingship," 296, note 82. For the prominent role of St. George on works associated with the personal patronage of the king, see Howe, "Divine Kingship," 278; and Samantha Riches, *St. George: Hero, Martyr, and Myth*, Stroud: Sutton, 2000, 107.
84. For the observation that St. George is represented like a companion of Edward's, see Howe, "Divine Kingship," 270 and 277. For the king's pilgrimage to Cologne in 1338 where he visited and made offerings at the shrine of the Three Kings, see W. M. Ormrod, "The Personal Religion of Edward III," *Speculum* 64 (1989): 860; and for the relevance of the three kings for Edward III, see Paul Binski, *Westminster Abbey and the Plantagenets, Kingship and the Representation of Power, 1200–1400*, New Haven, CT and London: Yale University Press, 1995, 183.
85. In the *Wilton Diptych* (London, National Gallery, c. 1395), it has been argued, Richard is portrayed as one of the three Magi before the Virgin. See S. Mitchell, "Richard II: Kingship and the Cult of Saints," in *The Regal Image of Richard II and the Wilton Diptych*, ed. Dillian Gordon, Lisa Monnas and Caroline Elam, London: Harvey Miller Publishers, 1997, 115–124; and O. Pujmanovà, "Portraits of Kings Depicted as Magi in Bohemian Painting," in *The Regal Image of Richard II and the Wilton Diptych*, ed., Dillian Gordon, Lisa Monnas and Caroline Elam, London: Harvey Miller Publishers, 1997, 247–266. For Richard and celebrations of the Epiphany, see Pamela M. King, *The York Mystery Cycle and the Worship of the City*, Cambridge: D. S. Brewer, 2006, 113.
86. His name, however, does not appear in any of the other Litanies original to the Bohun manuscripts.
87. In works made for a royal audience, the wall murals in St. Stephen's Chapel for example, the Magi could act as models for the devotions of their viewer. As in the Copenhagen Bohun Hours, the image of the bareheaded Magi kneeling before a regally-clad enthroned Virgin, who is supporting the standing Child, is depicted in St. Stephen's Chapel. These paintings, which are no longer extant, were in a fragmentary state before their destruction by fire in 1834. Their appearance was recorded in drawings by Richard Smirke. See Howe, "Divine Kingship," fig. 8. In the *Book of Hours of Etienne Chevalier* (Chantilly, Musée Condé, MS 71, 1452–1461), *trésorier* of France, the folio illuminated with the Adoration of the Magi includes a portrait of Charles VII. See *Les Heures d'Etienne Chevalier par Jean Fouquet: Les quarante enluminures du Musée Condé*, ed. Patricia Stirnemann, Marie-Thérèse Gousset, Claudia Rabel, and Emmanuelle Toulet, Chantilly and Paris: Musée Condé and Somogy, 2005, 10.
88. Ryan, trans., *The Golden Legend*, vol. 2, 155.
89. As pointed out by Glover in "Illustrations of the Miracles of the Virgin," 176, note 393, the Miracle of the Christ-Child as Hostage appears in only three of the thirty-six collections catalogued by Ward. See also Ward, *Catalogue of Romances*, 662, 673, and 681. See also Tubach, *Index exemplorum*, 83.
90. Glover, "Illustrations of the Miracles of the Virgin," 175–176.

91. The image of the liberation of the youth held captive by his enemies in this manuscript might even have had personal resonances. In 1381 Henry of Bolingbroke, who had sought refuge in the Tower of London, only narrowly escaped death from rebels who had killed many of his father's men. In an event that must have seemed nothing short of miraculous, a guard persuaded the mob to allow Henry to be let go. For a discussion of the effect the events might have had on Henry of Bolingbroke, see Mortimer, *The Fears of Henry IV*, 14–19.
92. See Ryan, trans., *The Golden Legend*, vol. 1, 147.
93. For paintings in which the Child reaches out towards his mother, see Hayden B. J. Maginnis, *Painting in the Age of Giotto*, University Park, PA: Pennsylvania State University Press, 1997, 138.
94. This summary is a succinct presentation and translation of the legend related in George F. Warner, ed., *Miracles de Nostre Dame, collected by Jean Miélot, Secretary to Philip the Good, Duke of Burgundy, reproduced in facsimile from Douce Manuscript 374 in the Bodleian Library*, Westminster: Nichols and Sons, 1885, 185–186. James, *The Bohun Manuscripts*, 61, pointed out similarities between the story illustrated in the Copenhagen Hours and Miélot's version of the legend. James stated that the legend depicted in the *bas-de-page* of Thott 547, 4° did not exactly agree with any of the versions of the tale known to him and judged that it represents a variant in which some points from a number of works occur. In addition to Miélot's account, James cites three other works which have episodes in common with those depicted in the *bas-de-page* and which conclude with the monk encountering a thief: a fourteenth-century manuscript (London, British Library, Egerton 1117), Johannes Herolt's *Promptuarium Discipuli de miraculis beatae Mariae Virginis*, MS 70, and a manuscript in Cambridge (Sidney Sussex College, MS 95, part iv, no. 39).
95. For this translation of this section of "Wie der Rosenkrantze ist funden" by Dominic of Prussia, see Anne Winston-Allen, *Stories of the Rose: The Making of the Rosary in the Middle Ages*, University Park, PA: Pennsylvania State University Press, 1998, 100–101.
96. James and Millar, *The Bohun Manuscripts*, 61.
97. Another work containing some of the same elements included in the Copenhagen manuscript is found in *Cantigas de Santa María*, a collection of 427 poems in honor of the Virgin, many probably by Alfonso X, King of Castile, Léon and Galicia (1221–1284). One of the *cantigas* (121) deals with a knight who promised to make a chaplet of roses for the Virgin daily. In the final stanzas the knight, who is out riding and about to be killed by enemies, dismounts from his horse and prays to the Virgin. A maiden then appears and helps the knight make a chaplet of roses, leading the men to decide against harming the knight. See Kathleen Kulp-Hill, *Songs of Holy Mary of Alfonso X, the Wise: A Translation of the Cantigas de Santa María*, Tempe: Arizona Center for Medieval and Renaissance Studies, 2000, 149. Another tale somewhat similar to the one represented in the Copenhagen Hours appears in a thirteenth-century manuscript (Paris, Bibliothèque nationale de France, latin 18134, f. 145v). In this legend a monk who was sent out on business with a sum of money was reciting his *Ave Marias* as he rode. Two thieves following him beheld a beautiful maiden riding at his side upon a white mule. Each *Ave* turned into a rose, which the maiden took from his lips and wove into a garland. The thieves were so overcome by this miracle that they fell at the monk's feet in repentance. See Beverly Boyd, "The Literary Background of Lydgate's The Legend of Dan Joos," *Modern Language Notes* 72 (1957): 84.
98. Transcribed in Johann Joseph Dobner, *Die mittelhochdeutsche Versnovelle Marien Rosenkranz*, Leipzig: Noske, 1928, 63–64. See also Boyd, "The Literary Background," 84–85.
99. de Hamel, "A New Bohun," 21.

100. Winston-Allen, *Stories of the Rose*, 98. A manuscript of St. Bernard's meditations was in the library at Pleshey, although it is not known when it entered the collection. See Dillon and St. John Hope, "Inventory of the Goods," 302.
101. The writings of Bernard of Clairvaux (1090–1153) were immensely influential in linking the Virgin with both the red and the white rose. Bernard wrote: "Mary was a rose, white by her virginity, red by her charity," See Winston-Allen, *Stories of the Rose*, 99. For the association of Mary with the rose of Jericho in *Sigillum sanctae Mariae*, the work of another twelfth-century theologian, Honorius Augustodunensis (d. c. 1151), see Rachel Fulton, *From Judgment to Passion: Devotion to Christ and the Virgin Mary, 800–1200*, New York: Columbia University Press, 263. For Gautier de Coinci frequently likening the Virgin to a rose in the *Miracles de Nostre Dame*, see Laurel Broughton, "The Rose, the Blessed Virgin Undefiled: Incarnational Piety in Gautier's *Miracles de Nostre Dame*," in *Gautier de Coinci: Miracles, Music and Manuscripts*, ed. Kathy M. Krause and Alison Stones, Turnhout: Brepols, 2006, 297. See also Jean C. Wilson, "'Richement et pompeusement parée': The Collier of Margaret of York and the Politics of Love in Late Medieval Burgundy," in *Excavating the Medieval Image: Manuscripts, Artists, Audiences: Essays in Honor of Sandra Hindman*, ed. David S. Areford and Nina Rowe, Aldershot: Ashgate 2004, 119.
102. For the meanings associated with this motif, see Mira Friedman, "The Falcon and the Hunt: Symbolic Love Imagery in Medieval and Renaissance Art," in *Poetics of Love in the Middle Ages*, ed. M. Lazar and N. J. Lacy, Fairfax, VA: George Mason University Press, 1989, 164. The representation of the monk crowning the Virgin with a garland may have been influenced by the imagery of fourteenth-century French ivories, like ones in which a lady bestows a chaplet on her lover, or those which show the God of Love crowning kneeling lovers at his feet. See, for example, Peter Barnet, ed., *Images in Ivory: Precious Objects of the Gothic Age*, Detroit: Detroit Institute of Arts in association with Princeton University, 1997, 227, and cat. 56, respectively.
103. Elements of the image – such as the passionate devotion to the Virgin, and the rose imagery – find parallels in poetry, for example in the *Cantigas de Santa Maria* (10): "Rose of beauty and fine appearance And flower of happiness and pleasure, Lady of most merciful bearing, And Lord for relieving all woes and cares; Rose of roses and flower of flowers, Lady of ladies lord of lords. 2. Such a Mistress everybody should love, For she can ward away any evil And she can pardon any sinner To create a better savor in this world. Rose of roses and flower of flowers. 3. We should love and serve her loyally, For she can guard us from falling; She makes us repent the errors That we have committed as sinners: Rose of roses and flower of flowers. 4. This lady whom I acknowledge as my Master And whose troubadour I'd gladly be, If I could in any way possess her love, I'd give up all my other lovers. Rose of roses and flower of flowers." See James J. Wilhelm, *Lyrics of the Middle Ages: An Anthology*, New York: Garland, 1990, 244.
104. See Ryan, trans., *The Golden Legend*, vol. 1, 148; Mary Clayton, *The Cult of the Virgin Mary in Anglo-Saxon England*, Cambridge and New York: Cambridge University Press, 1998, 22; and Rosa Maria Dessi and Marielle Lamy, "Saint Bernard et les controverse de l'Immaculée Conception," in *Vie et légendes de Saint Bernard de Clairvaux: Creation, diffusion, reception (XIXe-XXe siècles), Actes des Rencontres de Dijon, 7–8 juin 1991*, ed. Patrick Arabeyre, Jacques Berlioz, and Philippe Poirier, Cîteaux: Commentarii Cistercienses, 1993, 229–260.
105. See Ryan, trans., *The Golden Legend*, vol. 1, 148–149.
106. The Coronation is depicted in this manuscript, f. 28v.
107. The legend was represented in the *Madresfield Hours*, f. 31v and f. 32.

108. For Infancy cycles in English Books of Hours, see Sandler, *Gothic Manuscripts*, part 1, 39.
109. Books of Hours, in which the Little Office of the Virgin was illuminated with Christ's Passion and Resurrection, were popular with English patrons in the fifteenth century. See Janet Backhouse, *Books of Hours*, London: British Library, 1985, 36.
110. Amy Neff, "The Pain of Compassio: Mary's Labor at the Foot of the Cross," *Art Bulletin* 80 (1998): 266.
111. For the use of this type of hat for Jews, see Ruth Mellinkoff, *Outcasts: Signs of Otherness in Northern European Art of the Late Middle Ages*, Berkeley, CA: University of California Press, 1993, 59, 82, 83, etc.
112. The illustration of Christ giving up the Ghost (Luke 23:46) is found in another Bohun manuscript in the miniature of the Crucifixion with Witnesses at the opening of Hour of None of the Office of the Cross in the *Lichtenthal Psalter*, 162v. See Sandler, *The Lichtenthal Psalter*, plate 30.
113. Neff, "The Pain of Compassio," 265; for her discussion of the *Compassio* of the Virgin as an important theme in meditational literature, especially St. Bonaventura, see 257, 265, 271–273.
114. James wrote that the legend represented "the Miracle of the Usurer's (?) soul saved." See James and Millar, *The Bohun Manuscripts*, 50.
115. Caesarius of Heisterbach, *The Dialogue on Miracles*, vol. 1, 116–118. Caesarius recounts that there was once a man who had become rich through usury and who repented of this sin while he lay on his deathbed. He told the abbot who confessed him that he bequeathed all his goods to the monastery so that the abbot might pray for him and help save his soul. Upon his death his body was laid in the church. That night four devils took up their position on the left side of the coffin and an equal number of angels on the right. After a battle of words, the devils disappeared and the angels took the soul to heaven. Although they differ in the narrative details about how the usurer comes to the repenting of his sins and is ultimately welcomed in to heaven, the legend of the usurer in *The Dialogue on Miracles* and *La Vie des Peres* can be understood as suggesting to its audience that sins can be wiped away and that contrition leads to salvation. For the miracle in *La Vie des Pères*, see Lecoy, ed., *La Vie des Pères*, vol. 2, 196–209, and Tudor, *Tales of Vice and Virtue: The First Old French Vie des Pères*, Amsterdam and New York: Rodopi, 2005, 562–563. For these and other tales involving the death of a usurer, see Tubach, *Index exemplorum*, 380–383.
116. The inscription reads "Dieu uint a cist marcheant et ly tre pleda deu tut puissaunt" http://www.bl.uk/catalogues/illuminatedmanuscripts/ILLUMIN.ASP?Size=mid&IllID=29231
117. In the Lady Chapel at Ely, one of the niches is decorated with two scenes that have some commonalities with the Copenhagen *bas-de-pages*. In the first, an angel and the Virgin stand beside a sleeping man. The second scene is damaged but two figures can be discerned along with an angel holding scales and devils. See James, *The Sculptures in the Lady Chapel*, 22.
118. For devils and angels struggling over the deceased's soul, see Johannes Herolt, *Miracles of the Blessed Virgin Mary: (1435–1440)*, trans. C. C. Swinton Bland with an introduction by Eileen Power, London: Routledge, 1928, xxx.
119. For the Virgin appearing at the bedside of the mortally ill, see, for example, Caesarius of Heisterbach, *The Dialogue on Miracles*, vol. 1, 466; and for the Virgin curing the gravely sick, see, for example, Caesarius of Heisterbach, *The Dialogue on Miracles*, vol. 1, 487.
120. For the translation of this text, see *The Primer, or Office of the Blessed Virgin Marie, in Latin and English*, Antwerp: Arnold Conings, 1599, 84–85.

121. The Virgin's portrayal is reminiscent of ones in Last Judgment scenes, for example in the *Queen Mary Psalter*, f. 302v, and the *Taymouth Hours*, f. 137v, where she shows her breast, hoping to assuage the Lord's anger. For the association of the Virgin's breast with intercession, see Dorothy C. Shorr, "The Role of the Virgin in Giotto's Last Judgment," *Art Bulletin* 38 (1956): 212.
122. Head, ed., *Medieval Hagiography*, 643.
123. Ryan, trans., *The Golden Legend*, vol. 2, 88.
124. For the tale in London, British Library, MS Cotton Cleopatra C. X, f. 116v, see Ward, *Catalogue*, vol. 2, 604–605 and Neuhaus, *Die lateinischen Vorlagen*, 58–60. For the legend in William of Malmesbury's *De miraculis beatae virginis Mariae*, see Canal, ed., *El libro*, 98–99 in the Pez collection, see Crane, ed., *Liber*, 4–6. For Adgar's adaption of the legend, see Pierre Kunstmann, ed., *Le Gracial*, Ottawa: Éditions de l'Université d'Ottawa, 1982, 67–69; and Carl Neuhaus, *Adgar's Marienlegenden*, 1886, 40–49. For the version of the tale by Gautier de Coinci (I Mir 42), see Koenig, *Miracles*, vol. 3, 165–190. See also Tryon, "Miracles," 339; T. F. Crane, "Miracles of the Virgin," *The Romanic Review* 2 (1911): 248–250; Wilson, ed., *The Stella Maris*, 179; Warner, ed., *Miracles de Nostre Dame*, xxiii–xxv, 177–179; and Tubach, *Index exemplorum*, 388.
125. In the *Golden Legend*, the monk falls into the river before seeing his mistress, but in other versions he drowns afterwards. For the latter, see, for example, Miélot's account in Warner, ed., *Miracles de Nostre Dame*, 177.
126. In the Pez version of the tale, the Devil is described as having pushed the sacristan while he was crossing the river; in Adgar's poem, the devils cause him to fall. See Crane, ed., *Liber*, 5, and Kunstmann, ed., *Le Gracial*, 67.
127. For the Pez version of the events, see Crane, ed., *Liber*, 5.
128. In the versions in a Latin collection of the early thirteenth century (London, British Library, MS Royal 6 B. xiv, f. 91v), in the Pez collection, and in Miélot's *Miracles de Nostre Dame*, a young monk prayed for the drowned sacristan who was not permitted a Christian burial until he was visited by the Virgin and told that his prayers had saved the soul of his friend. See Ward, *Catalogue*, vol. 2, 640; Crane, ed., *Liber*, 64–74; and Warner, ed., *Miracles de Nostre Dame*, 177–179.
129. It was also represented in a series of paintings of the miracles of the Virgin in the Abbey Church of Bury St. Edmunds and in the spandrel of a niche in the Lady Chapel in Ely Cathedral. For the former see M.R. James, *On the Abbey of S. Edmund at Bury*, Cambridge: Cambridge Antiquarian Society, 1895, 143 and for the latter see James, *The Sculptures in the Lady Chapel*, 49. A slightly different version of this tale, perhaps the one narrated by Gautier de Coinci, was illustrated in the *Queen Mary Psalter*, f. 205v and f. 213v.
130. I am unsure whether the protagonist of this scene is a monk or nun. The habited figure is stocky like the monk represented in the Copenhagen manuscript; however, the face has more feminine features.
131. The Triumph of the Virgin was first represented in the tympanum of Notre Dame of Senlis, c. 1170–80. It later became a popular image in manuscripts and other visual arts. See F. Deuchler, *Der Ingeborgpsalter*, Berlin: de Gruyter, 1967, 65–66. For the imagery on English portals, see Carolyn Marino Malone, *Façade as Spectacle: Ritual and Ideology at Wells Cathedral*, Leiden: Brill, 2004.
132. For the *Sponsus/Sponsa* theme in Honorius Augustodunensis's *Sigillum sanctae Mariae* and in Bernard of Clairvaux's highly influential homilies on the Song of Songs, see, respectively, Fulton, *From Judgment to Passion*, 247–288, and Bernard of Clairvaux, *On the Song of Songs*, trans. Kilian Walsh, Kalamazoo: Cistercian Publications, 1981.

133. A grateful acknowledgment for the observation that the praying figure is right near the part of the text that implores God "to turn off [his] anger from us" is owed to Kathryn Smith.
134. This summary of the contents of the legend told by Adgar in *Le Gracial* is quoted from Shea, "Adgar's Gracial," 191.
135. For the origins of the story in Constantinople and its appearance in a sermon believed to date from the tenth century, see Tryon, "Miracles," 337, and James Parkes, *The Conflict of the Church and the Synagogue: A Study in the Origins of Anti-Semitism*, Cleveland, OH: World Publishing Company, 1961, 294. In the sermon, as well as in some later Latin versions – such as Johannes Monachus's *Liber de miraculis*, the Pez collection, Vincent de Beauvais's *Speculum historiale* (VII, 82), and Miélot's *Miracles de Nostre-Dame* – it is not the Virgin's image but the figure of Christ who reveals the debt has been paid. See *Johannes Monachus, Liber de miraculis: ein neuer Beitrag zur mittelalterlichen Mönchsliteratur*, ed. Michael Huber, Heidelberg: Carl Winter's Universitätsbuchhandlung, 1913, 30–31; Crane, ed., *Liber*, 44; and Warner, ed., *Miracles de Nostre Dame,* xxii–xxiii and 174. See also *Collectaneum exemplorum et visionum Clarevallense: e codice Trecensi 946*, ed. Olivier Legendre, Turnhout: Brepols, 2005, 354; Tryon, "Miracles," 337; and Wilson, ed., *The Stella Maris*, 173–174. In the *Cantigas de Santa Maria* (Walter Mettmann, ed., Madrid: Editorial Castalia, 1986–1989, no. 25) and Gonzalo de Berceo's *Milagros de Nuestra Senora* (E. Michael Gerli, ed., Madrid: Catedra, 1987, 175–87), the merchant uses the images of the Virgin and Christ as guarantors for his loan. In Berceo's version, Christ reveals that the Jew has lied, while in the *Cantigas* it is the Virgin who indicts him. See also Tubach, *Index exemplorum*, 220. For an overview of medieval works dealing with the legend of the merchant and the Jew, see Erik Boman, *Deux miracles de Gautier de Coinci: publiés d'après tous les manuscrits, avec une introduction, notes et glossaire*, Paris: E. Droz, 1935. For a miracle involving a Jew, a Christian, and an image of the Virgin in the Christian's home, see Koenig, ed., *Les Miracles de Nostre Dame*, vol. 2, 101.
136. It was represented in French illuminated manuscripts of Gautier de Coinci's, *Miracles de Nostre Dame,* for example, naf 24541(Paris, Bibliothèque Nationale de France), f. 165v, and in the Vernon manuscript (Bodleian Library, Oxford, MS Eng. Poet. A.1), f. 126, an English work of a later date than Thott 547, 4°. For the former, see Russakoff, "Imaging the Miraculous," 163–164; and for the latter, see *The Vernon Manuscript: A Facsimile of Bodleian Library, Oxford, Ms. Eng. Poet. A.*, intro. A. I. Doyle, Cambridge: Brewer, 1987, plate X.
137. For English works in which Theodore is prevented from sailing back to Constantinople due to a storm, see Canal, ed., *El libro*, 134; Neuhaus, *Adgar's Marienlegenden,* 182; Kjellman, *La deuxième collection,* 207; and Tryon, "Miracles," 337.
138. See Canal, ed., *El libro*, 135; Neuhaus, *Adgar's Marienlegenden*, 183; and Kjellman, *La deuxième collection*, 209.
139. Neuhaus, *Adgar's Marienlegenden*, 184. See also Canal, ed., *El libro*, 135.
140. Neuhaus, *Adgar's Marienlegenden*, 184.
141. The library at Pleshey contained books of law and government, including the Decretals, the Digests, the English statutes, and a copy of Giles of Rome's *De Regimine Principum*, a guidebook for princes. See Dillon and St. John Hope, "Inventory of the Goods," 301–302.
142. The composition of the third scene in the *bas-de-page* may be based on illuminations in Bolognese law books, with which the Bohun artists appear to have been familiar. For the influence of Bolognese painting on the Bohun atelier, see Dennison, "The Stylistic Sources," 241–245.

143. Peter Klein, "The Apocalypse in Medieval Art," in *The Apocalypse in the Middle Ages*, ed. Richard Kenneth Emmerson and Bernard McGinn, Ithaca, NY: Cornell University Press, 1992, 165–166.
144. Roger S. Wieck, *Painted Prayers: The Book of Hours in Medieval and Renaissance Art*, New York: George Braziller in association with the Pierpont Morgan Library, 1997, 91.
145. The theme of the Second Coming was linked with recompense for one's actions in Matthew (25:34–46).
146. Wieck, *Time Sanctified*, 97.
147. Morgan, "Texts and Images," 48–50.
148. The mid-fourteenth-century illumination of the Last Judgment was added to a twelfth-century manuscript (Oxford, Bodleian Library, MS Bodley 691) and appears on f. 1v. Below the image of the seated Christ, showing his wounds, flanked by angels holding instruments of the Passion, and inside the initial, is the standing, crowned Virgin, her arms extended, spreading her mantle above the Elect. She is flanked by the sun and moon. The miniature was executed between 1340 and 1360, probably at the behest of Bishop John Grandisson of Exeter (1327–1369). See http://icadb.princeton.edu:8991/F/BGHEUJQKCS5H5XJMF82GMXN19XKYSKGA7M2GEDHXYE9HM14PEI-00130?func=full-set-set&set_number=929945&set_entry=000001&format=999
149. In the *City of God*, as well as in other works, St. Augustine is concerned with what happens to the soul after it is separated from the body at death and the soul's experience of the *visio Dei*. See Janis Elliot, "Augustine and the New Augustinianism in the Choir Frescoes of the Eremitani, Padua," *Art and the Augustinian Order in Early Renaissance Italy*, ed. Louise Bourdua and Anne Dunlop, Aldershot: Ashgate, 2007, 115. For other theological works upon which this type of imagery might depend, see Harvey Stahl, "Heaven in View: The Place of the Elect in an Illuminated Book of Hours," in *Last Things: Death and the Apocalypse in the Middle Ages*, ed. Caroline Walker Bynum and Paul Freedman, Philadelphia, PA: University of Pennsylvania Press, 2000, 218–219; and for noblewomen's interest in the soul and heavenly rewards, see Sean L. Field, "Reflecting the Royal Soul: The *Speculum anime* Composed for Blanche of Castile," *Mediaeval Studies* 68 (2006): 1–42, and "Marie of Saint-Pol and Her Books," *English Historical Review* 125 (2010): 271–272. For Guillaume de Deguileville's works heavily influenced by St. Augustine, see Sarah Kay, *The Place of Thought: The Complexity of One in Late Medieval French Didactic Poetry*, Philadelphia, PA: University of Pennsylvania Press, 2007, 70–74. For the copy of the *Pèlerinage de vie humaine* given by Blanche de Bourgogne to her daughter, Jeanne, Duchess of Brittany, see Richard H. Rouse and Mary A. Rouse, *Manuscripts and their Makers: Commercial Book Producers in Medieval Paris, 1200–1500*, vol. 1, Turnhout: Harvey Miller, 2000, 243. For the anonymous English rendering of Deguileville's *Pilgrimage of the Soul* made for a great lady in 1413, and possibly by Thomas Hoccleve for Joan de Bohun, see Jessica Brantley, *Reading in the Wilderness: Private Devotion and Public Performance in Late Medieval England*, Chicago, IL: University of Chicago Press, 2007, 380, note 63.
150. At the Penitential Psalms in Egerton 3277, f. 133, scenes from the Last Judgement are situated in the border while scenes from the Passion are placed in the historiated initial. In the upper medalion of the initial "D," the enthroned, nimbed, bearded Christ, partially draped in a blue mantle, hands raised, displays his wounds. He is flanked by angels holding instruments of the Passion. To the right is a trumpeting angel and to the left souls make their way to heaven. Underneath them, the dead rise up from their coffins. Below them, lost souls are shown in the flames and the mouth of Hell. In the lower extension of the initial are the damned in a cauldron, attended by devils.

151. James and Millar, *The Bohun Manuscripts*, 52. See Ottosen, *The Responsories*, 53–62, and http://www.chd.dk/gui/thott547_OD_gui.html#OD
152. For the belief that women were more prone to gossip than men, see Derek G. Neal, *The Masculine Self in Late Medieval England*, Chicago and London: University of Chicago Press, 2008, 175.
153. For the view that women played a role in their own salvation, see Lewis, "Model Girls? Virgin-Martyrs and the Training of Young Women in late Medieval England, in *Young Medieval Women*," ed. Katherine J. Lewis, Noël James Menuge and Kim M. Philips, Stroud: Sutton, 1999, 30.
154. Surprisingly, unlike a number of other Bohun manuscripts, Thott 547, 4° does not include arms in the Seven Penitential Psalms or the Office of the Dead, sections of the manuscript which contain prayers for the dead. For the implications of armorials in devotional manuscripts, see Michael Michael, "The Privilege of 'Proximity': Towards a Re-definition of the Function of Armorials," *Journal of Medieval History* 23 (1997): 55–74.
155. For this observation with regard to devotional books, see Michael, "The Privilege," 73.
156. At Pleshey Castle there were copies of both the *Golden Legend* and Miracles of our Lady, both in French. The dates of these manuscripts are unknown. For the former, see Nichols, *A Collection of all the Wills*, 182; and for the latter, see Dillon and St. John Hope, "Inventory of the Goods," 300.
157. The subjects of the miracles in the Bodleian Psalter-Hours are: at Matins: Theophilus, f. 182; at Lauds: the Fallen Abbess, f. 188; at Prime: Beatrice the Nun, f. 200; at Tierce: the Jew of Bourges, f. 203v; at Sext: Amoras, f. 206v; at None: the Child image taken hostage, f. 209; at Vespers: the Child devoted to the devil, f. 211v; and at Compline: the Drowned Monk/Nun, f. 212v.
158. Eleanor de Bohun had four children: Humphrey (1382), Anne (c. 1383), Joan (1384), and Isabelle (c. 1385/1386).
159. Mary's surviving children, born in the 1380s, were Henry (1386 or 1387), Thomas (1387), and John (1389). She gave birth to three girls in the early 1390s.
160. See, for example, JGR, 1379–1383, vol. 1, no. 646, and vol. 2, no. 996.
161. Cy gist Alianore de Bohune, eisne(e) fille & un(e) des heires a l'Honorable Seigneur Mons. Humphry de Bohune, Compte de Hereford, d' Essex, & de Northampton, & Constable d Engleterre, femme a puissant & noble Prince Thomas de Wodestocke, fils a tresexcellent & tre(s) puissant Seigneur Edward Roy d' Engleterre, puis le conquestries Duc Gloucester, Compte d' Essex, de Buckingham, qui mourit le tier jour d'Octobre lan de (mil ccclxxxix). For the inscription, see John Hackett, *Select and Remarkable Epitaphs on Illustrious and Other Persons*, London: Printed for T. Osborne and J. Shipton, 1757, vol. 1, 249.
162. For the belief that an ancestor of the Bohuns was Lohengrin, the swan knight, son of Blanchefleur and Sir Perceval, see Lynn Staley, *Languages of Power in the Age of Richard II*, University Park, PA: Pennsylvania State University Press, 2005, 223.
163. The earldom of Hereford and Northampton was inherited by Mary, while that of Essex was inherited by Eleanor.
164. Joan's father, Richard Fitzalan, son of Alice de Warenne, succeeded in 1347 to the Earldom of Surrey, an estate of the house of Warenne, further increasing his great earldom. See McFarlane, *The Nobility of Later Medieval England*, 88.
165. For an analysis of women's funerary monuments of a slightly earlier period, see Loveday Lewes Gee, *Women, Art and Patronage from Henry III to Edward III, 1216–1377*, Woodbridge: Boydell Press, 2002.

166. That the Bohuns retained two artists is an indication of the importance they placed on book production and of their wealth. In the fourteenth century it was mostly royal households, like that of Philippa of Hainault, Edward III's queen, or Charles V of France and his close family, who retained an illuminator or illuminators. For the miniaturist Master Robert, employed by Queen Philippa, and Jean de Montmartre who worked for the French king, Jean II, see Alexander, *Medieval Illuminators*, 27. For Robert, see also Michael A. Michael, "A Manuscript Wedding Gift from Philippa of Hainault to Edward III," *The Burlington Magazine* 127 (1985): 589; and Juliet Vale, *Edward III and Chivalry: Chivalrous Society and its Context, 1270–1350*, Woodbridge: Boydell Press, 1982, 47. For the workshop employed in the late thirteenth century by Eleanor of Castile, Edward I's queen, see John Carmi Parsons, "Of Queens, Courts and Books: Reflections on the Literary Patronage of Thirteenth-Century Plantagenet Queens," in *The Cultural Patronage of Medieval Women*, ed. June Hall McCash, Athens, GA: University of Georgia Press, 1996, 178. For the king's painters, Gilbert Prince and Thomas Litlington, see Jonathan J. G. Alexander, "The Portrait of Richard II in Westminster Abbey," in *The Regal Image of Richard II and the Wilton Diptych*, ed. Dillian Gordon, Lisa Monnas and Caroline Elam, London: Harvey Miller Publishers, 1997, 204. For Jean Susanne, who worked for Jean II of France, see Rouse and Rouse, *Manuscripts and their Makers*, 2, 87. For Jean Bondol, "pictor regis" in the service of Charles V, see Rouse and Rouse, *Manuscripts and their Makers*, 2, 64.

Part Two

Chapter Three: Description of Thott 517, 4°

1. See Appendix.
2. For the distinction made between legendaries, collections of non-martyrs' lives, and passionaries, collections of martyrs' lives, providing information about saints arranged according to the liturgical year, which collapsed fairly early on, see Sheila Delany, *The Naked Text: Chaucer's Legend of Good Women*, Berkeley, CA: University of California Press, 1994, 64.
3. Leslie Ross, *Text, Image, Message: Saints in Medieval Manuscript Illuminations*, Westport, CT: Greenwood Press, 1994, 2–4, 68.
4. See Sandler, "Mary de Bohun's 'Livret de saintes' in Copenhagen," 65.
5. Dennison, "The Stylistic Sources," 174, and Sandler, *The Lichtenthal Psalter*, 119–121.
6. Dennison, "The Stylistic Sources," 165 and 342.
7. Foot, "An Eighteenth-Century Dutch Patron," 204.
8. There are a number of manuscripts made for the Bohun family that are similar in format to the volumes in Copenhagen. *The Lichtenthal Psalter*, like Thott 547, 4° and Thott 517, 4°, has twenty lines of text. The Bodleian Library's Psalter-Hours and the Fitzwilliam Museum's Psalter have text-blocks comprising 18 lines, while the Pommersfelden volume has twenty-two lines.
9. Olsen and Nordenfalk, *Gyldne Bøger*, 61; and Sandler, *Gothic Manuscripts*, part 2, 162.
10. Sandler, *Gothic Manuscripts*, part 2, 162.
11. Dennison, "The Stylistic Sources," 175; and Sandler, *The Lichtenthal Psalter*, 153.
12. Dennison, "The Stylistic Sources," 175.

Chapter Four:
Principal Texts and Illuminations in Thott 517, 4°

1. Before the Reformation, numerous monastic houses were dedicated to these three saints. Among female saints, the Virgin ranks number one, Margaret number two, and the Magdalene number three. See Theresa Coletti, *Mary Magdalene and the Drama of Saints: Theater, Gender, and Religion*, Philadelphia, PA: University of Pennsylvania Press, 2006, 250, note 35.
2. Dennison, "The Stylistic Sources," 173–174; Sandler, *The Lichtenthal Psalter*, 126, and "Mary de Bohun's 'Livret de saintes' in Copenhagen," 65.
3. The manuscripts most often contain events from the life and posthumous miracles of a saint whose relics were kept or venerated at the monastery where the book was housed, as well as hymns, prayers, masses, and other cult material. For a discussion of these manuscripts, see Francis Wormald, "Some Illustrated Manuscripts of the Lives of Saints," *Bulletin of the John Rylands Library* 35 (1952): 248–266.
4. An example of a book of small size, written in the vernacular and made for a specific group of readers, is the so-called Katherine Group, a collection of five thirteenth-century Middle English texts, including three lives of female saints – Juliana of Nicomedia, Margaret of Antioch, and Catherine of Alexandria – copied for a group of anchoresses. The two other texts preserved in the manuscript MS Bodley 34 (Oxford, Bodleian Library, 15.4 × 10.8 cm) are the sermon Hali Meiðhad (holy maidenhood), and the allegory Sawles Warde (refuge of the souls). Jocelyn Wogan-Browne has called the manuscript a "specialized miniature female legendary, see *Saints' Lives and Women's Literary Culture, 1150–1300: Virginity and its Authorizations*, Oxford and New York: Oxford University Press, 2001, 6. See also Wogan-Browne's "The Apple's Message: Some Post-Conquest Accounts of Textual Transmission," in *Late Medieval Religious Texts and their Transmission: Essays in Honour of A. I. Doyle*, ed. A. J. Minnis, Cambridge: D. S. Brewer, 1994, 45.
5. The life of the Magdalene and the *Transitus* appear together in a large thirteenth-century hagiographic collection (Brussels, Bibliothèque Royale de Belgique, MS 10326). See Meyer, "Légendes hagiographiques," 403–404.
6. For the English origins and date of MS Additional 6524, see Jacques Lemaire, "Edition de quelques vies de saints d'après le texte des manuscrits Bruxelles, B.R., 10236, Paris, B.N. nouv. acq. franç. 10128, Paris, Bibl. Sainte Geneviève, 588, Londres, B.M. Add. 6524," Mémoire présenté pour l'obtention du grade de licencié en Philologie Romane, Université libre de Bruxelles, 1968–1969, 26.
7. Dillon and St. John Hope, "Inventory of the Goods," 300–303. For the relationship of Thott 517, 4° to MS Additional 6524, see Smith, ed., *The Lives*, xx.
8. Nichols, *A Collection of all the Wills*, 182–183; and Bigelow, "The Bohun Wills, II," 648–649.
9. There are two versions of the Transitus of Pseudo Melito, designated Transitus B1 and Transitus B2. The text in the Copenhagen manuscript is an Anglo-Norman translation of the former. For the Transitus B1 text, see C. Tischendorf, *Apocalypses apocryphae Mosis, Esdrae, Pauli, Johannis, item Mariae dormitio, additis Evangeliorum et Actuum apocryphorum supplementis / maximam partem nunc primum edidit*, Leipzig: Herm. Mendelssohn, 1866, 124–136; and Mary Clayton, *The Cult of the Virgin Mary in Anglo-Saxon England*, Cambridge and New York: Cambridge University Press, 1998. For Transitus B2, see Monika Haibach-Reinisch, *Melito Ein neuer Transitus Mariae des Pseudo-Melito: Textkritische Ausgabe und Darlegung der Bedeutung dieser ursprünglicheren Fassung für Apokryphenforschung*

und lateinische und deutsche Dichtung des Mittelalters, Rome: Pontificia Academia Mariana Internationalis, 1962.

10. For the dating of the text, see Simon Claude Mimouni, *Dormition et Assomption de Marie: histoire des traditions anciennes*, Paris: Beauchesne, 1995, 272; Clayton, *The Cult of the Virgin Mary*, 85; and Stephen J. Shoemaker, *Ancient Traditions of the Virgin Mary's Dormition and Assumption*, Oxford and New York: Oxford University Press, 2002, 35–36, note 72.
11. The Transitus text in French found in Thott 517, 4° is also present in a number of other manuscripts, including an Anglo-Norman translation made earlier than the one in the Copenhagen manuscript. See Meyer, "Légendes hagiographiques," 443, note 6 and above p. 174, note 6.
12. This summary was made with the help of the translation of the *Transitus mariae* in Montague Rhodes James, *The Apocryphal New Testament*, Oxford: Oxford University Press, 1924, 209–216.
13. Shoemaker, *Ancient Traditions*, 2.
14. See Thott 517, 4°, f. 9v.
15. See Boninus Mombritius, *Sanctuarium seu Vitae Sanctorum*, vol. 2, Hildesheim: Georg Olms Verlag, 1978, 190–196.
16. Elizabeth A. Francis, "A Hitherto Unprinted Version of the Passio Sanctae Margaritae with Some Observations on Vernacular Derivatives," *Publications of the Modern Language Association of America* 42 (1927): 96.
17. See Mary Clayton and Hugh Magennis, *The Old English Lives of St. Margaret*, Cambridge: Cambridge University Press, 1994, 7–9, and Chapter 3.
18. Brigitte Cazelles, ed., *The Lady as Saint: A Collection of French Hagiographic Romances of the Thirteenth Century*, Philadelphia, PA: University of Pennsylvania Press, 1991, 216, 228–229, 231–237; and *Seinte Marherete the meiden ant martyr: Re-ed. from MS. Bodley 34, Oxford, and MS. Royal 17A XXVII, British Museum*, ed. Frances M. Mack, London: Oxford University Press, 1934, xxiv.
19. See Meyer, "Légendes hagiographiques," 443.
20. For earlier sources for this imagery, see Clayton and Magennis, *The Old English Lives*, 32.
21. The prologue, an important aspect of the Mombritius recension, which introduces Theotimus, the chronicler of the legend, is not found in the Copenhagen manuscript. Nor is Theotimus mentioned as accompanying the nurse to the prison where Margaret is kept. Teochinus/Theotimus makes his first appearance at the end of the legend, f. 22.
22. The first mention of protection of mothers was in a twelfth-century legend in the vernacular by the Anglo-Norman poet Wace. See *Wace: La vie de sainte Marguerite*, ed. Elizabeth A. Francis, Paris: Librairie Ancienne Edouard Champion, 1932, 48–49. For Margaret's plea to the Lord on behalf of pregnant women in the Katherine group, see *Anchoritic Spirituality: Ancrene Wisse and Associated Works*, trans. and with an introduction by Anne Savage and Nicholas Watson, New York: Paulist Press, 1991, 303. For expectant mothers being promised that they will not suffer and will give birth to healthy children in a version of the legend composed in England and preserved in a single manuscript (York Cathedral, MS 16.K.13), see F. Spencer, "The Legend of St. Margaret. III. The York MS 16.K.13," *Modern Language Notes* 5 (1890): 110. For the version preserved in a single manuscript (Cambridge, University Library, MS Ee 6.11), see F. Spencer, "The Legend of St. Margaret. II," *Modern Language Notes* 5 (1890): 75. For Margaret's plea for women in childbirth in the *South English Legendary*, see Wendy R. Larson, "Three Thirteenth-Century Lives of St Margaret of Antioch," in *Medieval Hagiography: An Anthology*, ed. T. Head, New York and London: Routledge, 2001, 690.

23. The Mombritius Latin text reads: "scripserit passionem meam: uel qui de suo labore comparauerit codicem passionis meæ" (whoever writes my passion or from his labor provides a manuscript of my passion). For birthing amulets as works of professional scribes, see Don C. Skemer, *Binding Words: Textual Amulets in the Middle Ages*, University Park, PA: Pennsylvania State University Press, 242. For these texts that were written usually on parchment, placed inside a satchel, purse, or similar object, and suspended from the devotee's girdle or neck, see A. Aymar, "Le sachet accoucheur et ses mysteres," *Annales du Midi* 38 (1926): 273–347; Wendy R. Larson, "Who Is the Master of This Narrative? Maternal Patronage of the Cult of St. Margaret," in *Gendering the Master Narrative: Women and Power in the Middle Ages*, ed. Mary C. Erler and Maryanne Kowaleski, Ithaca, NY and London: Cornell University Press, 2003, 100–101; and Skemer, *Binding Words*, 242 and 244.

24. "un tablet dor ove une ymage de Seinte Margarete garnise ove diverse perles et balys, par nous donez meisme le jour de lan renoef a nostre soer de Bokyngham." See JGR 1379–1383, vol. 1, May 6, 1382, 232. Anne was first married to Edmund Mortimer (d. 1425), with whom she did not have any children, and after the earl's death, she wed John de Holland. Her first child was born around 1430. For the date of John Lydgate's work, see Katherine J. Lewis, "Model Girls?", 25. For the dedication to Lady March, "Remembre, O virgyne vpon that other side, On hir that caused, oonly for thi sake, Thyn holy lyf me to compile and make, – My Lady Marche I mene, whiche of entent Yafe firste to me in commaundement," see *The Minor Poems of John Lydgate*, ed. Henry Noble MacCracken, vol. 1, London: Oxford University Press, 1961–1962, 176.

25. The inclusion of a life of St. Margaret in the *Hours of Jeanne II of Navarre* has been pointed out by Sandler, *Gothic Manuscripts*, part 2, 163. The French text, although a much abbreviated account of the saint's legend, includes an appeal on behalf of pregnant women. The Book of Hours contains the arms of Navarre, Evreux, and Bourgogne, but not those of Champagne. Therefore it must date after 1336, the year when King Philip VI gave Jeanne the kingdom of Navarre in return for her ceding her rights to the County of Champagne. See *Les Fastes du Gothique. Le siècle de Charles V*, Paris: Galeries nationales du Grand Palais, 1981, no. 265. For the payment to Robert de Fontaines on August 20, 1398, for illuminating the work for Queen Isabeau, see Rouse and Rouse, *Manuscripts and their Makers*, vol. 2, 129.

26. This observation was made by Sandler, *Gothic Manuscripts*, part 2, 163. The antiphon, versicle and prayer in Thott 517, 4° are the same as the ones found in the *memoriae* in the Office of the Virgin in the British Library's Psalter-Hours, MS Egerton *3277*, f. 120, while the same antiphon and prayer are located in the *memoriae* following Lauds in the Copenhagen Hours, f. 14, and after Vespers in the Bodleian Library's Psalter-Hours, f. 218v.

27. See Smith, ed., *The Lives*, xxi–xxii. From a combined Latin text version of the two parts a French translation was made. For a discussion of the gradual process of the combination of the two parts which led to the French translation, see Smith, ed., *The Lives*, xx–xxiii.

28. For the Latin text (BHL 5457) corresponding to part 1 of Thott 517, 4°, ff. 22v–31v, see Smith, ed., *The Lives*, xxiii; and Sandler, "Mary de Bohun's 'Livret de saintes' in Copenhagen," 66, note 8, citing *Catalogus codicum hagiographicorum latinorum antiquiorum saeculo xvi qui asservantur in bibliotheca nationali parisiensi*, ed. Socii Bollandiani, Subsidia hagiographica, vol. 3, Brussels, 1889–1893, 525–530, edited from a fourteenth-century text (Paris, Bibliothèque nationale de France, MS lat. 803, ff. 225–234).

29. For the Latin source for part 2 of Thott 517, 4°, ff. 31v–38, see Smith, ed., *The Lives*, xxi–xxiii, citing BHL 5443; and Sandler, "Mary de Bohun's 'Livret de saintes' in

Copenhagen," 66, note 8, citing É.-M. Faillon, *Monuments inédits sur l'apostolat de Sainte Marie Madeleine en Provence et sur les autres apôtres de cette contrée, Saint Lazare, Saint Maximin, Sainte Marthe, les Saintes Maries Jacobé et Salomé, etc.*, vol. 2, Paris: J.-P. Migne, 1859, cols. 433–436, 445–451.

30. For the mendicants who saw something of themselves in the Magdalene, see Katherine Ludwig Jansen, *The Making of the Magdalen: Preaching and Popular Devotion in the later Middle Ages*, Princeton, NJ: Princeton University Press, 2001, 76. For the copy of the life in the Burgundian ducal library, see Andrea Pearson, *Envisioning Gender in Burgundian Devotional Art, 1350–1530: Experience, Authority, Resistance: Women and Gender in the Early Modern World*, Aldershot: Ashgate, 2005, 44. For Blanche of Savoy's (d. 1386) veneration of the Magdelene, see Pellegrin, *La Bibliothèque des Visconti*, 253, no. 811. For a vernacular life of the Magdalene by Guillaume le Clerc (fl. c.1210–c.1238), mostly devoted to the miracle of Marseille, in a collection owned by nuns and possibly commissioned by Isabella, Countess of Arundel, see Wogan-Browne, *Saints' Lives*, 6–7, 170–176. For the life of the Magdalene by the Franciscan friar Nicholas Bozon, preserved in a manuscript (London, British Library, MS Cotton Domitian A. XI) and probably intended for a female audience, see Wogan-Browne, *Saints' Lives*, 143; and Mary Elizabeth Long, "Reading Female Sanctity: English Legendaries of Women, ca. 1200–1650," Ph.D. thesis, University of Massachusetts, Amherst, 2004, 81–82, 95–100.
31. Images of the Magdalene's authority, her sacramental role in anointing Christ with oil, and the risen Lord appearing to her before all others, appealed to women. For the depiction of the Magdalene informing the apostles that Christ has risen in the *St. Albans Psalter* (Hildesheim, St. Godehard), which may have been made for Christina of Markyate, see Jane Geddes, *The St Albans Psalter: A Book for Christina of Markyate*, London: British Library, 2005, 20, 55, and 102. Other illustrations of this type appear in the *Gospel Book of Henry the Lion* (Wolfenbüttel, Herzog August Bibliothek, Codex Guelf. 105 Noviss. 2), made for Henry, Duke of Saxony and his wife, Matilda of England (m. 1168); the *Ingeborg Psalter* (Chantilly, Musée Condé, MS 1695), owned by Ingeborg of Denmark, second wife of Philip II Augustus of France; and the *Queen Mary Psalter*, probably made for Isabelle of France, wife of Edward II of England.
32. *A Legend of Holy Women: A Translation of Osbern Bokenham's Legends of Holy Women*, trans. and with an introduction by Sheila Delany, Notre Dame, IN: University of Notre Dame Press, 1992, 102.
33. *Three Chapters of Letters Relating to the Suppression of Monasteries*, ed. Thomas Wright, London: John Bowyer Nichols and Son, 1843, 59; and *The Victoria History of the Counties of England: A History of the County of Wiltshire*, ed. R. B. Pugh and Elizabeth Crittall, vol. 3, London: Published for the Institute of Historical Research by Oxford University Press, 1956, 263.
34. Pugh and Crittall, eds., *A History of the County of Wiltshire*, vol. 3, 263–265.
35. CCR, Richard II, vol. 1, 1380, 394.
36. For Henry of Bolingbroke's grant to Thomas, Duke of Gloucester, for the term of Henry's life, of the advowson of Llanthony Priory in exchange for the advowsons of Farley Priory, Wix Priory, and of the churches of Tilbrock, Kettleston, and Barnsley for the term of Thomas's life, see London, National Archives, Piece reference DL 27/312.
37. The *memoriae* to Mary Magdalene are present in the Exeter manuscript, f. 123; the Egerton manuscript, ff. 119v and 164; the Bodleian Library's Psalter-Hours, f. 198v and f. 218v; and in the Copenhagen Hours, f. 13v. In the initial in the Bodleian Library's Psalter-Hours, f. 218v, and in the Exeter College Psalter, f. 123, Mary is nimbed and holds her attribute, an ungent jar. In the Egerton Psalter-Hours, she is represented

twice: in the *memoriae* after Lauds, f.119v, her commemoration is illustrated with a scene showing the Noli me tangere; and on f. 164, Mary is depicted crowned, blessing with her right hand, and holding a covered cup in her left hand. In the Copenhagen Hours, the commemoration is introduced with an ornamental letter.

38. For the pictorial tables of saints in MS Auct.D.4.4, f. 238, see James and Millar, *Bohun Manuscripts*, pl. xxxvii a; and in MS 348, f. 10, see Joachim M. Plotzek, *Andachtsbücher des Mittelalters aus Privatbesitz: Katalog zur Ausstellung im Schnütgen-Museum Köln*, Cologne: Schnütgen-Museum, 1987, 92, nr. 12, f. 10.
39. Sandler, *Gothic Manuscripts*, part 2, 158.
40. The text in Thott 517, 4° on f. 32 reads: "De cestui (seint Maximin) sa copaigna la benoite magdaleine ausi come la uirge a seinte iehn leungeliste a qui nre sires la uoit comandee et purce il se uidrent ensemble."
41. See James, *The Apocryphal New Testament*, 215–216.
42. For the pictorial tradition of the Assumption, see Gold, *The Lady and the Virgin*, 54–55, and 59–60.
43. For earlier English representations of Margaret transfixing the dragon with a cross-spear, see, for example, the *Alphonso Psalter* (London, British Library, MS Add. 24686), f. 2v; and the *Queen Mary Psalter*, f. 112v.
44. In Thott 547, 4°, f. 14, depicted inside the initial at the opening of the prayer is a bird. For the pictorial tables of saints in the Psalter-Hours in the Bodleian Library, f. 238, see James and Millar, *Bohun Manuscripts*, pl. xxxvii a and in the Book of Hours in Pommersfelden, f. 10, see Plotzek, *Andachtsbücher*, 92.
45. See, for example, the prefatory image of Margaret receiving the crown from an angel in an English Psalter of the second half of the thirteenth century (New York, Pierpont Morgan Library, M. 679), f. 15v.
46. For images of Margaret fighting the demon with a scourge or stick, see Lois Drewer, "Margaret of Antioch the Demon-Slayer, East and West: The Iconography of the Predella of the Boston Mystic Marriage of St. Catherine," *Gesta* 32 (1993): 11. For an English example of St. Margaret with a scourge, see the thirteenth-century *Huth Psalter* (London, British Library, MS Add. 38116), f. 13.
47. For Mary Magdalene and St. Margaret in the sequence of virgins in the Litanies of manuscripts belonging to the Bohun family, see Dennison, "The Stylistic Sources," 310–311; and Sandler, *The Lichtenthal Psalter*, 31. The intercessory powers of Mary Magdalene are invoked in the *memoriae* of the Office of the Virgin in Thott 547, 4°, f. 13v, and in the Bodleian Library's Psalter-Hours, f. 218v: Grant to us, most merciful Father, that just as the blessed Mary Magdalene obtained pardon for her sins by loving our Lord Jesus Christ above all things, so she may obtain for us in the presence of thine eternal mercy a blessing. Through the same, our Lord Jesus Christ thy Son. For *memoriae* to St. Margaret see above p. 176, note 26.
48. Dennison, "British Library, Egerton MS 3277," 141–142. Other manuscripts and literary works connected to Thomas of Woodstock are a copy of Higden's *Polychronicon* (Oxford, Bodleian Library, MS Bodley 316), which was presented by him to the college he founded at Pleshey, a two-volume Bible in English (London British Library, MS Egerton 617 and 618), a *Somme le Roi* (Reims, Bibliothèque municipale, MS 570), and "The Dialogue between a Secular and a Friar," found in a collection of miscellaneous Wycliffite tracts (Dublin, Trinity College MS 244) dedicated to the Duke of Gloucester. For the Bible, see A. I. Doyle, "English Books In and Out of Court from Edward III to Henry VII," in *English Court Culture in the Later Middle Ages*, ed. V. J. Scattergood and J. W. Sherborne, London: Duckworth, 1983, 168. For the Reims *Somme le Roi*, containing heraldic evidence, pointing to the ownership of Thomas of Woodstock,

see Jenny Stratford, "La Somme le Roi (Reims, Bibliothèque municipale, MS 570), the Manuscripts of Thomas of Woodstock, Duke of Gloucester, and the Scribe, John Upton," in *Le statut du scripteur au Moyen Âge. Actes du XIIe colloque scientifique du Comité international de paléographie latine (Cluny, 17–20 juillet 1998)*, ed. Marie-Clotilde Hubert, Emmanuel Poulle, and Marc H. Smith, Paris: Ecole des Chartes, 2000, 267–282. For the dedication to the Duke of Gloucester in MS 244, f. 212v, see *Four Wycliffite Dialogues: Dialogue between Jon and Richard, Dialogue between a Friar and a Secular, Dialogue between Reson and Gabbyng, Dialogue between a Clerk and a Knight*, ed. Fiona Somerset, Oxford: Oxford University Press, 2009, 32. For the Psalter-Hours, illuminated by a London artist for Eleanor, probably in the 1390s (Edinburgh, National Library of Scotland, MS Adv. 18.6.5), see Sandler, *Gothic Manuscripts*, part 2, 164. Based on ex-libris inscriptions, it can also be concluded that Thomas of Woodstock acquired manuscripts from the collections of other book owners. These manuscripts are: a *Roman de la Rose* (London, British Library, Royal MS 19 B. XIII); a copy of Brunetto Latini's *Livre du Trésor* (Oxford, Bodleian Library, MS Douce 319); and a Processional with music for his chapel (London, British Library, MS Harley 2942). See Stratford, "La Somme le Roi," 270.

49. For her connections to the Luttrell Psalter (London, British Library, MS Add. 42130) in which her obituary appears, see *The Luttrell Psalter: Two Plates in Colour and One Hundred and Eighty-Three in Monochrome from the Additional Manuscript 42130 in the British Museum*, intro. by Eric George Millar, London: printed for the trustees, 1932, 5. For the two scarcely legible words, which some have read as "joan boun" in the middle of the lower margin on f. 91 of the *Simeon manuscript*, an anthology of religious and instructional verse and prose, mainly in English, see Doyle, ed., *The Vernon Manuscript*, 15.
50. In a manuscript (San Marino, Huntington Library, HM 111), written after Joan's death in 1419, the translation of the poem is attributed to the dowager countess of Hereford: "Ceste conpleynte paramont feust translatee commandement de ma dame de Hereford, que dieu pardoynt." See H. C. Schulz, "Thomas Hoccleve, Scribe," *Speculum* 12 (1937): 80. The female patron may be significant, according to Jennifer Bryan, for the way the Virgin is presented in the poem. Although much of Hoccleve's devotional verse honors Mary, the Complaint of the Virgin, Bryan observes, is the only poem in which she appears as the speaking subject rather than the object of the sinful poet's pleas for mercy and remembrance. See Jennifer Bryan, *Looking Inward: Devotional Reading and the Private Self in Late Medieval England*, Philadelphia, PA: University of Pennsylvania Press, 2007, 187.
51. See Thomas Rymer, *Foedera, conventiones, literae et cujuscunque generis acta publica, inter reges Angliæ, et alios quosvis imperatores, reges, pontifices, principes, vel communitates, ab ineunte sæculo duodecimo, viz, ab anno 1101, ad nostra usque tempora, habita aut tractata, ex autographis, infra secretiores archivorum regiorum thesaurarias, per multa sæcula reconditis, fideliter exscripta*, vol. 9, London: J. Tonson, 1729, 291, for Henry V's will in which it states: "Missale & Portophorium quæ habuimus de Dono, Charissimæ Aviæ nostræ, Comitissæ Herefordia & sunt ejusdem Scripturæ." For Joan's books purchased from her executors by Henry V, see Cavanaugh, "A Study of Books Privately Owned," 346.
52. Sandler, *The Lichthenthal Psalter*, 148; and for additional reasons to attribute the *Lichthenthal Psalter* to Mary's collection, see 151–152.
53. On f. 169 at the Seven Penitential Psalms, below the main miniature on the right border, are the arms of England with *a label three points azore flory or* above Bohun.
54. Sandler, *Gothic Manuscripts*, part 2, 161.
55. For his interest in books, see Jeanne E. Krochalis, "The Books and Reading of Henry V and His Circle," *The Chaucer Review* 23 (1988): 54–55; Henry Summerson, "An English Bible and Other Books Belonging to Henry IV," *Bulletin of the John Rylands*

Library 79 (1997): 109–115; and Mortimer, *The Fears of Henry IV*, 41, 45, 46, 118, 220, and 322. For John Gower rededicating *Confessio Amantis* to Henry, Count of Derby, in 1393, see *Confessio amantis / John Gower*, ed. Russell A. Peck, Toronto, Buffalo, and London: University of Toronto Press, in association with the Medieval Academy of America, 1980, xxxii. For Chaucer and Henry IV, see V. J. Scattergood, "Literary Culture at the Court of Richard II," in *English Court Culture in the later Middle Ages*, ed. V. J. Scattergood and J. W. Sherborne, London: Duckworth, 1983, 30. For his interest in Christine de Pisan, see Krochalis, "The Books," 55.

56. For his gift of missals in 1403 to Richard II's queen, Isabella, and his own children, see J. J. G. Alexander, "Painting and Manuscript Illumination for Royal Patrons in the Later Middle Ages," in *English Court Culture in the later Middle Ages*, ed. V. J. Scattergood and J. W. Sherborne, London: Duckworth, 1983, 158. For Henry's manuscripts, see Summerson, "An English Bible," 109–115.
57. A legend ("legentt"), probably used in the liturgy in connection with saints' feast days, was listed in the inventory of books for Thomas of Woodstock's chapel. See Dillon and St. John Hope, "Inventory of the Goods," 298.
58. For the romances in their collection see Dillon and St. John Hope, "Inventory of the Goods," 300–302. 59. For the relevance of the lives of female saints for women, see Jocelyn Wogan-Browne, "Saints' Lives and the Female Reader," *Forum for Modern Language Studies* 27 (1991): 314.
60. For *La Vie de sainte Geneviève de Paris* composed for a "dame de Valois," possibly Eleanor of Vermandois (d. 1214), who had a special devotion to the saint, see Meyer, "Légendes hagiographiques," 350–351; and Lennart Bohm, *La Vie de sainte Geneviève de Paris. Poème religieux*, Uppsala: Almqvist och Wiksell, 1955, 51–57. For a prose version "en ro[m]anz" of Saint Geneviève's life, commissioned between 1185 and 1310 for "[La] dame de Flanders," see *La vie de Sainte Geneviève: Cinq versions en prose des XIVe et XVe siècles*, ed. Anders Bengtsson, Stockholm: Regia Universitatis Stockholmiensis, 2006, x and 1. According to Bohm, an inscription in a juvenile hand, "Marguerite escrit bien," in a manuscript containing *La Vie de sainte Geneviève* (Paris, Bibliothèque Mazarine, MS 1716) indicates that one of its readers was a member of the French royal family called Marguerite. See Bohm, *La Vie de sainte Geneviève*, 25–26. For *La vie de Sainte Marthe* translated into vernacular for Margaret, Countess of Flanders and Hainault, daughter of Marie de Champagne (1202–1280), or her daughter, Jeanne, see Wogan-Browne, *Saints' Lives*, 149. For *La vie de sainte Elysabel, fille du roi de Hongrie* by the French poet Rutebeuf, dedicated to Isabelle (1241–1271), a daughter of Louis IX and wife of Thibaut, King of Navarre, see Meyer, "Légendes hagiographiques," 347; and *Oeuvres complètes de Rutebeuf*, ed. Edmond Faral and Julia Bastin, vol. 2, Paris: Éditions A. et J. Picard et Cie., 1959–1960, 101. It is likely that a good number of these vernacular hagiographies were originally composed for oral delivery.
61. For example, Isabella de Warenne, Countess of Arundel (d. 1282), is associated with a number of manuscripts of male hagiographies. The *Life of St Edmund of Abingdon*, a translation into Anglo-Norman French by Matthew Paris of his own Latin life of the saint, and the Latin *vita* of St. Richard of Chichester by Ralph of Bocking, are dedicated to her. She borrowed and most likely read a manuscript containing the life of Thomas Beckett by Matthew Paris and the illustrated Life of Edward the Confessor. She may also have read a manuscript containing hagiographic material devoted to Sts. Alban and Amphibalus, including a verse passion of St. Alban translated into Anglo-Norman French by Matthew Paris. A note on a flyleaf in the manuscript (Dublin, Trinity College, MS 177, E i 40) reads: "G send please to the lady countess of Arundel, Isabel, that she is to send you the book about St. Thomas the Martyr which I translated and

illustrated and which the lady countess of Cornwall may keep until Whitsuntide." Bocking says about Isabella that the lives of the saints "... are plentifully represented in your library." See David Jones, "St. Richard of Chichester: The Sources for his Life," *Sussex Record Society* 79 (1995): 8. For Isabella's interest in hagiographic biographies, see Wogan-Browne, *Saints' Lives,* 168–170. For Eleanor of Castile, Edward I's queen, who had her workshop execute a life of St. Thomas as well as a Life of St. Edward, see Parsons, "Of Queens, Courts and Books," 178.

62. Larson, "Who Is the Master of This Narrative?" 97.
63. In the life of Mary Magdalene in the *Golden Legend,* Jacobus de Voragine recounts a posthumous miracle in which Mary saves a pregnant woman from drowning. See Ryan, ed., *The Golden Legend,* vol. 1, 382.
64. Jansen, *The Making of the Magdalen,* 295.
65. Jansen, *The Making of the Magdalen,* 295.
66. Jansen, *The Making of the Magdalen,* 296.
67. For a discussion on the church and the canonization of mothers, see Anneke Mulder-Bakker, ed., *Sanctity and Motherhood: Essays on Holy Mothers in the Middle Ages,* New York: Garland, 1995, 4.
68. For Mary giving birth without pain, see, for example, Ryan, ed., *The Golden Legend,* vol. 1, 198.
69. For the Virgin's girdle kept at Westminster, Chartres, Paris, Prato, and Assisi, see Brendan Cassidy, "A Relic, Some Pictures and the Mothers of Florence in the Late Fourteenth Century," *Gesta* 30 (1991): 99, note 17. For the girdle brought to English queens during their confinement, see Nicholas Vincent, *The Holy Blood: King Henry III and the Westminster Blood Relic,* Cambridge: Cambridge University Press, 2001, 169–170. For a discussion of the Westminster relic of the Virgin's girdle in relation to an image of the Assumption that shows St. Thomas receiving the girdle in the De Lisle Hours, f. 162v, see K. Smith, *Art, Identity, and Devotion,* 252–256.
70. Eleanor proved her age (14) by June 1380, while Mary proved hers in December 1384. See CCR, Richard II, vol.1, June 22, 1380, 390 and June 22, 1380, 394; and CCR, Richard II, vol. 2, December 22, 1384, 512–516, respectively.
71. *The Victoria History of the Counties of England: A History of the County of Essex,* ed. William Page, London: Archibald Constable and Company Limited, 1907, vol. 2, 110–113. Since the early fourteenth century, the Bohuns, earls of Essex, were the principal patrons of this abbey. William de Bohun, Earl of Northampton, and Elizabeth, his wife, granted land to the abbey in return for prayers for their souls. They were also buried there. See Karen Stöber, *Late Medieval Monasteries and their Patrons: England and Wales, c. 1300–1540,* Woodbridge: Boydell Press, 2007, 124. Humphrey de Bohun, the sixth earl, who died in 1361, made a cloister and gave an expensive Gospel book and other gifts as well as paying for a golden crown to be placed on the statue of the Virgin. See Bigelow, "The Bohun Wills, II," 633. Six members of the Bohun family, including Joan's husband, were buried there. See Stöber, *Late Medieval Monasteries,* 124. The dowager countess was responsible for repairing, adorning, and rebuilding the church. She had the altars adorned with ornaments, sculptures made for the nave, had it roofed with lead, gave vestments and a reliquary, and had a new belfry built. She also helped the works of the house, gave food and wine at festivals, and procured the grant of wine from Henry IV. See Page, ed., *A History of the County of Essex,* vol. 2, 112.
72. CCR Edward III, vol. 14, May 10, 1374, 26.
73. Thomas Hoccleve claimed that he undertook for her his devotional poem *The Complaint of the Virgin,* a translation into English of a section of Guillaume de Deguileville's

allegorical *Le Pèlerinage de l'âme*. The poem appeared in 1413. In a manuscript of a later date (San Marino, Huntington Library, HM 111), the translation of the poem is attributed to the Lady Hereford: "Ceste conpleynte paramont feust translatee commandement de ma dame de Hereford, que dieu pardoynt." The Huntington Library manuscript was written after Joan's death in 1419 since her name is followed by "que dieu pardoynt." See Schulz, "Thomas Hoccleve, Scribe," 80. The content of the work is similar to Guillaume's but the structure is different. See Bryan, *Looking Inward*, 187. The female patron may be significant, according to Bryan, for the way the Virgin is presented in the poem. Although much of Hoccleve's devotional verse honors Mary, the Complaint of the Virgin, as Bryan points out, is the only poem in which she appears as the speaking subject, rather than the object of the sinful poet's pleas for mercy and remembrance.

74. See p. 180, note 60 above for an example of a young female reader of a female saint's life (Paris, Bibliothèque Mazarine 1716). Although we do not know much about the circumstances of the Bohun sisters' education, we can find evidence of the value Eleanor, as well as Thomas of Woodstock and Henry of Bolingbroke, placed on the devotional literacy of their daughters and sons. A manuscript which Eleanor could have studied as a child is one mentioned in her will: "a book having the psalter, primer and other devotions with two gold clasps enameled with my arms which [...] I have much used." This type of book was used in the instruction of children. For the books Thomas of Woodstock studied as a child, see Nicholas Orme, "The Education of the Courtier," in *English Court Culture in the Later Middle Ages*, ed. V. J. Scattergood and J. W. Sherborne, London: Duckworth, 1983, 81. Amongst the books in Eleanor and Thomas's London house were reading material appropriate for children, such as a Psalter and primer, and a *Meistre des Istoires*. See Krochalis, "The Books," 51. Eleanor de Bohun bequeathed her personal collection of books to her daughters and son. In 1397, when Henry of Bolingbrokes's two daughters, Blanche and Philippa, were about seven and five respectively, they were given their ABCs. This type of book contained elementary prayers and teachings (Pater, Ave, Ten Commandments, Credo, graces), slightly more advanced material in the Psalter, and the primer (Book of Hours). See Orme, "The Education," 80; and Phillips, *Medieval Maidens*, 64. For female tutors (mistresses) appointed to Mary and Henry's children, see Jennifer C. Ward, *English Noblewomen in the Later Middle Ages*, London: Longman, 1992, 69. For Katherine Waterton, Philippa of Lancaster's mistress, see Orme, "The Education," 72. For Henry of Bolingbroke's governess and his father's lover, Katherine Swynford, who was part of Mary de Bohun's household, see Ward, *English Noblewomen*, 63.

Appendix

Thott 547, 4°

Physical Make-up

66 folios, 129 × 179 mm.

Collation

1(8)+2(8)+3(8)+4(8)+5(8)+6(8)+7(8)+8(8)+9(2)

Text block

67/68 × 108/9 mm. The pages are ruled and support twenty lines of text, written in one column.

Condition

The condition of the manuscript is good. Only a few miniatures have been damaged and suffered loss of paint. For example, f. 43.

Contents

ff. 1–31v, The Hours of the Virgin (Sarum Use).
ff. 32v–38v, Seven Penitential Psalms.
ff. 38v–41v, Litany.
ff. 42–42v, Preces.
ff. 42v–66v, Office of the Dead.

Illuminations at the Major Liturgical Divisions

f. 1. Historiated Initial "D" at Matins: Annunciation. Borders: Portrait of the Book Owner, Angel Musicians. *Bas-de-Page*: Legend of the Unchaste Abbess.

f. 6v. Historiated Initial "D" at Lauds: Visitation. Two-line initial "D": Shield with the Bohun Arms, Earls of Hereford and Essex. *Bas-de-Page*: Legend of Theophilus.

f. 14v. *Haut-de-Page*: Annunciation to the Shepherds. Historiated Initial "D" at Prime: Nativity. Three-line initial "D": Shield with the Bohun Arms. Borders: Seven Medallions with Angel Musicians. *Bas-de-Page*: Legend of the Jew of Bourges.

f. 18. Historiated Initial "D" at Terce: Adoration of the Magi. *Bas-de-Page*: Legend of the Child Image taken Hostage.

f. 20. Historiated Initial "D" at Sext: Presentation of the Child in the

Temple and Purification of the Virgin. *Bas-de-Page*: Legend of the Monk and the Roses.

f. 22v. Historiated Initial "D" at None: Crucifixion. *Bas-de-Page*: Miracle of the Soul Saved. Borders: Longinus, Two Angels, Head of God.

f. 24v. Historiated Initial "D" at Vespers: Resurrection. *Bas-de-Page*: the Legend of the Drowned Sacristan. Border: Soldier Guarding Christ's Sepulcher.

f. 28v. Historiated Initial "C" at Compline: Coronation of the Virgin. *Bas-de-Page*: Legend of the Jew and the Merchant. Border: Angel Musicians.

f. 32v. *Haut-de-Page*: The Just in the New Jerusalem. Historiated Initial "D" at the Seven Penitential Psalms: Last Judgement, Christ Displays His Wounds. *Bas-de-Page*: The Dead are Raised. Separation of the Saved from the Damned. Borders: Angels, Souls, Devils.

Heraldry

Bohun, Earls of Hereford and Essex (*azure a bend argent two cotises and between six lions rampart or*): f. 1, 6v, 14v, f. 28.
Pre-1340 arms of England: f 1.
Post-1340 arms of England: 6v.
Heir apparent (post-1340 arms of England with a label *argent*): f. 6v.
St. George (*argent a cross gules*): f. 17v.

Scribal hands

Scribe One: 1v–66v.
Scribe Two: f. 1.

Illuminators

Hand One: all the historiated initials, the *haut-* and *bas-de-page*, as well as the borders on the folios at the liturgical divisions.
Hand Two: painted the decorative initials and borders on the rest of the folios of the manuscript.

Provenance
Female member of the Bohun family
Samuel van Huls
Count Otto Thott

Binding
Gold-tooled red morocco binding, late seventeenth century to the early eighteenth century

Martyrs, Confessors, and Virgins Named in the Litany
Martyrs: f. 39v, Stephen, Linus, Cletus, Clement, Sixtus, Cornelius, Cyprian, Laurence, Vincent, Fabian, Sebastian, Dionysius and companions, Alban, Eustace and companions, Edmund, Thomas, f. 40, George, Quintin, Oswald, Alphege, Gervase, Prothase.

Confessors: Silvester Hilary, Remigius, Martin, Nicholas, Gregory, Francis, Dominic, Ambrose, Germanus, Dunstan, Cuthbert, Julian, f. 40v, Benedict, Giles, Botulph, Leonard, Blaise.

Virgins: Mary Magdalene, Mary of Egypt, Felicity, Perpetua, Agatha, Agnes, Cecilia, Lucy, Thecla, Scolastica, Radegund, Margaret, Katherine, Christina, f. 41, Juliana, Fides, Spes, Caritas.

Commemoration of Saints at Lauds
f. 12, Trinity, f. 12v Cross, Michael, John the Baptist, f. 13 Peter & Paul, John the Evangelist, f. 13v, Mary Magdalene, Katherine, f. 14, Margaret, All Saints, f. 14v [De Pace].

Thott 517, 4°

Physical Make-up
38 folios. 176 × 130 mm. The folios have been trimmed.

Collation
1(8)+2(8)+3(8)+4(8)+5(6)
1–8v, 9–16v, 17–24v, 25–32v, 33–38v

Text block
111 × 70 mm. The pages are ruled and support twenty lines of text, written in one column.

Condition

The condition of the manuscript is good.

Contents

ff. 1–10v, Passing of Mary.
ff. 10v–22v, Life and Passion of St. Margaret.
ff. 22v–38, Apostolic and Eremitic Life of Mary Magdalene.

Major Illuminations

f. 1. Historiated Initial "Q": Assumption of the Virgin.
f. 10v. Historiated Initial "S": St. Margaret Delivered from the Dragon.
f. 22v. Historiated Initial "A": Mary Magdalene Borne Up by Angels.

Scribe

Text written by one scribe.

Illuminators

Hand One: historiated initials and borders on the folios at the beginning of each life.
Hand Two: decorative initials and borders, with the exception of folios 1, 10v and 22v.

Provenance

Bohun family
Samuel van Huls
Count Otto Thott

Binding

Gold-tooled red morocco binding, late seventeenth century to the early eighteenth century, by same book binder as Thott 547, 4°. None of the stamps used to decorate the binding of Thott 547, 4° were applied to Thott 517 4°.

Bibliography

Abbreviations

CCR Calendar of the Close Rolls
CFR Calendar of the Fine Rolls
CPR Calendar of the Patent Rolls
CIPM Calendar of the Inquisitions Post Mortem
JGR John of Gaunt's Register

Abrahams, N. C. L. *Description des manuscrits français du moyen âge de la Bibliothèque Royale de Copenhague.* Copenhagen: Imprimerie de Thiele, 1844.

Alexander, Jonathan J. G. "Painting and Manuscript Illumination for Royal Patrons in the Later Middle Ages." *English Court Culture in the Later Middle Ages.* Edited by V. J. Scattergood and J. W. Sherborne, 141–162. London: Duckworth, 1983.

Alexander, Jonathan J. G. *Medieval Illuminators and their Methods of Work.* New Haven, CT: Yale University Press, 1992.

Alexander, Jonathan J. G. "The Portrait of Richard II in Westminster Abbey." In *The Regal Image of Richard II and the Wilton Diptych*, edited by Dillian Gordon, Lisa Monnas and Caroline Elam, 197–206. London: Harvey Miller Publishers, 1997.

Alexander, Jonathan J. G., and Paul Binski, eds. *Age of Chivalry Art in Plantagenet England 1200–1400.* London: Royal Academy of Arts, 1987.

Archer, Rowena E. "Rich Old Ladies: The Problem of Late Medieval Dowagers." In *Property and Politics: Essays in Later Medieval English History*, edited by Anthony James Pollard, 15–35. Gloucester: Sutton, 1984.

Archer, Rowena E., and B. E. Ferme, "Testamentary Procedure with Special Reference to the Executrix." *Reading Medieval Studies* 15 (1989): 3–34.

Armitage-Smith, Sydney, ed. *John of Gaunt's Register.* 2 vols. London: Camden Society, 1911.

Arnold, Janet. "The Jupon or Coat-Armour of the Black Prince in Canterbury Cathedral." *Church Monuments* 8 (1993): 12–24.

Aston, Margaret. *Thomas Arundel: A Study of Church Life in the Reign of Richard II.* Oxford: Oxford University Press, 1967.

Augustine, St. *Œuvres de Saint Augustin.* Vol. 3. L'ascétisme chrétien. Paris: Desclée de Brouwer, 1949.

Aymar, A. "Le sachet accoucheur et ses mysteres." *Annales du Midi* 38 (1926): 273–347.

Backhouse, Janet. *Books of Hours.* London: British Library, 1985.

Bailey, B. Gregory, Meaghan E. Bernard, Gregory Carrier, Cherise L. Elliott, John Langdon, Natalie Leishman, Michal Mlynarz, Oksana Mykhed, and Lindsay C. Sidders. "Coming of Age and the Family in Medieval England." *Journal of Family History* 33 (2008): 41–60.

Banks, Mary Macleod, ed. *An Alphabet of Tales: An English Fifteenth-Century Translation of the Alphabetum narrationum of Etienne de Besançon, from Additional MS. 25,719 of the British Museum.* London: Kegan Paul, Trench, Trübner and Co., 1904.

Barnet, Peter ed. *Images in Ivory: Precious Objects of the Gothic Age.* Detroit: Detroit Institute of Arts in association with Princeton University, 1997.

Bengtsson, Anders, ed. *La vie de Sainte Geneviève: Cinq versions en prose des XIVe et XVe siècles.* Stockholm: Regia Universitatis Stockholmiensis, 2006.

Bennett, Adelaide. "A Thirteenth-Century French Book of Hours for Marie." *The Journal of the Walters Art Gallery* 54 (1996): 21–50.

Bennett, Adelaide. "Leaves of a Fourteenth-Century Franco-Flemish Antiphonary Owned by John Ruskin (1819–1900)." In *Tributes to Lucy Freeman Sandler: Studies in Illuminated Manuscripts*, edited by Kathryn A. Smith and Carol H. Krinsky, 235–251. London and Turnhout: 2007.

Bennett, Michael J. "Edward III's Entail and the Succession to the Crown, 1376–1471." *English Historical Review* 103 (1998): 580–609.

Bernard of Clairvaux. *On the Song of Songs.* Trans. Kilian Walsh. Kalamazoo: Cistercian Publications, 1981.

Bigelow, M. M. "The Bohun Wills, I." *American Historical Review* 1 (1896): 415–441.

Bigelow, M. M. "The Bohun Wills, II." *American Historical Review* 1 (1896): 631–649.

Binski, Paul. *Westminster Abbey and the Plantagenets, Kingship and the Representation of Power, 1200–1400.* New Haven, CT and London: Yale University Press, 1995.

Binski, Paul, and Stella Panayotova, eds. *The Cambridge Illuminations: Ten Centuries of Book Production in the Medieval West.* London: Harvey Miller, 2005.

Blaess, M. "Les Manuscrits français dans les monastères anglais au moyen âge." *Romania* 94 (1973): 321–358.

Blumenfeld-Kosinski, Renate, trans. "Gautier de Coincy, Miracles of the Virgin Mary." In *Medieval Hagiography: An Anthology*, edited by Thomas Head, 627–633. New York: Garland, 1999.

Bohm, Lennart. *La Vie de sainte Geneviève de Paris. Poème religieux.* Uppsala: Almqvist och Wiksell, 1955.

Boman, Erik. *Deux miracles de Gautier de Coinci: publiés d'après tous les manuscrits, avec une introduction, notes et glossaire.* Paris: E. Droz, 1935.

Bothwell, James S. "'Escheat with Heir': Guardianship, Upward Mobility, and Political Reconciliation in the Reign of Edward III." *Canadian Journal of History* 35 (2000): 241–273.

Bothwell, James S. *Edward III and the English Peerage: Royal Patronage, Social Mobility, and Political Control in Fourteenth-Century England.* Woodbridge: The Boydell Press, 2004.

Boutell, Charles. *A Manual of Heraldry, Historical and Popular.* London: Winsor and Newton, 1863.

Boyd, Beverly. "The Literary Background of Lydgate's The Legend of Dan Joos." *Modern Language Notes* 72 (1957): 81–87.

Brantley, Jessica. *Reading in the Wilderness: Private Devotion and Public Performance in Late Medieval England.* Chicago, IL: University of Chicago Press, 2007.

Brooke, Christopher N. L. *The Medieval Idea of Marriage.* Oxford: Oxford University Press, 1989.

Broughton, Laurel. "The Rose, the Blessed Virgin Undefiled: Incarnational Piety in Gautier's *Miracles de Nostre Dame*." In *Gautier de Coinci: Miracles, Music and Manuscripts*, edited by Kathy M. Krause and Alison Stones. Turnhout: Brepols, 2006.

Brundage, James A. *Law, Sex and Christian Society in Medieval Europe.* Chicago, IL: University of Chicago Press, 1987.

Bruun, C. "De illuminerede Haandskrifter fra Middelalderen i Det store kongelige Bibliotek." *Aarsberetninger og Meddelelser fra Det store kongelige Bibliotek.* Copenhagen: Gyldendal, 1870–1902.

Bryan, Jennifer. *Looking Inward: Devotional Reading and the Private Self in Late Medieval England.* Philadelphia, PA: University of Pennsylvania Press, 2007.

Bunt, Gerrit Hendrik Volken, ed. *William of Palerne: An Alliterative Romance.* Groningen: Bouma's Boekhuis, 1985.

Bynum, Caroline Walker. *Holy Feast and Holy Fast: The Religious Significance of Food to Medieval Women.* Berkeley, CA: University of California Press, 1987.

Caesarius of Heisterbach. *The Dialogue on Miracles.* Trans. H. von E. Scott and C. C. Swinton Bland, intro. G. G. Coulton. 2 vols. London: Routledge, 1929.

Calendar of the Close Rolls preserved in the Public Record Office: Prepared under the Superintendence of the Deputy Keeper of the Records, Edward III. 14 vols. London: For Her Majesty's Stationery Office, 1896–1913.

Calendar of Entries in the Papal Registers Relating to Great Britain and Ireland: Papal Letters, 1342–1362. Ed. W. H. Bliss. Vol. 3. London: For Her Majesty's Stationery Office, 1897.

Calendar of Inquisitions post mortem and other Analogous Documents preserved in the Public Record Office: Prepared under the Superintendence of the Deputy Keeper of the Records. Vol. 13–14: Edward III, 1370–1377, Vol. 15: Richard II, 1377–1384, Vol. 16: Richard II, 1384–1392 and Vol. 17: Richard II, 1393–1399. London: For Her Majesty's Stationery Office, 1952–1988.

Calendar of the Patent Rolls preserved Record Office: Prepared under the Superintendence of the Deputy Keeper of the Records, Edward III. 16 vols. London: For Her Majesty's Stationery Office, 1891–1916.

Calendar of the Patent Rolls preserved Record Office: Prepared under the Superintendence of the Deputy Keeper of the Records, Richard II. 6 vols. London: For Her Majesty's Stationery Office, 1895–1909.

Camille, Michael. *Mirror in Parchment: The Luttrell Psalter and the Making of Medieval England.* London: Reaktion Books, 1998.

Canal, J. M., ed. *El libro 'De laudibus et miraculis sanctae mariae' de Guillermo de Malmesbury, estudio y texto.* Rome: Alma Roma Libreria Editrice and Edizioni Ephem. Mariol., 1968.

Carpenter, D. A. *The Minority of Henry III.* London: Methuen, 1990.

Carter, Peter. "The Historical Content of William of Malmesbury's Miracles." In *The Writing of History in the Middle Ages: Essays Presented to Richard William Southern*, edited by R. H. C. Davis and J. M. Wallace-Hadrill, with the assistance of R. J. A. I. Catto and M. H. Keen. Oxford: Clarendon Press, 1981.

Cassidy, Brendan. "A Relic, Some Pictures and the Mothers of Florence in the Late Fourteenth Century." *Gesta* 30 (1991): 91–99.

Cavanaugh, Susan H. "A Study of Books Privately Owned in England: 1300–1450." Ph.D. thesis, University of Pennsylvania, 1980.

Caviness, Madeline. *The Early Stained Glass of Canterbury Cathedral, ca. 1175–1220.* Princeton, NJ: Princeton University Press, 1977.

Cazelles, Brigitte, ed. *The Lady as Saint: A Collection of French Hagiographic Romances of the Thirteenth Century*. Philadelphia, PA: University of Pennsylvania Press, 1991.

Chavannes-Mazel, Claudine A. "The Miroir Historial of Jean le Bon: The Leiden Manuscript and Its Related Copies." Ph.D. thesis, University of Leiden, 1988.

Clayton, Mary. *The Cult of the Virgin Mary in Anglo-Saxon England.* Cambridge and New York: Cambridge University Press, 1998.

Clayton, Mary, and Hugh Magennis. *The Old English Lives of St. Margaret.* Cambridge: Cambridge University Press, 1994.

Cokayne, George Edward. *The Complete Peerage of England, Scotland, Ireland, Great Britain and the United Kingdom, Extant, Extinct or Dormant.* 14 vols. New ed., revised and enlarged by Vicary Gibbs et al. London: St Catherine's Press, 1910–59.

Coletti, Theresa. *Mary Magdalene and the Drama of Saints: Theater, Gender, and Religion.* Philadelphia, PA: University of Pennsylvania Press, 2006.

Corona, Gabriella, ed. *Ælfric's Life of Saint Basil the Great: Background and Context.* Woodbridge, UK and Rochester, NY: D. S. Brewer, 2006.

Crane, Thomas Frederick. "Miracles of the Virgin." *Romanic Review* 2 (1911): 235–279.

Crane, Thomas Frederick, ed. *Liber de miraculis sanctae Dei genitricis Mariae.* Ithaca, NY: Cornell University, 1925.

Dean, R., and M. B. M. Boulton. *Anglo-Norman Literature: A Guide to Texts and Manuscripts.* London: Anglo-Norman Text Society, 1999.

Delany, Sheila, trans. and intro. *A Legend of Holy Women: A Translation of Osbern Bokenham's Legends of Holy Women.* Notre Dame, IN: University of Notre Dame Press, 1992.

Delany, Sheila. *The Naked Text: Chaucer's Legend of Good Women.* Berkeley, CA: University of California Press, 1994.

Delisle, Léopold. *Recherches sur la librairie de Charles V.* 2 vols. Paris, H. Champion, 1907.

Dennison, Lynda. "The Fitzwarin Psalter and its Allies: A Reappraisal." In *England in the Fourteenth Century: Proceedings of the 1985 Harlaxton Symposium,* edited by W. M. Ormrod, 42–66. Woodbridge: Boydell Press, 1986.

Dennison, Lynda. "The Stylistic Sources, Dating and Development of the Bohun Workshop." Ph.D. thesis, University of London, 1988.

Dennison, Lynda. "Oxford, Exeter College MS 47: The Importance of Stylistic and Codicological Analysis in its Dating and Localization." In *Medieval Book Production: Assessing the Evidence: Proceedings of the Second Conference of the Seminar in the History of the Book to 1500, Oxford, July 1988,* edited by L. L. Brownrigg, 41–59. Los Altos Hills: Anderson-Lovelace, 1990.

Dennison, Lynda. "British Library, Egerton MS 3277: A Fourteenth-Century Psalter-Hours and the Question of Bohun Family Ownership." In *Proceedings of the 1997 Symposium: Family and Dynasty in Late Medieval England,* edited by Richard Eales and Shaun Tyas, 122–155. (Harlaxton Medieval Studies, n.s., 9). Donington: Shaun Tyas, 2003.

Dennison, Lynda. "Transformation, Interaction and Integration: The Career and Collaboration of a Fourteenth Century Flemish Illuminator." In *Manuscripts in Transition: Recycling Manuscripts, Texts and Images: Proceedings of the International Congress held in Brussels (5–9 November 2002),* edited by Brigitte Dekeyzer and Jan Van der Stock, 173–191. Paris: Uit geverij Peeters, 2005.

Despres, Denise L. "Mary of the Eucharist: Cultic Anti-Judaism in Some Fourteenth-Century English Devotional Manuscripts." In *From Witness to Witchcraft: Jews and Judaism in Medieval Christian Thought,* edited by Jeremy Cohen, 375–401. Wiesbaden: Harrassowitz, 1996.

Dessi, Rosa Maria, and Marielle Lamy. "Saint Bernard et les controverse de l'Immaculée Conception." In *Vie et legends de Saint Bernard de Clairvaux: Creation, diffusion, reception (XIXe–XXe siècles), Actes des Rencontres de Dijon, 7–8 juin 1991,* edited by Patrick Arabeyre, Jacques Berlioz, and Philippe Poirier. Cîteaux: Commentarii Cistercienses, 1993.

Deuchler, F. *Der Ingeborgpsalter.* Berlin: de Gruyter, 1967.

Dillon, J., and W. H. St. John Hope. "Inventory of the Goods and Chattels Belonging to Thomas, Duke of Gloucester, and Seized in His Castle at Pleshy, Co. Essex, 21 Richard II (1397); with Their Values, as Shown in the Escheator's Accounts." *Archaeological Journal* 54 (1897): 275–308.

Dobner, Johann Joseph. *Die mittelhochdeutsche Versnovelle Marien Rosenkranz.* Leipzig: Noske, 1928.

Donahue, Jr., Charles. "The Canon Law on the Formation of Marriage and Social Practice in the Later Middle Ages." *Journal of Family History* 8 (1983): 144–158.

Donovan, Claire. *The De Brailes Hours: Shaping the Book of Hours in Thirteenth-Century Oxford.* London: The British Library, 1991.

Doyle, A. I. "English Books In and Out of Court from Edward III to Henry VII." In *English Court Culture in the Later Middle Ages,* edited by V. J. Scattergood and J. W. Sherborne, 163–182. London: Duckworth, 1983.

Doyle, A. I. *The Vernon Manuscript: A Facsimile of Bodleian Library, Oxford, Ms. Eng. Poet. A.* Cambridge: Brewer, 1987.

Drewer, Lois. "Margaret of Antioch the Demon-Slayer, East and West: The Iconography of the Predella of the Boston Mystic Marriage of St. Catherine." *Gesta* 32 (1993): 11–20.

Duffy, Eamon. *Marking the Hours: English People and their Prayers, 1240–1570: The Riddell Lectures 2002.* New Haven, CT: Yale University Press, 2006.

Elliot, Janis. "Augustine and the New Augustinianism in the Choir Frescoes of the Eremitani, Padua." In *Art and the Augustinian Order in Early Renaissance Italy,* edited by Louise Bourdua and Anne Dunlop, 99–126. Aldershot: Ashgate, 2007.

Ellis, Roger H. *Catalogue of Seals in the Public Record Office: Personal Seals.* 2 vols. London: For Her Majesty's Stationery Office, 1978 and 1981.

Everard, J. A. *Brittany and the Angevins, Province and Empire, 1158–1203.* Cambridge: Cambridge University Press, 2000.

Faillon, É.-M. *Monuments inédits sur l'apostolat de Sainte Marie Madeleine en Provence et sur les autres apôtres de cette contrée, Saint Lazare, Saint Maximin, Sainte Marthe, les Saintes Maries Jacobé et Salomé, etc.* Vol. 2. Paris: J.-P. Migne, 1859.

Faral, Edmond, and Julia Bastin, eds. *Oeuvres complètes de Rutebeuf.* Paris: Éditions A. et J. Picard et Cie., 1959–1960.

Les Fastes du Gothique. Le siècle de Charles V. Paris: Galeries nationales du Grand Palais, 1981.

Field, Sean L. "Reflecting the Royal Soul: The *Speculum anime* Composed for Blanche of Castile." *Mediaeval Studies* 68 (2006): 1–42.

Field, Sean L. "Marie of Saint-Pol and Her Books." *English Historical Review* 125 (2010): 271–272.

Foot, Mirjam M. "An Eighteenth-Century Dutch Patron of Bookbinding." *Quaerendo* 41 (2011): 193–207.

Forsyth, Ilene H. *The Throne of Wisdom: Wood Sculptures of the Madonna in Romanesque France.* Princeton, NJ: Princeton University Press, 1972.

Francis, Elizabeth A. "A Hitherto Unprinted Version of the Passio Sanctae Margaritae with Some Observations on Vernacular Derivatives." *Publications of the Modern Language Association of America* 42 (1927): 87–105.

Francis, Elizabeth A., ed. *Wace: La vie de sainte Marguerite.* Paris: Librairie Ancienne Edouard Champion, 1932.

Friedman, Mira. "The Falcon and the Hunt: Symbolic Love Imagery in Medieval and Renaissance Art." In *Poetics of Love in the Middle Ages,* edited by M. Lazar and N. J. Lacy, 157–183. Fairfax, VA: George Mason University Press, 1989.

Froissart, Jean. *Chronicles of England France and Spain: and the Adjoining Countries, From the Latter Part of the Reign of Edward II, to the Coronation of Henry IV.* Trans. Thomas Johnes. London: William Smith, 1839.

Fulton, Rachel. *From Judgment to Passion: Devotion to Christ and the Virgin Mary, 800–1200.* New York: Columbia University Press, 2002.

Geddes, Jane. *The St Albans Psalter: A Book for Christina of Markyate.* London: British Library, 2005.

Given-Wilson, Chris. *The English Nobility in the Late Middle Ages: The Fourteenth-Century Political Community.* London: Routledge & Kegan Paul, 1987.

Glover, Sarah. "Illustrations of the Miracles of the Virgin in English Books of Hours, c. 1200–1400." Ph.D. thesis, University of Virginia, 2003.

Gold, Penny Schine. *The Lady and the Virgin: Image, Attitude, and Experience in Twelfth-Century France.* Chicago, IL: University of Chicago Press, 1985.

Gonzalo de Berceo. *Milagros de Nuestra Senora.* Edited by E. Michael Gerli. Madrid: Catedra, 1987.

Goodman, Anthony. *The Loyal Conspiracy: The Lords Appellant under Richard II.* London: Kegan Paul, 1971.

Gwynn, Aubrey. *The English Austin Friars in the Time of Wyclif.* London: Humphrey Milford, 1940.

Hackett, John. *Select and Remarkable Epitaphs on Illustrious and Other Persons.* 2 vols. London: Printed for T. Osborne and J. Shipton, 1757.

Hahn, Cynthia. "'Joseph Will Perfect, Mary Enlighten and Jesus Save Thee': The Holy Family as Marriage Model in the Mérode Triptych." *Art Bulletin* 68 (1986): 54–66.

Haibach-Reinisch, Monika. *Melito Ein neuer Transitus Mariae des Pseudo-Melito: Textkritische Ausgabe und Darlegung der Bedeutung dieser ursprünglicheren Fassung für Apokryphenforschung und lateinische und deutsche Dichtung des Mittelalters.* Rome: Pontificia Academia Mariana Internationalis, 1962.

de Hamel, Christopher. *A History of Illuminated Manuscripts.* Oxford: Phaidon, 1986.

de Hamel, Christopher. "A New *Bohun.*" In *The English Medieval Book: Studies in Memory of Jeremy Griffiths,* edited by A. S. G. Edwards, Ralph Hanna, and Vincent Gillespie. London: British Library, 2000, 19–26.

Hartmann, Arnulfus, ed. *Bartholomæi Veneti O.S.A: Registra generalatus, 1383–1393*. Rome: Institutum Historicum Augustinianum, 1996.

Head, Thomas, ed. *Medieval Hagiography: An Anthology*. New York: Garland, 1999.

Heinzer, Felix. "Un témoin inconnu des Bohun Manuscripts: le MS. 2 des Archives de l'abbaye de Lichtenthal." *Scriptorium* 43 (1989): 259–266.

Herbert, J. A. "A New Manuscript of Adgar's Mary-legends." *Romania* 32 (1903): 415–421.

Herolt, Johannes. *Miracles of the Blessed Virgin Mary: (1435–1440)*. Trans. C. C. Swinton Bland and intro. Eileen Power. London: Routledge, 1928.

Hirsch, Theodor, Max Toeppen, and Ernst Strehlke, eds. *Scriptores rerum Prussicarum. Die Geschichtquellen der preussischen Vorzeit bis zum Untergange der Ordensherrschaft*. Vol. 2. Leipzig: Hirzel, 1863.

Holmes, Megan. "Disrobing the Virgin: The Madonna Lactans in Fifteenth-Century Florentine Art." In *Picturing Women in Renaissance and Baroque Italy*, edited by Geraldine A. Johnson and Sara F. Matthews Grieco, 167–195. Cambridge: Cambridge University Press, 1997.

Holt, Richard. "Thomas of Woodstock and Events at Gloucester in 1381." *Historical Research* 58 (1985): 237–242.

Howe, Emily. "Divine Kingship and Dynastic Display: The Altar Wall Murals of St. Stephen's Chapel, Westminster." *Antiquaries Journal* 81 (2001): 259–303.

Howlett, D. R. *The English Origins of Old French Literature*. Dublin: Four Courts Press, 1996.

Huber, Michael, ed. *Johannes Monachus, Liber de miraculis. Ein neuer Beitrag zur mittelalterlichen Mönchsliteratur*. Heidelberg: Carl Winter's Universitätsbuchhandlung, 1913.

Hughes, Muriel J. "The Library of Philip the Bold and Margaret of Flanders, First Valois Duke and Duchess of Burgundy." *Journal of Medieval History* 4 (1978): 145–188.

Ilsøe, Harald. "Hvordan så Otto Thotts bøger ud?" *Fund og Forskning* 35 (1996): 65–94.

Jacobus de Voragine. *The Golden Legend: Readings on the Saints*. Trans. William Granger Ryan. 2 vols. Princeton, NJ: Princeton University Press, 1993.

James, Montague Rhodes. *On the Abbey of S. Edmund at Bury*. Cambridge: Cambridge Antiquarian Society, 1895.

James, Montague Rhodes. *The Sculptures in the Lady Chapel at Ely*. London: D. Nutt, 1895.

James, Montague Rhodes. *A Descriptive Catalogue of the Second Series of Fifty Manuscripts (Nos. 51 to 100) in the Collection of Henry Yates Thompson*. Cambridge: Cambridge University Press, 1902.

James, Montague Rhodes. *The Apocryphal New Testament*. Oxford: Oxford University Press, 1924.

James, Montague Rhodes, and Eric George Millar. *The Bohun Manuscripts: A Group of Five Manuscripts Executed in England about 1370 for Members of the Bohun Family*. Oxford: Printed for the Roxburghe Club by J. Johnson at the University Press, 1936.

Jansen, Katherine Ludwig. *The Making of the Magdalen: Preaching and Popular Devotion in the Later Middle Ages*. Princeton, NJ: Princeton University Press, 2001.

Jennings, J. C. "The Writings of Prior Dominic of Evesham." *English Historical Review* (1962): 298–304.

Jones, David. "St. Richard of Chichester: The Sources for his Life." *Sussex Record Society* 79 (1995): 83–159.

Jørgensen, Ellen. *Catalogus codicum latinorum mediiaevi Bibliothecae Regiæ Hafniensis.* Copenhagen: Prostat in aedibus Gyldendalianis, 1926.

Kay, Sarah. *The Place of Thought: The Complexity of One in Late Medieval French Didactic Poetry.* Philadelphia, PA: University of Pennsylvania Press, 2007.

King, Pamela M. *The York Mystery Cycle and the Worship of the City.* Cambridge: D. S. Brewer, 2006.

Kjellman, Hilding. *La deuxième collection anglo-normande des miracles de la Sainte Vierge et son original latin.* Paris and Uppsala: Edouard Champion and A.-B Akademiska Bokhandeln, 1922.

Klein, Peter. "The Apocalypse in Medieval Art." In *The Apocalypse in the Middle Ages,* edited by Richard Kenneth Emmerson and Bernard McGinn. Ithaca, NY: Cornell University Press, 1992, 159–199.

Koenig, V. Frederic, ed. *Gautier de Coincy. Les miracles de Nostre Dame.* 4 vols. Geneva: Droz, 1955–70.

Krause, Kathy M., and Alison Stones, eds. *Gautier de Coinci: Miracles, Music and Manuscripts.* Turnhout: Brepols, 2006.

Krochalis, Jeanne E. "The Books and Reading of Henry V and His Circle." *The Chaucer Review* 23 (1988): 50–77.

Kulp-Hill, Kathleen. *Songs of Holy Mary of Alfonso X, the Wise: A Translation of the Cantigas de Santa María.* Tempe: Arizona Center for Medieval and Renaissance Studies, 2000.

Kunstmann, Perre, ed. *Le Gracial.* Ottawa: Éditions de l'Université d'Ottawa, 1982.

Larson, Wendy R. "Three Thirteenth-Century Lives of St Margaret of Antioch." In *Medieval Hagiography: An Anthology,* edited by T. Head, 675–708. New York and London: Routledge, 2001.

Larson, Wendy R. "The Role of Patronage and Audience in the Cults of Sts Margaret and Marina of Antioch." In *Gender and Holiness: Men, Women and Saints in Late Medieval Europe,* edited by Samantha J. E. Riches and Sarah Salih, 23–35. London: Routledge, 2002.

Larson, Wendy R. "Who Is the Master of This Narrative? Maternal Patronage of the Cult of St. Margaret." In *Gendering the Master Narrative: Women and Power in the Middle Ages,* edited by Mary C. Erler and Maryanne Kowaleski, 94–104. Ithaca, NY, and London: Cornell University Press, 2003.

Lecoy, Félix, ed. *La vie des pères.* 3 vols. Paris: Société des anciens textes français, 1987.

Legendre, Olivier, ed. *Collectaneum exemplorum et visionum Clarevallense: e codice Trecensi 946.* Turnhout: Brepols, 2005.

Legge, M. Dominica, ed. *Anglo-Norman Letters and Petitions from All Souls Ms. 182.* Oxford: Blackwell, 1941.

Legge, M. Dominica. "William the Marshal and Arthur of Brittany." *Historical Research* 55 (1982): 18–24.

Lemaire, Jacques. "Edition de quelques vies de saints d'après le texte des manuscrits Bruxelles, B.R., 10236, Paris, B.N. nouv.acq. franc., 10128, Paris, Bibl. Sainte Geneviève, 588, Londres, B.M. Add. 6524." Mémoire présenté pour l'obtention du grade de licencié en Philologie Romane, Université libre de Bruxelles, 1968–1969.

Lewes Gee, Loveday. *Women, Art and Patronage from Henry III to Edward III, 1216–1377.* Woodbridge: Boydell Press, 2002.

Lewis, Katherine J. “Model Girls? Virgin-Martyrs and the Training of Young Women in Late Medieval England.” In *Young Medieval Women,* edited by Katherine J. Lewis, Noël James Menuge, and Kim M. Philips, 25–46. Stroud: Sutton, 1999.

Lodge, Eleanor C., and Robert Somerville, eds. *John of Gaunt's Register, 1379–1383.* 2 vols. London: Offices of the Society, 1937.

Long, Mary Elizabeth. “Reading Female Sanctity: English Legendaries of Women, ca. 1200–1650.” Ph.D. thesis, University of Massachusetts, Amherst, 2004.

Lundgren, Anders Hugo Hjalmar. *Studier öfver Theophiluslegendens romanska varianter.* Uppsala: K.W. Appelbergs Boktryckeri, 1913.

MacCracken, Henry Noble, ed. *The Minor Poems of John Lydgate.* London: Oxford University Press, 1961.

MacFarlane, K. B. *The Nobility of Later Medieval England.* Oxford: Clarendon Press, 1973.

Mack, Frances M., ed. *Seinte Marherete the meiden ant martyr: Re-ed. from MS. Bodley 34, Oxford, and MS. Royal 17A XXVII, British Museum.* London: Oxford University Press, 1934.

Madan, F. “The Localization of Manuscripts.” In *Essays in History Presented to Reginald Lane Poole,* edited by H. W. C. Davis, 5–29. Oxford: Clarendon Press, 1927.

Maginnis, Hayden B. J. *Painting in the Age of Giotto.* University Park, PA: Pennsylvania State University Press, 1997.

Malone, Carolyn Marino. *Façade as Spectacle: Ritual and Ideology at Wells Cathedral.* Leiden: Brill, 2004.

Marks, Richard. *Stained Glass in England during the Middle Ages.* London: Routledge, 1993.

Melletier, Jean Le. *Les Seigneurs de Bohon, illustre famille anglo-normande, originaire du Cotentin.* Coutances: Arnaud-Bellée, 1978.

Mellinkoff, Ruth. *Outcasts: Signs of Otherness in Northern European Art of the Late Middle Ages.* Berkeley, CA: University of California Press, 1993.

Mettmann, Walter ed. *Cantigas de Santa Maria.* 3 vols. Madrid: Editorial Castalia, 1986–1989.

Meyer, Paul. “Légendes hagiographiques en Français.” *Histoire littéraire de la France* 33. Paris: Imprimerie nationale, 1906, 328–458.

Michael, Michael. “The Privilege of ‘Proximity’: Towards a Re-definition of the Function of Armorials.” *Journal of Medieval History* 23 (1997): 55–74.

Michael, Michael A. “A Manuscript Wedding Gift from Philippa of Hainault to Edward III.” *The Burlington Magazine* 127 (1985): 582–599.

Millar, Eric George. *The Luttrell Psalter: Two Plates in Colour and One Hundred and Eighty-Three in Monochrome from the Additional Manuscript 42130 in the British Museum.* London: Printed for the trustees, 1932.

Mimouni, Simon Claude. *Dormition et Assomption de Marie. Histoire des traditions anciennes.* Paris: Beauchesne, 1995.

Mitchell, S. “Richard II: Kingship and the Cult of Saints.” In *The Regal Image of Richard II and the Wilton Diptych,* edited by Dillian Gordon, Lisa Monnas, and Caroline Elam, 115–124. London: Harvey Miller Publishers, 1997.

Mombritius, Boninus. *Sanctuarium seu Vitae Sanctorum.* 2 vols. Hildesheim: Georg Olms Verlag, 1978.

Morgan, D.A.L. “The Banner-Bearer of Christ and Our Lady's Knight: How God Became an Englishman Revisited.” In *St. George's Chapel, Windsor, in the Fourteenth Century,* edited by Nigel Saul, 51–61. Woodbridge: Boydell Press, 2005.

Morgan, Nigel J. *The Medieval Painted Glass of Lincoln Cathedral.* London: Oxford University Press, 1983.

Morgan, Nigel J. "Texts and Images of Marian Devotion in Fourteenth-Century England." In *England in the Fourteenth Century: Proceedings of the 1991 Harlaxton Symposium*, 34–57. Stamford: Paul Watkins Medieval Studies, 1993.

Morgan, Nigel J. "Patrons and their Devotions in the Historiated Initials and Full-Page Miniatures of 13th-Century English Psalters." In *The Illuminated Psalter: Studies in the Content, Purpose and Placement of Its Images*, edited F. O. Büttner, 309–322. Turnhout: Brepols, 2004.

Morganstern, Anne McGee, and John A. Goodall. *Gothic Tombs of Kinship in France, the Low Countries and England.* University Park, PA: Pennsylvania State University Press, 2000.

Mortimer, Ian. "Richard II and the Succession to the Crown." *History* 91 (2006): 320–336.

Mortimer, Ian. *The Fears of Henry IV. The Life of England's Self-Made King.* London: Vintage, 2007.

Mulder-Bakker, Anneke, ed. *Sanctity and Motherhood: Essays on Holy Mothers in the Middle Ages.* New York: Garland, 1995.

Murray, Peter, and Linda Murray. *A Dictionary of Christian Art.* Oxford and New York: Oxford University Press, 2004.

Mussafia, Adolf. "Studien zu den mittelalterlichen Marienlegenden." *Sitzungsberichte der kaiserlichen Akademie der Wissenschaften in Wien, Philosophisch-historische Klasse* 113 (1886): 917–994; 115 (1887): 5–93; 119 (1889): 1–66; 123 (1890): 1–85; 139 and (1898): 1–74.

Neal, Derek G. *The Masculine Self in Late Medieval England.* Chicago, IL and London: University of Chicago Press, 2008.

Neff, Amy. "The Pain of Compassio: Mary's Labor at the Foot of the Cross." *Art Bulletin* 80 (1998): 266.

Neuhaus, Carl, ed. *Adgar's Marienlegenden nach der Londoner Handschrift Egerton 612.* Heilbronn: Henninger, 1886.

Neuhaus, Carl. *Die Lateinischen Vorlagen zu den alt-franzosischen Adgar'schen Marienlegende.* Aschersleben: H. C. Bestehorn, 1886–1887.

Nichols, John. *A Collection of All the Wills, Now Known to Be Extant, of the Kings and Queens of England, Princes and Princesses of Wales, and Every Branch of the Blood Royal, From the Reign of William the Conqueror to that of Henry the Seventh Exclusive: with Explanatory Notes, and a Glossary.* London: Printed by J. Nichols, 1780.

Olsen, Kåre, and Carl Nordenfalk. *Gyldne Bøger: Illuminerede middelalderlige håndskrifter i Danmark og Sverige.* Copenhagen: Nationalmuseet, 1952.

Orme, Nicholas. "The Education of the Courtier." In *English Court Culture in the Later Middle Ages*, edited by V. J. Scattergood and J. W. Sherborne, 63–85. London: Duckworth, 1983.

Ormrod, W. M. "The Personal Religion of Edward III." *Speculum* 64 (1989): 849–877.

Ormrod, W. M. *The Reign of Edward III: Crown and Political Society in England 1327–1377.* New Haven, CT and London: Yale University Press, 1990.

Ottosen, Knud. *The Responsories and Versicles of the Latin Office of the Dead.* Aarhus: Aarhus University Press, 1993.

Page, William, and H. Arthur Doubleday, eds. *The Victoria History of the Counties of England: A History of the County of Essex.* 5 vols. London: Archibald Constable and Company Limited, 1903–1966.

Parkes, James. *The Conflict of the Church and the Synagogue: A Study in the Origins of Anti-Semitism.* Cleveland, OH: World Publishing Company, 1961.

Parsons, John Carmi. "Of Queens, Courts and Books: Reflections on the Literary Patronage of Thirteenth-Century Plantagenet Queens." In *The Cultural Patronage of Medieval Women,* edited by June Hall McCash, 175–201. Athens, GA: University of Georgia Press, 1996.

Parsons, John Carmi. "Mothers, Daughters, Marriage, Power: Some Plantagenet Evidence, 1150–1500." In *Medieval Queenship,* edited by John Carmi Parsons, 63–78, 206–209. New York, St. Martin's Press, 1998.

Pearson, Andrea. *Envisioning Gender in Burgundian Devotional Art, 1350–1530: Experience, Authority, Resistance: Women and Gender in the Early Modern World.* Aldershot: Ashgate, 2005.

Peck, Russell A., ed. *Confessio amantis / John Gower.* Toronto, Buffalo and London: University of Toronto Press in association with the Medieval Academy of America, 1980.

Pellegrin, Elisabeth. *La bibliothèque des Visconti et des Sforza, ducs de Milan.* Paris: CNRS, 1955.

Phillips, Kim M. "Maidenhood as the Perfect Age of Woman's Life." In *Young Medieval Women,* edited by Katherine J. Lewis, Noël James Menuge, and Kim M. Philips, 1–24. Stroud: Sutton, 1999.

Phillips, Kim M. *Medieval Maidens: Young Women and Gender in England, 1270–1540.* Manchester: Manchester University Press, 2003.

Pinches, J. H., and R. V. *The Royal Heraldry of England,* London: Heraldry Today, 1974.

Plotzek, Joachim M. *Andachtsbücher des Mittelalters aus Privatbesitz: Katalog zur Ausstellung im Schnütgen-Museum Köln.* Cologne: Schnütgen-Museum, 1987.

Poncelet, Albert. "Index miraculorum B.V. Mariae quae saec. VI–XV latine conscripta sunt." *Analecta Bollandiana* 21 (1902): 242–360.

Procter, Francis, and Christophor Wordsworth, eds. *Breviarium ad usum insignis ecclesiae Sarum.* 3 vols. Cambridge: Cambridge University Press, 1879–1886.

Pugh, R. B., and Elizabeth Crittall. *The Victoria History of the Counties of England: A History of the County of Wiltshire.* Vol. 3. London: Published for the Institute of Historical Research by Oxford University Press, 1956.

Pujmanovà, O. "Portraits of Kings Depicted as Magi in Bohemian Painting." In *The Regal Image of Richard II and the Wilton Diptych,* edited by Dillian Gordon, Lisa Monnas, and Caroline Elam, 247–266. London: Harvey Miller Publishers, 1997.

Ragusa, Isa, and Rosalie B. Green, eds. *Meditations on the Life of Christ: An Illustrated Manuscript of the Fourteenth Century, Paris, Bibliothèque nationale, Ms. ital. 115.* Princeton, NJ: Princeton University Press, 1977.

Register of Edward the Black Prince Preserved in the Public Record Office. Part 3 (Palatinate of Chester), A.D. 1351–1365. Edited by Michael Charles Burdett Dawe and H. C. Johnson. London: Stationery Office, 1932.

Riches, Samantha. *St. George: Hero, Martyr, and Myth.* Stroud: Sutton, 2000.

Riches, Samantha. "Hagiography in Context: Images, Miracles, Shrines and Festivals." In *A Companion to Middle English Hagiography*, edited by Sarah Salih, 25–46. Cambridge: D. S. Brewer, 2006.

Rickert, Margaret. *Painting in Britain: The Middle Ages*. Harmondsworth: Penguin, 1954.

Rosenthal, Joel T. *Patriarchy and Families of Privilege in Fifteenth-Century England*. Philadelphia, PA: University of Pennsylvania Press, 1991.

Ross, Leslie. *Text, Image, Message: Saints in Medieval Manuscript Illumination*. Westport, CT: Greenwood Press, 1994.

Roth, Francis. *The English Austin Friars*. 2 vols. New York: Augustinian Historical Institute, 1961.

Rouse, Richard H., and Mary A. Rouse. *Manuscripts and their Makers: Commercial Book Producers in Medieval Paris, 1200–1500*. 2 vols. Turnhout: Harvey Miller, 2000.

Rubin, Miri. *Gentile Tales: The Narrative Assault on Late Medieval Jews*. New Haven, CT: Yale University Press, 1999.

Russakoff, Anna. "Imaging the Miraculous: Les Miracles de Notre Dame, Paris, BnF, n.acq.fr. 24541." Ph.D. thesis, New York University, 2006.

Rymer, Thomas. *Foedera, conventiones, literae et cujuscunque generis acta publica, inter reges Angliæ, et alios quosvis imperatores, reges, pontifices, principes, vel communitates, ab ineunte sæculo duodecimo, viz, ab anno 1101, ad nostra usque tempora, habita aut tractata, ex autographis, infra secretiores archivorum regiorum thesaurarias, per multa sæcula reconditis, fideliter exscripta*. London: J. Tonson, 1729.

Sandler, Lucy Freeman. "A Note on the Illuminators of the Bohun Manuscripts." *Speculum* 60 (1985): 364–372.

Sandler, Lucy Freeman. *Gothic Manuscripts 1285–1385*. Edited by J. J. G. Alexander. *Survey of Manuscripts Illuminated in the British Isles*. Vol. 5. Parts 1 and 2. London: Harvey Miller, 1986.

Sandler, Lucy Freeman. "Political Imagery in the Bohun Manuscripts." In *Decoration and Illustration in Medieval English Manuscripts. English Manuscript Studies 1100–1700,* edited by A. S. G. Edwards, 114–153. London: British Library, 2002.

Sandler, Lucy Freeman. "The Illustration of the Psalms in Fourteenth-Century English Manuscripts: Three Psalters of the Bohun Family." In *Reading Texts and Images: Essays on Medieval and Renaissance Art and Patronage in Honour of Margaret M. Manion,* edited by Bernard J. Muir, 123–151. Exeter: University of Exeter Press, 2002.

Sandler, Lucy Freeman. "Lancastrian Heraldry in the Bohun Manuscripts." In *The Lancastrian Court: Proceedings of the 2001 Harlaxton Symposium,* edited by Jenny Stratford, 221–232. Donington: Shaun Tyas, 2003.

Sandler, Lucy Freeman. *The Lichtenthal Psalter and the Manuscript Patronage of the Bohun Family*. London: H. Miller, 2004.

Sandler, Lucy Freeman. "Word Imagery in English Gothic Psalters: The Case of the Vienna Bohun Manuscript: ÖNB, cod. 1826." In *The Illuminated Psalter: Studies in the Content, Purpose and Placement of its Images,* edited by F. O. Buttner. Turnhout, 387–395. Brepols, 2005.

Sandler, Lucy Freeman. "Bared: The Writing Bear in the British Library Bohun Psalter." In *Tributes to Jonathan J. G. Alexander: The Making and Meaning of Illuminated Medieval and Renaissance Manuscripts, Art and Architecture,* edited by Gerald B. Guest and Susan L'Engle, 269–282. London: Harvey Miller/Brepols, 2006.

Sandler, Lucy Freeman. "Mary de Bohun's 'Livret de saintes' in Copenhagen." In *Tributes to Nigel Morgan: Contexts of Medieval Art; Images, Objects & Ideas,* edited by Julian M. Luxford and M. A. Michael, 65–76. Turnhout: Brepols, 2010.

Sandler, Lucy Freeman. "One Hundred and Fifty Years of Study of the Illuminated Book in England: The Bohun Manuscripts from the Nineteenth Century to the Present." *Gothic Art & Thought in the Later Medieval Period,* edited by Colum Hourihane, 243–283. University Park, PA, 2011.

Saul, Nigel, ed. *St. George's Chapel, Windsor, in the Fourteenth Century.* Woodbridge: Boydell Press, 2005.

Savage, Anne, and Nicholas Watson, trans. and intro. *Anchoritic Spirituality: Ancrene Wisse and Associated Works.* New York: Paulist Press, 1991.

Scattergood, V. J. "Literary Culture at the Court of Richard II." *English Court Culture in the Later Middle Ages.* Edited by V. J. Scattergood and J. W. Sherborne, 29–44. London: Duckworth, 1983.

Shorr, Dorothy C. "The Role of the Virgin in Giotto's Last Judgment." *Art Bulletin* 38 (1956): 207–214.

Schulz, H. C. "Thomas Hoccleve, Scribe." *Speculum* 12 (1937): 71–81.

Scott-Stokes, Charity. *Women's Books of Hours in Medieval England: Selected Texts Translated from Latin, Anglo-Norman French, and Middle English.* Woodbridge, UK and Rochester, NY: D. S. Brewer, 2006.

Seward, Barbara. *The Symbolic Rose.* New York: Columbia University Press, 1960.

Shea, Jennifer. "Adgar's Gracial and Christian Images of Jews in Twelfth-Century Vernacular Literature." *Journal of Medieval History* 33 (2007): 181–196.

Sherborne, James. *War, Politics and Culture in Fourteenth-Century England.* London: Hambledon Press, 1994.

Shoemaker, Stephen J. *Ancient Traditions of the Virgin Mary's Dormition and Assumption.* Oxford and New York: Oxford University Press, 2002.

Simpson, Amanda. *The Connections between English and Bohemian Painting during the Second Half of the Fourteenth Century.* Outstanding Theses from the Courtauld Institute of Art. New York: Garland Publishing, 1984.

Sinanoglou, Leah. "The Christ Child as Sacrifice: A Medieval Tradition and the Corpus Christi Plays." *Speculum* 48 (1973): 491–509.

Skemer, Don C. *Binding Words: Textual Amulets in the Middle Ages.* University Park, PA: Pennsylvania State University Press, 2006.

Smith, John Rees, ed. *The Lives of St Mary Magdalene and St. Martha (MS Esc. H-I-13).* Exeter: University of Exeter Press, 1989.

Smith, John Thomas. *Antiquities of Westminster, The Old Palace, St. Stephen's Chapel.* London: Printed for J. T. Smith and sold by R. Rejan and J. Manson, 1807.

Smith, Kathryn A. *Art, Identity, and Devotion in Fourteenth Century England: Three Women and their Books of Hours.* Toronto: University of Toronto Press, 2003.

Smith, Lesley. "Scriba, Femina: Medieval Depictions of Women Writing." In *Women and the Book: Assessing the Visual Evidence,* edited by Lesley Smith and Jane H. M. Taylor, 21–44. London and Toronto: British Library and University of Toronto Press, 1997.

Socii Bollandiani, ed. *Catalogus codicum hagiographicorum latinorum antiquiorum saeculo xvi qui asservantur in bibliotheca nationali parisiensi.* Vol. 3. Brussels: Apud editors, 1889–1893.

Somerset, Fiona, ed. *Four Wycliffite Dialogues: Dialogue between Jon and Richard, Dialogue between a Friar and a Secular, Dialogue between Reson and Gabbyng, Dialogue between a Clerk and a Knight.* Oxford: Oxford University Press, 2009.

Somerville, Robert. *History of the Duchy of Lancaster: 1265–1603.* Vol. 1. London: The Chancellor and Council of the Duchy of Lancaster, 1953.

Southern, Richard W. "The English Origins of the 'Miracles of the Virgin.'" *Mediaeval and Renaissance Studies* 4 (1958): 176–216.

Spencer, F. "The Legend of St. Margaret." *Modern Language Notes* 4 (1889): 197–201.

Spencer, F. "The Legend of St. Margaret. II." *Modern Language Notes* 5 (1890): 142–150.

Spencer, F. "The Legend of St. Margaret. III. The York MS 16.K.13," *Modern Language Notes* 5 (1890): 107–111.

Stahl, Harvey. "Heaven in View: The Place of the Elect in an Illuminated Book of Hours." In *Last Things: Death and the Apocalypse in the Middle Ages,* edited by Caroline Walker Bynum and Paul Freedman, 205–232. Philadelphia, PA: University of Pennsylvania Press, 2000.

Staley, Lynn. *Languages of Power in the Age of Richard II.* University Park, PA: Pennsylvania State University Press, 2005.

Stanton, Anne Rudloff. *The Queen Mary Psalter: A Study of Affect and Audience.* Philadelphia, PA: American Philosophical Society, 2001.

Steinberg, Leo. "'How Shall This Be?' Reflections on Filippo Lippi's Annunciation in London." *Artibus et Historiae* 16 (1987): 25–44.

Stirnemann, Patricia, Marie-Thérèse Gousset, Claudia Rabel, and Emmanuelle Toulet, eds. *Les Heures d'Etienne Chevalier par Jean Fouque. Les quarante enluminures du Musée Condé.* Chantilly and Paris: Musée Condé and Somogy, 2005.

Stöber, Karen. *Late Medieval Monasteries and their Patrons: England and Wales, c. 1300–1540.* Woodbridge: Boydell Press, 2007.

Stone, Carole. "Anti-Semitism in the Miracle Tales of the Virgin." *Medieval Encounters* 5 (1999): 368–370.

Stratford, Jenny. "La Somme le Roi (Reims, Bibliothèque municipale, MS. 570), the Manuscripts of Thomas of Woodstock, Duke of Gloucester, and the Scribe, John Upton." In *Le statut du scripteur au Moyen Âge. Actes du XIIe colloque scientifique du Comité international de paléographie latine (Cluny, 17–20 juillet 1998),* edited by Marie-Clotilde Hubert, Emmanuel Poulle, and Marc H. Smith, 267–282. Paris: Ecole des Chartes, 2000.

Summerson, Henry. "An English Bible and Other Books Belonging to Henry IV." *Bulletin of the John Rylands Library* 79 (1997): 109–115.

Tarayre, Michel. *La Vierge et le miracle. Le Speculum historiale de Vincent de Beauvais.* Paris: Honoré Champion, 1999.

Tischendorf, C. *Apocalypses apocryphae Mosis, Esdrae, Pauli, Johannis, item Mariae dormitio, additis Evangeliorum et Actuum apocryphorum supplementis / maximam partem nunc primum edidit.* Leipzig: Herm. Mendelssohn, 1866.

Tout, Thomas Frederick. *Chapters in the Administrative History of Medieval England: The Wardrobe, The Chambers and the Small Seals.* Vol. 5. Manchester: University of Manchester Press, 1930.

Tristram, E. W. *English Wall Painting: The Fourteenth Century.* London: Routledge & Kegan Paul, 1955.

Tryon, Ruth Wilson. "Miracles of Our Lady in Middle English Verse." *PMLA* 38 (1923): 308–388.

Tubach, Frederic C. *Index exemplorum: A Handbook of Medieval Religious Tales*. Helsinki: Suomalainen Tiedeakatemia, 1969.

Tuck, Anthony. *Richard II and the English Nobility*. London: Edward Arnold, 1973.

Tudor, Adrian P. *Tales of Vice and Virtue: The First Old French Vie des Peres*. Amsterdam and New York: Rodopi, 2005.

Tudor, Adrian P. "Telling the Same Tale? Gautier de Coinci's *Miracles de Nostre Dame* and the first *Vie de Pères*." In *Gautier de Coinci: Miracles, Music and Manuscripts,* edited by Kathy M. Krause and Alison Stones, 301–330. Turnhout: Brepols, 2006.

Vale, Juliet. *Edward III and Chivalry: Chivalrous Society and its Context, 1270–1350*. Woodbridge: Boydell Press, 1982.

Vidas, Marina. "Representation and Reception: Women in the Copenhagen Bohun Hours (Royal Library, Ms Thott 547, 4°)." *Fund og Forskning i Det Kongelige Biblioteks Samlinger* 50 (2011): 77–126.

Vincent, Nicholas. *The Holy Blood: King Henry III and the Westminster Blood Relic*. Cambridge: Cambridge University Press, 2001.

Walford, Weston Styleman. "On Some Marks of Cadency Borne by the Sons of King Edward III, and by Others of the Family of Plantagenet." *Archaeological Journal* 7 (1850): 156–165.

Walker, Simon. *The Lancastrian Affinity 1361–1399*. Oxford: Clarendon, 1990.

Walker, Sue Sheridan. "Proof of Age of Feudal Heirs in Medieval England." *Mediaeval Studies* 35 (1973): 306–323.

Walker, Sue Sheridan. "Widow and Ward: The Feudal Law of Child Custody in Medieval England." *Feminist Studies* 3 (1976): 104–116.

Walker, Sue Sheridan. "Feudal Constraint and Free Consent in the Making of Marriages in Medieval England: Widows in the King's Gift." *Historical Papers* 14 (1979): 9–110.

Ward, H. L. D. *Catalogue of Romances in the Department of Manuscripts in the British Museum*. Vol. 2. London: British Museum, 1893.

Ward, Jennifer C. *English Noblewomen in the Later Middle Ages*. London: Longman, 1992.

Ward, Jennifer C. trans. and ed. *Women of the English Nobility and Gentry, 1066–1500*. Manchester: Manchester University Press, 1995.

Warner, George F. *Queen Mary's Psalter: Miniatures and Drawings by an English Artist of the 14th Century, Reproduced from Royal Ms. 2 B VII in the British Museum*. London: The British Museum, 1912.

Warner, George F., ed. *Miracles de Nostre Dame, collected by Jean Miélot, Secretary to Philip the Good, Duke of Burgundy, Reproduced in facsimile from Douce Manuscript 374 in the Bodleian Library*. Westminster: Nichols and Sons, 1885.

Watson, A. *The Early Iconography of the Tree of Jesse*. Oxford: Oxford University Press, 1934.

Waugh, Scott L. *The Lordship of England: Royal Wardships and Marriages in English Society and Politics, 1217–1327*. Princeton, NJ: Princeton University Press, 1988.

Welter, J.-Th. *L'Exemplum dans la litterature religieuse et didactique du moyen âge*. Paris and Toulouse: Occitania, 1927.

Wieck, Roger S. *Time Sanctified: The Book of Hours in Medieval Art and Life*. New York: George Braziller, in association with the Walters Art Gallery, 1988.

Wieck, Roger S. *Painted Prayers: The Book of Hours in Medieval and Renaissance Art.* New York: George Braziller in association with the Pierpont Morgan Library, 1997.
Wilhelm, James J. *Lyrics of the Middle Ages: An Anthology.* New York: Garland, 1990.
Williamson, Beth. *Christian Art: A Very Short Introduction.* New York: Oxford University Press, 2004.
Williamson, Beth. *The Madonna of Humility: Development, Dissemination and Reception, c. 1340–1400.* Woodbridge: Boydell Press, 2009.
Wilson, Evelyn Faye, ed. *The Stella Maris of John of Garland.* Cambridge, MA: Medieval Academy of America, 1946.
Wilson, Jean C. "'Richement et pompeusement parée': The Collier of Margaret of York and the Politics of Love in Late Medieval Burgundy." In *Excavating the Medieval Image: Manuscripts, Artists, Audiences: Essays in Honor of Sandra Hindman,* edited by David S. Areford and Nina Rowe, 109–134. Aldershot: Ashgate 2004.
Winston-Allen, Anne. *Stories of the Rose: The Making of the Rosary in the Middle Ages.* University Park, PA: Pennsylvania State University Press, 1998.
Wogan-Browne, Jocelyn. "Saints' Lives and the Female Reader." *Forum for Modern Language Studies* 27 (1991): 314–332.
Wogan-Browne, Jocelyn. "The Apple's Message: Some Post-Conquest Accounts of Textual Transmission." In *Late Medieval Religious Texts and their Transmission: Essays in Honour of A.I. Doyle,* edited by A. J. Minnis, 39–53. Cambridge: D.S. Brewer, 1994.
Wogan-Browne, Jocelyn. *Saints' Lives and Women's Literary Culture, 1150–1300: Virginity and its Authorizations.* Oxford and New York: Oxford University Press, 2001.
Wormald, Francis. "Some Illustrated Manuscripts of the Lives of Saints." *Bulletin of the John Rylands Library* 35 (1952): 218 266.
Wright, Thomas, ed. *Three Chapters of Letters Relating to the Suppression of Monasteries.* London: John Bowyer Nichols and Son, 1843.
Wylie, James Hamilton. *History of England under Henry the Fourth.* 4 vols. London: Longmans, Green and Co., 1896.
Ziolkowski, Jan, ed. *Nigel of Canterbury: Miracles of the Virgin Mary in Verse.* Toronto: Published for the Centre of Medieval Studies by the Pontifical Institute of Mediaeval Studies, 1986.

Index of Names, Places, and Manuscripts

Abelard 162n50
Adgar, William 52, 69, 90, 91, 92, 158n8, 161n41, 161n42, 163n56, 169n124, 169n26, 170n134
Ælfric 157n2, 162n56
Agnes de Sutton 160n33
Alberic, Master 52
Alfonso X, King of Castile, Léon, Galicia 166n97
Alice Fitzalan, Countess of Kent 23, 29, 148n2
Alice Plantagenet, co-heiress of Thomas Brotherton, Earl of Norfolk 150n43
Alice de Warenne, Countess of Arundel 172n164
Anne Plantagenet, Countess of Stafford 122, 172n158
Anne Stafford, Countess of March 129, 176n24
Anselm the Younger, Abbot of Bury St. Edmunds 52, 157n3
Arthur I, Duke of Brittany 152n63

Barking, convent 150n43
Barnsley, church 177n36
Blanche d'Artois, Queen of Navarre 15
Blanche de Bourgogne 171n49, 179n41
Blanche Plantagenet, Duchess of Lancaster 26, 28, 30, 150n33
Blanche Plantagenet, daughter of Mary de Bohun and Henry IV 28, 182n74
Beatrice le Scrope 160n33
Bede 157n2
Beauvais, Vincent de 53, 60, 64, 69, 159n17, 161n41, 163n56, 163n64, 170n135
Bennett, Michael 31, 152n62, 152n64
Berderfeld, Geoffrey 153n14
Bokenham, Osbern 131
Bohun family 15, 16, 18, 26, 33, 49, 72, 90, 122, 131, 132, 137, 141,145n1, 146n18, 161n37, 173n8, 178n47, 181n71, 185, 186
Bondol, Jean 173n166
Bradefeld, Brother Thomas de 154n16
Bricett Priory 153n15
Bruun, Christian 16, 17, 51, 145n3
Bury St. Edmunds, abbey 52, 169n129

Caesarius of Heisterbach 52, 84, 168n115
Canterbury Cathedral 158n15
Chalfont St. Giles, Buckinghamshire 158n15
Charles V, King of France 35, 154n21, 173n166
Charles VII, King of France 165n87
Christ 46, 52, 53, 54, 55, 56, 62, 64, 65, 66, 67, 69, 70, 71, 72, 73, 74, 75, 76, 77, 78, 81, 82, 83, 84, 85, 86, 87, 88, 89, 90, 93, 95, 97, 101, 102, 103, 104, 121, 122, 123, 124, 125, 126, 127, 128, 130, 131, 132, 133, 134, 141, 158n16, 159n18, 161n37, 162n48, 163n61, 164n68, 165n87, 166n89, 166n93, 168n109, 168n112, 170n135, 171n148, 171n150, 172n157, 177n31, 178n47, 184
Coinci, Gautier de 52, 53, 58, 60, 64, 69, 85, 159n17, 167n101, 169n124, 169n129, 170n136

David, King of Israel 54, 55, 56, 65, 96, 160n27
Deguileville, Guillaume de 138, 171n149, 182n73
Dennison, Lynda 17, 18, 33, 35, 115, 119, 121, 138, 146n15, 152n1, 153n10
Dominic, Prior of Evesham 52, 157n4, 161n41, 163n56
Drigsdahl, Erik 20, 156n22

Edmund Plantagenet "Crouchback," Earl of Lancaster 15

Edmund Plantagenet (of Langley), Duke of York 26, 31
Edmund Plantagenet (of Woodstock), Earl of Kent 31
Edward I, King of England 15, 31, 58
Edward II (of Carnarvon), King of England 177n31
Edward III, King of England 15, 23, 24, 25, 26, 27, 31, 63, 72, 106, 107, 148n6, 150n43, 160n35, 165n83, 165n84, 173n166
Edward of Woodstock, "the Black Prince" 31, 63
Eleanor of Castile, Queen of England 173n166, 181n61
Eleanor of Provence, Queen of England 140
Eleanor de Bohun, Duchess of Gloucester 15, 21, 23, 24, 25, 26, 27, 28, 29, 33, 35, 58, 73, 106, 107, 122, 129, 131, 132, 138, 141, 149n27, 151n52, 154n16, 154n18, 162n50, 172n158, 172n161, 172n163, 179n48, 181n70, 182n74
Eleanor de Mautravers 23
Eleanor Plantagenet, Countess of Arundel 23, 151n59
Elizabeth de Bohun, Countess of Arundel 23, 25
Elizabeth de Burgh, Countess of Ulster and Duchess of Clarence 26, 149n32
Elizabeth Plantagenet (of Rhuddlan), Countess of Hereford 58, 149n24, 161n39
Ely Cathedral 158n15, 168n17, 169n29
"English Artist" 18, 33, 152n1, 153n10
Eric of Pomerania, King of Denmark, Norway, and Sweden 156n30

Farleigh Priory (Farley) 132, 177n36
"Flemish Hand" 18, 33, 146n15, 152n1
Fontaine, Robert de 176n25
Foot, Mirjam 49, 148n34
Froissart, Jean 27, 28, 29, 30

Gelting, Michael H. 151n52
Geoffrey de Mandeville, Earl of Essex 140
Glover, Sarah 19, 71, 166n89

The Hague 49
Heinzer, Felix 18
Henry, Duke of Saxony 177n31
Henry III, King of England 15, 30, 140, 151n53, 152n63
Henry IV (of Bolingbroke), King of England 15, 16, 19, 28, 29, 30, 31, 32, 36, 58, 132, 138, 141, 151n52, 152n65, 153n16, 160n36, 166n91, 177n36, 180n55, 180n56, 182n71, 182n74
Henry V, King of England, son of Mary de Bohun and Henry IV 28, 138, 172n159, 179n51
Henry Bouchier, Count of Eu 131
Hoccleve, Thomas 138, 141, 171n149, 179n50, 182n73
Holy Spirit 40, 54, 61, 72, 76, 82, 84, 88, 118, 125, 126, 136
Hood, Henry 17, 18, 34, 153n8
Honorius of Autun (Honorius Augustodunensis) 163n64, 167n101, 170n132
Hugh de Courtenay 72
Huls, Samuel van 49, 185, 186
Humphrey III de Bohun 132
Humphrey VII de Bohun, 4th Earl of Hereford 15, 58, 161n39
Humphrey de Bohun, 6th Earl of Hereford 33, 34, 143, 154n16, 181n71
Humphrey de Bohun, 7th Earl of Hereford 15, 17, 19, 23, 24, 25, 26, 27, 35, 72, 106, 143, 148n6, 151n60, 154n18, 172n161
Humphrey Plantagenet, Duke of Buckingham, son of Eleanor de Bohun and Thomas of Woodstock 25, 172n158

Humphrey Plantagenet, Duke of Gloucester, son of Mary de Bohun and Henry IV 28

Ingeborg of Denmark, Queen of France 177n31
Isabeau de Bavière, Queen of France 129, 176n25
Isabel Plantagenet, Countess of Eu 131
Isabella de Warenne, Countess of Arundel 177n30, 180n61
Isabelle de France, (Isabella) Queen of England, wife of Edward II 154n21
Isabelle de France, (Isabella) Queen of England, wife of Richard II 180n56
Isabelle de France, Queen of Navarre 180n60
Isabelle Plantagenet, nun, daughter of Eleanor de Bohun and Thomas of Woodstock 30, 122, 172n158

James, M.R. 16, 17, 51, 80, 84, 155n10, 166n94, 168n114
Jean II, King of France 173n166
Jeanne, Duchess of Brittany 171n149
Jeanne II, Queen of Navarre 129, 176n25
Jeanne de Dampierre 180n160
Joan de Bohun née Fitzalan, Countess of Hereford 15, 19, 23, 24, 26, 27, 29, 30, 31, 32, 35, 36, 106, 138, 140, 141, 149n20, 151n56, 151n59, 153n15, 161n39, 171n149, 172n164, 179n49, 179n50, 179n51, 181n71, 182n73
Joan Clifford of Frampton 57
Joan de Mountagu 150n43
Joan Plantagenet, daughter of Eleanor de Bohun and Thomas of Woodstock 172n158
Job 98, 99, 100, 101, 143
John Fitzalan, son of Richard Fitzalan and Eleanor Plantagenet 23
John Plantagenet, son of Edward I 31
John Plantagenet, Duke of Bedford, son of Mary de Bohun and Henry IV 172n159
John Plantagenet (of Gaunt), Duke of Lancaster 19, 25, 26, 27, 28, 29, 30, 31, 129, 149n20, 160n36,
John de Pabenham 57
John de Segrave 150n33
Joseph 54, 67, 69, 70, 77, 78, 160n27, 164n70

Kettleston, church 177n36

Lionel Plantagenet (of Antwerp), Duke of Clarence 26, 31, 140, 149n32, 151n61
Litlington, Thomas 173n166
Llanthony, priory 35, 153n14, 153–154n16, 157n1, 177n36
London 24, 27, 33, 153n14, 182n74
Lords Apellant 32
Lydgate, John 129, 176n24

Magi 72, 73, 74, 75, 118, 155n14, 165n84, 165n87, 184
Malachus 126
Manuscripts
- Brussels, Bibliothèque Royale de Belgique, MS 10326 146n6, 174n5
- Baden-Baden, Lichtenthal Abbey, *Lichtenthal Psalter*, Archiv, MS 2 18, 19, 20, 33, 97, 105, 115, 119, 138, 145n1, 168n112
- Cambridge, Fitzwilliam Museum, Psalter, MS 38–1950 17, 18, 19, 33, 97, 138, 145n1, 173n8
- Cambridge, Fitzwilliam Museum, *Carew-Poyntz Hours*, MS 48 53, 164n78, 165n81
- Cambridge, Fitzwilliam Museum, *Pabenham-Clifford Hours*, formerly Grey-Fitzpayn Hours, MS 242 57
- Cambridge, Fitzwilliam Museum, Psalter, MS 330 158n16
- Cambridge, Sidney Sussex College, MS 95 166n94

Cambridge, University Library, MS Ee 6.11 176n22
Chantilly, Musée Condé, *Book of Hours of Etienne Chevalier*, MS 71 165n87
Chantilly, Musée Condé, *Ingeborg Psalter*, MS 1695 177n31
Copenhagen, Det Kongelige Bibliotek (Royal Library), Saints' Lives, MS Thott 517, 4° 15, 16, 17, 18, 19, 20, 21, 80, 111–119, 121–141, 143, 145n1, 145n5, 146n6, 148n34, 156n30, 173n8, 174n7, 175n11, 176n26, 176n28, 177n29, 178n40, 185–186
Copenhagen, Det Kongelige Bibliotek (Royal Library), Hours, MS Thott 547, 4° 15, 16, 17, 18, 19, 20, 21, 39–49, 51–107, 111, 112, 113, 114, 115, 116, 117, 118, 119, 141, 143, 145n1, 145n3, 146n10, 147n26, 148n34, 155n9, 156n16, 156n21, 156n30, 166n94, 170n136, 172n154, 173n8, 178n44, 178n47, 183–185, 186
Dublin, Trinity College, Life of St. Alban and other works, MS 177 (E i 40) 181n61
Dublin, Trinity College, MS 244 179n48
Edinburgh, National Library of Scotland, MS Adv. 18.6.5 179n48
Hildesheim, Dombibliothek, *Saint Albans Psalter*, MS St. Godehard 1 162n51, 177n31
Leiden, Bibliotheek der Universiteit, *Leiden Psalter*, MS 76 A 162n51
London, British Library, MS Additional 6524 122, 146n6, 174n6, 174n7
London, British Library, *Huth Psalter*, MS Additional 38116 178n46
London, British Library, *Luttrell Psalter*, MS Additional 42130 159n18, 160n33, 163n62, 179n49
London, British Library, *De Brailes Hours*, MS Additional 49999 and Dyson Perrins 4 158n16, 162n51, 163n59
London, British Library, MS Cotton Cleopatra C. X 157n2, 163n64, 169n124
London, British Library, MS Cotton Domitian A. XI 177n30
London, British Library, *Winchester Psalter*, MS Cotton Nero.C.IV 162n51
London, British Library, Bible, MS Egerton 617 178n48
London, British Library, MS Egerton 1117 166n94
London, British Library, *Neville of Hornby Hours*, MS Egerton 2781 53, 163n59
London, British Library, Psalter-Hours, MS Egerton 3277 18, 19, 33, 34, 36, 41, 45, 53, 65, 73, 85, 132, 145n1, 152n2, 156n22, 171n150, 176n26, 178n37
London, British Library, Processional, MS Harley 2942 179n48
London, British Library, *Queen Mary Psalter*, MS Royal 2.B.VII 53, 159n19, 162n48, 162n51, 163n62, 164n78, 169n121, 169n129, 177n31, 178n43
London, British Library, MS Royal 6 B. XIV 169n128
London, British Library, *Smithfield Decretals*, MS Royal 10. E. IV 159n18
London, British Library, *Roman de la Rose*, MS Royal 19 B. XIII 179n48
London, British Library, *Romance of Lancelot*, MS Royal 20.D.IV 33, 145n1, 152n2
London, British Library, *Taymouth Hours*, MS Yates Thompson 13 53, 84, 159n20, 162n46, 163n59, 165n81, 169n121

London, Lambeth Palace Library, *Lambeth Apocalypse*, MS 209 158n15
Madresfield Court, *Madresfield Hours*, MS M 53, 159n19, 165n85, 168n107
Munich, Bayerische Staatsbibliothek, Cod. lat. 5927 80
New York, New York Public Library, *Tickhill Psalter*, MS Spencer 26 153n12
New York, Pierpont Morgan Library, *Tiptoft Missal*, M.107 134
New York, Pierpont Morgan Library, *Ramsey Psalter*, M.302 159n18
New York, Pierpont Morgan Library, Psalter, M.679 178n45
Oxford, Balliol College Library, Miscellanea, MS 240 163n64
Oxford, Bodleian Library, Psalter-Hours, MS Auct.D.4.4. 17, 18, 19, 33, 36, 41, 53, 58, 65, 71, 73, 76, 81, 86, 88, 93, 97, 98, 101, 105, 115, 132, 136, 138, 145n1, 152n2, 155n10, 162n48, 172n157, 173n8, 176n26, 178n37, 178n38, 178n44
Oxford, Bodleian Library, MS Bodley 34 174n4
Oxford, Bodleian Library, Higden's *Polychronicon*, MS Bodley 316 178n48
Oxford, Bodleian Library, MS Bodley 691 171n148
Oxford, Bodleian Library, Religious Miscellany, MS Douce 79 134
Oxford, Bodleian Library, Brunetto Latini's Livre du Trésor, MS Douce 319 179n48
Oxford, Bodleian Library, Vernon Manuscript, MS Eng. Poet. A.1 170n136
Oxford, Exeter College, Psalter, MS 47 17, 18, 19, 33, 35, 41, 132, 145n1, 152n3, 154n23, 155n10, 178n37
Paris, Bibliothèque Mazarine, *Vie de sainte Geneviève*, MS 1716 180n60
Paris, Bibliothèque Nationale de France, MS latin 803 177n28
Paris, Bibliothèque Nationale de France, MS français 6447 146n6
Paris, Bibliothèque Nationale de France, MS français 17229 146n6
Paris, Bibliothèque Nationale de France, MS Miscellaneous texts, français 25532 16
Paris, Bibliothèque Nationale de France, MS latin 18134 166n97
Paris, Bibliothèque Nationale de France, MS naf 24541 170n136
Paris, Bibliothèque Nationale de France, *Hours of Jeanne II of Navarre*, MS nal 3145 129, 176n25
Private Collection, Book of Hours 41, 145n1, 146n18, 155n8, 155n9
Pommersfelden, Kunstsammlungen Graf von Schönborn, MS 348 18, 19, 33, 35, 41, 73, 115, 132, 136, 145n1, 173n8, 178n44
Reims, Bibliothèque municipale, Somme le Roi MS 570 178n48
San Marino, Huntington Library, Hoccleve's Poems, HM 111 179n50, 182n73
Toulouse, Bibliothèque de la ville de Toulouse, MS 482 157n2
Vienna, Österreichische Nationalbibliothek, Psalter, MS 1826 16, 17, 18, 19, 33, 35, 97, 98, 145n1, 152n1, 154n23, 156n21, 161n39
York, York Cathedral, MS 16.K.13 175n22
Margaret II, Countess of Flanders, daughter of Marie de Champagne 180n60
Margaret III, Countess of Flanders 26
Margaret de Courtenay, née Bohun 72, 161n39
Marseille 130, 131, 140, 177n30
Mary de Bohun, Countess of Derby 15, 16, 17, 19, 20, 21, 23, 24, 25, 26, 27, 28, 29, 30, 32, 33, 36, 106, 138, 141,

148n7, 150n52, 151n52, 151n56, 153n16, 154n18, 156n30, 160n34, 172n159, 172n163, 179n48, 181n70, 182n74
Matilda, Empress 132
Matilda of England, Duchess of Saxony 177n31
Maud de Bohun 132
Maud de Chaworth 23
Maud de Mandeville 107
Maud de Mountagu 150n43
Maud Plantagenet, Countess of Leicester 26
Melito of Sardis 122
Meyer, Paul 16, 146n6
Miélot, Jean 78, 80, 166n94, 169n125
Millar, Eric 17
Milton, William 153n15
Mombrizio, Bonino (Mombritius, Boninus) 124
Monachus, Johannes 170n135
Monkelane, William de 33
Montmartre, Jean de 173n166
Mortimer, Ian 31, 32, 151n52, 152n65, 152n66
Mussafia, Adolfo 157n2, 157n3

Nordenfalk, Carl 118

Olibrius 125, 126, 127, 128, 130

Paris, Matthew 180–181n61
Paul, the Deacon of Naples 162n56
Pleshey (Pleshy) Castle 17, 18, 24, 26, 27, 28, 29, 30, 33, 34, 35, 122, 138, 154n18, 157n1, 167n100, 170n141, 172n156, 178n48
Philip the Bold, Duke of Burgundy 154n21
Philip VI, King of France 176n25
Philip II Augustus, King of France 177n31
Philippa of Hainault, Queen of England 27, 28, 63, 140, 149n32, 162n55, 173n166,
Philippa Plantagenet, Queen of Denmark, Norway, and Sweden 156n30, 182n74
Philippa Plantagenet (of Clarence), Countess of Ulster 31
Prince, Gilbert 173n166

Radbertus, Paschasius 163n64
Ralph of Bocking 180n61
Richard I, King of England 152n63
Richard II (of Bordeaux), King of England 23, 26, 31, 32, 63, 72, 73, 122, 151n61, 152n65, 152n66, 165n85, 180n56
Richard Fitzalan, Earl of Arundel, son of Edmund Fitzalan and Alice de Warenne 23, 24
Richard Fitzalan, Earl of Arundel, son of Richard Fitzalan and Eleanor Plantagenet 23, 28, 29
Robert, miniaturist 173n166
Robert de Ufford 150n43
Rochford, manor 29, 150–151n52
Roger Mortimer, Earl of March and of Ulster 31, 151n61
Rome 33, 130
Rosenthal, Joel T. 24
Rutebeuf, poet 180n60
Roth, Francis 17, 34

Saints
- Alphege of Canterbury 47, 185
- Ambrose 47, 185
- Augustine of Hippo 47, 97, 153n14, 156n21, 162n47, 171n149
- Benedict of Nursia 47, 156n22, 185
- Bernard of Clairvaux 81, 167n100, 167n101, 170n132
- Bonaventure 81, 168n113
- Botulph of Icanho 47, 185
- Cuthbert of Lindisfarne 47, 185
- Dominic 47, 156n21, 156n22, 185
- Dunstan of Canterbury 47, 185
- Edmund, King of East Anglia 47, 185

Elizabeth 54, 61, 62, 65
Ethelreda 132
Francis of Assisi 47, 156n21, 156n22, 185
Gabriel, Archangel 54, 55, 118, 124, 134
Geneviève 180n60
George 44, 47, 51, 71, 72, 73, 156n23, 165n81, 165n82, 165n83, 165n84, 184, 185
Gregory of Tours 157n2, 163n64
John the Baptist 46, 185
John the Evangelist 122, 185
Longinus 82, 83
Margaret 15, 16, 47, 111, 121, 122, 124, 125, 126, 127, 128, 129, 130, 132, 133, 135, 136, 137, 139, 140, 143, 174n1, 174n4, 175n21, 175–176n22, 176n24, 176n25, 178n43, 178n45, 178n46, 178n47, 185, 186
Mary Magdalene 15, 16, 19, 83, 111, 117, 118, 121, 130, 131, 132, 133, 136, 137, 139, 140, 161n37, 174n1, 174n5, 177n30, 177n31, 178n37, 178n47, 181n63, 185, 186
Maximin 131, 133, 178n38
Michael, Archangel 84, 123, 124, 134, 185
Oswald of York 47, 185
Peter 123, 124, 131, 134, 185
Tecla 126
Thomas Becket, Archbishop of Canterbury 47, 180–181n81
St. Paul's, London 52
St. Stephen's Chapel, Westminster 58, 72, 160n35, 165n87
Salisbury, Cathedral 40
Sandler, Lucy Freeman 17, 19, 20, 33, 34, 35, 41, 63, 105, 118, 119, 121, 132, 138, 143, 145n1, 147n21, 147n34, 153n10, 153n12, 154n23, 156n20, 156n26, 156n27, 160n34, 162n49, 176n25, 176n26, 179n52
Smith, John Rees 18
Smith, Kathryn A. 162n46, 163n62, 164n70, 170n133
Solomon, King 55
Swynford, Katherine 182n74

Teye, John de 17, 20, 33, 34, 36, 153n8, 153n10
Theodosius 127
Theophilus 53, 63, 64, 65, 71, 103, 104, 157n2, 158n15, 158n16, 159n20, 159n21, 162n56, 163n88, 172n157, 183
Theotimus 126, 175n21
Thomas Fitzalan (Arundel), Bishop, son of Richard Fitzalan and Eleanor Plantagenet 23, 32,
Thomas Holland, Earl of Kent 23
Thomas Plantagenet (of Brotherton), Earl of Norfolk 150n43
Thomas Plantagenet (of Woodstock), Earl of Essex and Buckingham, Duke of Gloucester 15, 25, 26, 27, 29, 30, 31, 32, 35, 36, 58, 73, 106, 107, 122, 132, 138, 140, 141, 150n46, 151n55, 153n16, 160n35, 172n161, 177n36, 178–179n48, 180n57, 182n74
Thomas Plantagenet, Duke of Clarence, son of Mary de Bohun and Henry IV 28, 172n15
Thott, Count Otto 49, 185, 186
Tickhill, John 153n12
Tilbrock, church 177n36

Virgin Mary 15, 19, 39, 40, 41, 42, 43, 44, 45, 46, 51, 52, 53, 54, 55, 56, 57, 59, 60, 61, 62, 63, 64, 65, 66, 67, 68, 69, 70, 71, 72, 73, 74, 75, 76, 77, 78, 79, 80, 81, 82, 83, 84, 85, 86, 87, 88, 89, 90, 91, 92, 93, 96, 97, 101, 102, 103, 104, 105, 106, 107, 111, 117, 118, 119, 121, 122, 123, 124, 125, 132, 133, 134, 135, 137, 140, 141, 143, 144, 146n6, 155n14, 157n1, 157n2, 157n5, 158n15, 158n16, 159n18, 159n21, 160n27, 161n37, 161n41, 162n46, 162n47, 162n48, 162n56, 163n59, 163n62, 163n63, 164n67, 164n71, 165n81,

165n85, 165n87, 166n97, 167n101, 167n102, 167n103, 168n109, 168n113, 168n117, 169n119, 169n121, 169n128, 169n129, 169n131,170n135, 171n148, 174n1, 176n26, 178n47, 179n50, 181n69, 181n71, 182n73, 183, 184, 186
Visconti, Gian Galeazzo, Duke of Milan 35
Voragine, Jacobus de 53, 64, 69, 74, 75, 87, 163n57, 181n63

Walden Abbey 140, 141, 181–182n71
Walmgate, St. Denys, church 158n15
Waterton, Hugh de 151n52
Waterton, Katherine 182n74
Wilhale, William 153n14
William, poet 154n22
William de Bohun, Earl of Northampton 23, 72, 181n71
William de Burgh, Earl of Ulster 26
William of Malmesbury 52, 157n5, 163n56, 169n124
Wix Priory 177n36
Worksop Priory 153n12